D0562787

Our
Canada
Our Country
Our Stories

Inspirational Tales From the Heart and Soul of This Great Land

From the Editors and Contributors of *Our Canada*

Foreword by Gary George

Our Canada, Our Country, Our Stories

Inspirational Tales From the Heart and Soul of This Great Land
From the Editors and Contributors of *Our Canada*
Foreword by Gary George

ISBN 978-1-62145-409-0
E-Pub 978-1-62145-411-3

Our Canada and ***More of Our Canada*** are reader-written publications of The Reader's Digest Magazines Canada Limited, Montreal, QC. We are interested in receiving your comments on the content of this book. Submit your comments at **ourcanada.ca** or write to:
Our Canada c/o ***Reader's Digest***
5101 Rue Buchan, Suite 300
Montreal, QC H4P 1S4

Printed in the United States for The Reader's Digest Association (Canada) ULC, by LSC Communications
1 3 5 7 9 10 8 6 4 2a

CONTRIBUTING PHOTOGRAPHERS

FRONT COVER

Jana O'Neil, Tantallon, Nova Scotia

Originally from Moncton, New Brunswick, Jana moved to Nova Scotia more than two decades ago. She discovered her zest for photography in her early 30s while out and about enjoying nature. Jana gravitates towards capturing the everyday beauty that surrounds us, from dandelions and forest beds of wildflowers to stunning sunrises and sunsets. She feels very lucky to live in a country where we experience four majestic seasons—yes, even snowy winters! Jana's other passions include kayaking, hiking, camping and exploring new places with family, friends and her "fur babies." She has a wonderful son who shares in her love of photography. She is a firm believer in living life to its fullest and is always up for an adventure.

Jana snapped this photo at Graves Island Provincial Park, Nova Scotia, on a magnificent, chilly fall day.

FAMILY (p.15)

Bill L. Knibbs, Medicine Hat, Alberta
Bill shares this great picture of his brothers, the Knibbs "Leafs" hockey team, at the rink back in 1937.

KINDNESS (p.51)

Andrea Hamilton, Pointe Claire, Quebec
Andrea sent along this heartwarming photo of her son Ryan and his beloved dog Blu taken at Boom Lake in Banff National Park, Alberta.

VALOUR (p.101)

Catherine MacKenzie, Fall Lake, Nova Scotia
Catherine shares a great shot of her grandfather Harry Thompson MacKenzie leading the troops as a member of the Canadian Armed Forces Reserves.

MEMORIES (p.149)

Liz Youngman, Ottawa, Ontario
Liz shares this peaceful image snapped by her partner Barb Gray, by the lake in Bowman, Quebec.

ADVENTURE (p.191)

Tyler Dixon, Calgary, Alberta
Tyler enjoying the beautiful view at Sunshine Village Ski Resort in Banff, Alberta.

COMMUNITY (p.227)

Leanne Smith, Calgary, Alberta
Leanne snapped this awesome picture of the Indian Village while attending the Calgary Stampede several years ago.

TALENT (p.277)

Timothy Mohan, Elliot Lake, Ontario
Tim shares one of his incredible pieces of art called "Two of Us."

BACK COVER

Edwood Brooker, Burlington, Ontario

FOREWORD

Long Story Short

Hi there! I'm the lead editor of *Our Canada* magazine and I'm absolutely thrilled that you're holding our new book in your hands. If you're an avid reader with a passion for this great land we so proudly call home, I think you're in for a treat. I've been editing *Our Canada* since 2006 and, prior to that, I spent two years writing promotional material in support of the then newly minted "reader-written magazine" published by Reader's Digest Magazines Canada.

If there's one thing I've come to appreciate over the years, it's that the old saying is true—everyone does indeed have at least one great story to tell. You'll see what I mean as soon as you dive into the 120-plus story selections that follow, all of which were originally published in *Our Canada* or its companion magazine, *More of Our Canada,* during the past five years.

But before you do, I'd like to share *Our Canada*'s story with you—well, the condensed version at least.

Our Canada was launched as a bimonthly publication in January 2004, following an overwhelmingly successful "Show Us Your Canada" contest held in *Reader's Digest* magazine the previous year. The *Reader's Digest* editorial team at the time waded through all of the contest entries, and then selected and fleshed out the content that appeared in *Our Canada*'s highly successful premier issue. With that original blueprint in place, a small editorial team dedicated to *Our Canada* was created and the magazine was off to the races in earnest. By September 2005, *Our Canada* had grown from zero subscriptions to 250,000, becoming in the process one of the most successful Canadian magazine launches of that era. In a nutshell, the new magazine "written by Canadians, for Canadians" went viral in print, long before "going viral" became a phenomenon on the Internet.

In September 2008, responding to a growing number of subscribers who wished to receive *Our Canada* 12 times a year instead of the usual six, we introduced *More of Our Canada,* a subscriber-only publication scheduled for delivery during the "in-between months" of *Our Canada*'s bimonthly publication calendar.

Moving forward from that point, we solidified our online presence on www.ourcanada.ca, where most of the incoming submissions are accepted and categorized, and jumped onto the growing social-media bandwagon, primarily via our Facebook page. While generating ongoing momentum for our two magazine publications, and engaging with a highly active and loyal social media following, we also produced two hardcover books of photography and collaborated on a third one about travel in Canada. In 2014, we started up our iPad edition and more recently we've been accepted onto popular digital magazine platforms such as Texture, Google Play, PressReader and Zinio.

Fuelling the magazines' ongoing popularity to this very day is a steady flow of reader-written stories and photo submissions sent in to us by everyday Canadians from across the country, representing a wide range of age groups, walks of life, cultural backgrounds, interests and pursuits. From rural hamlets to major urban centres, remote northern outposts to southern border towns, fishing villages in the Maritimes and Newfoundland and Labrador to the First Nations cultural sanctuary of Haida Gwaii, B.C.—and everywhere in between—*Our Canada* is above all a gathering place for all Canadians. We strive to be a venue where everyone is welcome and invited to share their memories and experiences, hopes and aspirations, and love for this wonderful country of ours.

Being "reader-written," we do not engage the services of professional writers but rather select and polish written submissions sent in to us by the everyday people of Canada, regular folks just like you and me. And therein lie two of my favourite aspects of the job that my colleague, Senior Editor Maryanne Gallagher, and I are privileged to perform: firstly, reading through all of the amazing stories sent our way, which number in the thousands, and, secondly, reaching out to those individuals whose submissions are selected to appear in an upcoming issue and working with them to make their story the best it can possibly be. Editorially, our aim here is to point out and see that any gaps in a submission are filled; make sure the facts being presented are accurate; and edit for length as well as consistency of writing style and grammar—all the while maintaining the contributor's natural tone of voice and turn of phrase.

For our readers, from one issue to the next, the end result is a wonderful snapshot of Canada on any given day, focusing on shared memories and adventures; family, culture and community; talents, hobbies and interests; and an overall love of Canada and its people, places and wildlife. As a gesture of thanks for their participation, selected contributors receive a free copy of the issue in which their submission appears and a free one-year gift subscription. More importantly, I believe, our published contributors reap the satisfaction of seeing their work through to completion—and of being able to share it not only with their inner circle of family, friends and neighbours but also with a national audience of well over one million Canadians.

On the following pages, with the collaboration of book editor Pamela Johnson, designer Olena Lytvyn and proofreader Joan Page McKenna, we've compiled a representative sampling of the type of stories we present in every issue of *Our Canada* and *More of Our Canada.* Drawing upon content from our core departments, we've structured the book along thematic lines, focusing on values and topics to which most Canadians can relate: Family, Kindness, Valour, Memories, Adventure, Community and Talent. As you'll soon see, the stories span the country and generations of life in Canada, touching upon many of the cultures and traditions that make up our great Canadian mosaic.

Being able to share with you in book form for the first time these wonderfully down-to-earth, inspiring, funny, and at times very moving submissions is both an honour and a pleasure for all of us here at *Our Canada.* Enjoy!

—***Gary George***, *Editor-in-Chief,* **Our Canada** *magazine*

TABLE OF CONTENTS

FAMILY

It's what makes us resilient
and keeps us strong—
the joys, sorrows, humour
and wisdom of family life

Tapping the Trees

Fond memories of time spent with Dad in the sugar snow

Big, fat flakes land on my upturned face. I stick out my tongue and taste the moist sugar snow. Instantly, I am transported back to when I was eight years old on our farm in the Eastern Townships of Quebec. The sap was running—my favourite time of year!

I was outside with my little brother, Billy, when I noticed the shed door open and ran to see what Dad was doing. He was sitting on a small stool, surrounded by wooden sap buckets, holding each one up towards the window and peering inside.

"What are you doing, Daddy? Are we going to put the sap buckets on the trees today?"

"As soon as I finish checking for cracks," he said. "See, when I hold them up to the window, the light shines through the cracks—so far, only two. I'll put those in water and the wood will expand, filling in the cracks, and then they're as good as new."

"Can I come? I can help." He looked at me, reached over and touched the top of my head,

"Oh, you think you can help, do you? What can you do?"

"I can hand you those little things you put in the trees."

"Okay, but first go and tell your mother, so she can watch Billy."

After taking Billy to Mom, I went to the barn, where Dad was hitching June and Sandy to the big sleigh with sides that he used for hauling logs from the bush. We placed the buckets in the back of the sleigh and I scrambled onto the front seat, close to Dad, as he started the horses with his usual: "Hey there, giddup." Starting out, Dad kept saying: "Whoa there, slow down, easy, easy. They want to run, Shirl. It's been a long winter; getting out in the warm spring air makes them frisky. Whoa, Sandy, take it easy."

Dad always spoke softly to the horses, I guess much like he did with us. A quiet, gentle man, my father, wanting only enough to feed and clothe his family. Independent, willing to help his neighbours in times of need, but mostly content to stay on his own farm, working with his animals and reading in the quiet evenings. On cold winter nights, my sisters and brothers and I would curl up beside him on the couch and listen to stories from the Bible while Mom sat in the rocker with her knitting or mending.

We reached the sugar bush, stopping at the first maple tree. Dad began drilling a tiny hole in the trunk of the tree, just about even with the top of my head. Setting the drill aside, he picked up his hammer and I handed him one of the spouts, which he hammered in place.

The spouts had a little hook on the bottom where he placed the metal handle of the bucket. Instantly, the sap started dripping with a delightful splash as it hit the bottom.

"I like sap better than when it turns into maple syrup, don't you, Dad? Can I taste some now?"

"Not yet. When we get back from tapping the rest of the trees, there'll be enough sap in here and we'll both have a good drink."

Back to the sleigh, on to the next tree, weaving our way through the sugar bush, the branches brushing against us, the snow filtering down softly through the billowy tree tops. It's a wonderful memory that returns to me every March, when the sugar snow lands on my tongue and I remember the sweet, mapley taste of sap.

*—by **Shirley Davidson Bonic**, Regina, Saskatchewan*

The Curling Kettle

Getting a handle on this popular winter pastime just takes a little imagination

About eight years ago, when I was in Grade 4, two of my 12 siblings—Joline and Jason—and I joined our school's Little Rockers Curling Club. After attending our first practice, we were so pleased with it that we decided we needed to curl every day of the week. Unfortunately, a farm in rural Saskatchewan does not have too many curling rinks waiting to be used—unless, of course, you use your imagination.

First off, we needed ice. It must have been our lucky day, because we discovered a frozen slough out in the pasture that was pretty smooth. Even better, it had no snow on it, thanks to the howling Saskatchewan winds.

We rushed to the house with excitement and grabbed our brooms, planning to head out to curl. Then we remembered that we didn't have sliders—but that didn't stop us. We took care of the problem by putting generous amounts of duct tape on the bottom of our boots. Now we were ready to curl. Then we realized that there was still a gaping hole in our plan. We didn't have any curling rocks.

What could we use? We started to search through the house. Yes! Mom's kettle would do wonderfully. It was the next best thing to a curling rock. We took off out of the house with the kettle in tow and slid out onto the slough. Much to our dismay, it was too windy for the kettle to do anything but blow off course.

Well, we were determined, so we put our heads together. If we filled it with water, we thought, surely it would be heavy enough. When that was put to the test, the water kept sloshing out of the top. So now what? We still had one last idea to try. We filled the kettle with water once more and froze it before trying again. This time, it worked like a charm. Our curling rink was a success and we spent many hours out on that slough.

Eventually, the novelty began to wear off and before long we abandoned our game. The slough became covered with hard snowdrifts and we moved on to more exciting winter activities.

Spring came, our curling rink melted and the kettle sank to the bottom of the slough. Oops. Mom had to buy herself a new kettle. From time to time, she still wonders what happened to the original kettle. Personally, I think it made one of the finest curling rocks ever!

*— by **Lynnae Ylioja**, Macrorie, Saskatchewan*

The Debonaire

Classy and timeless, this "old" boat is still a part of the family

I was taking the kids fishing for the evening. Approaching the docks, fishing rods and tackle boxes in hand, my son's friend asked, "Which boat is yours?"

"You see that fancy orange one that says 'Moomba'?" I replied.

The boy's eyes widened, his mouth beginning to form the words, "No waa..."

"Ours is behind that one," I said.

Back in the summer of 1979, my dad decided our family needed a boat, and I recall the exact instant when this decision formed in his mind. We'd been out fishing on a big Manitoba lake in a friend's 12-foot fishing boat with an ancient sputtering engine when a summer storm blew in. Miles from the boat launch and with nowhere to take shelter, we proceeded to drive headlong into the wind and waves—as you are supposed to do, my dad assured us—for what seemed an eternity.

Somewhere between trying to keep his cigarette lit and ordering us to sit in a way to balance the tiny boat—which miraculously seemed to keep the three-foot swells from spilling over the bow and gunnels—the thought must have crystalized in my dad's head. "We need a bigger boat."

In 1980, a "bigger boat" meant something different than it does today. Back then, for our family of four, a bigger boat meant a 16-foot aluminum boat with a 20-horsepower engine equipped with—and I cannot overstate the importance that this feature held for my older brother Darrin and me—a steering wheel.

My dad pulled the shiny metal miracle into the driveway one cool spring evening and the impression it left on me has never waned. The boat glimmered. Made entirely of polished and buffed aluminum, it reflected light like a kaleidoscope. It had a windshield, bow, steering wheel, a gear and throttle control console, and a canopy with zip-out windows. On the "dashboard" was riveted a stylish bronze crest that said "Aroliner."

That evening, Darrin and I crawled all over the boat. We looked under the bow, sat in each of the possible places to sit, and, though the boat was on a trailer in the driveway, we fought desperately over who got to "drive." We took turns making engine sounds and steering the wheel—avoiding imagined icebergs, tidal waves and bad guys. I remember asking, "Can we sleep in it?"

"Maybe some night, but not tonight," my dad said.

We were shuffled off inside wondering when that night would be. As my brother and I made our way to bed, we looked out at the boat. Now it was his turn. My dad crawled all over the boat, looked under the bow and sat in each of the seats. Then he sat in the driver's seat—I remind you that the boat was on a trailer in our driveway. We watched him light a cigarette, then dangle it off the side while placing his other hand on the steering wheel and practiced slow graceful turns. I always imagined he was making engine sounds.

The Aroliner Boat Company manufactured aluminum boats in its St. Boniface shop in Winnipeg from the 1930s through to the early 1990s. I recall passing the boat shop as a kid and seeing all the boats in stock neatly organized, stood on end and leaning on each other like men standing in a line. The boats came in a variety of styles and names, each connoting a certain characteristic of the design. Our boat was from the Debonaire line. "It means classy," my dad said.

Docked humbly in the shadow of today's brightly painted and more garish vessels, there continues to be a subtle class to the old Debonaire. With timeless, smart lines, the Debonaire was the everyman's entry into the world of boating. Humble. Smart. Practical. Classiness is like that. Debonair remains the best word to describe the old boat that again sits smartly among its louder, larger, often tattooed descendants.

We used the Debonaire for a number of years—the important years. My uncles bought similar boats and for about a decade we would make an annual fishing trip somewhere in Manitoba or northern Ontario. An extended family fishing derby was established and I recall the thrill of the convoy as three or four carloads of uncles, aunts and cousins—shiny aluminum boats in tow—would rendezvous, then wind its way from the Prairies to the dark forests of Whiteshell and Nopiming parks.

On a return trip to the Manitoba lake where the idea to get a bigger boat initially took shape, we set up a day camp on a small island. Fishing from the shore with Darrin and Mom, I remember watching Dad repeatedly cruise towards us at full speed, turning away at what seemed like the last minute, leaving a generous, frothy trail in his wake.

I couldn't figure out what he was doing. I wondered if something was wrong with the engine or if he was testing to make sure the steering was working. "He's having so much fun," Mom said. Fun. Oh, right. It wasn't a word we often associated with my dad, but as he sped past again, I could see him smiling, one hand on the wheel, the other dangling a cigarette over the side. Fun. So that's what it looked like. We didn't say anything. We just stood and watched and smiled with him.

Long before I would be able to drive a car, I'd honed the careful art of steering and navigating a boat: Careful, intentional, planned. Nothing jerky, nothing sudden. Once the criteria of learning to prime and pull-start the 20-horsepower Evinrude was mastered, permission was a mere formality. Learning to drive the boat on my own was a bigger rite of passage than getting my driver's licence. Probably because I was only 13 years old, the significance of being trusted by my parents to take the boat from shore to a fishing hole for an hour or two was a form of freedom that is hard to explain. But Darrin and I experienced it often. We took the boat. We fished. We smoked.

We caught a lot of fish in that boat and we confidently navigated many stretches of rough waters, laughing as it bumped and rocked its way to many ports of call. But, with time, the boat eventually frequented the waters less and less. Like many "old boats," it became a bit of a yard fixture, a default storage container for life's odds and ends, the buffed aluminum hidden for years beneath raggedy blue tarpaulins.

"You should come and get it if you want it," my dad said a few years back in a moment of downsizing. "If you don't want it, we'll probably just sell it." We made the epic late-summer journey from our home near Saskatoon to Winnipeg to retrieve the old boat. Our Debonaire was built in 1964. We'd bought it in 1980. It was a classy boat in its day. It served us well. I wondered if times had changed. I wondered if I had. Did I really want the boat? Would it serve my new family well?

The Debonaire's new port of call is just east of Prince Albert National Park. Its motor still starts in a single pull. After dropping my kids off at the dock, I often take it out for a solo cruise. I cut smooth, steady curves and occasionally look back at the s-shaped wake that slowly disappears into the surface waves, the boat's signature, its past. If I still smoked, I'd dangle my cigarette over the edge.

*—by **Brad Nichol**, Rosthern, Saskatchewan*

An Occasion Fit for a Queen

Owning the first television on the block made for an anxious but thrilling Tuesday afternoon in 1953

We got our very first television set in 1953, the year of Queen Elizabeth II's coronation. For weeks, Mom, desperate to watch the ceremony, had cajoled, nagged and begged Dad to buy a TV. Being a frugal man, he had put up a good fight, but we all knew that in the end he would lose.

My two sisters, Elaine and Joan, and I jumped for joy at the 17-inch black-and-white monster. We felt pretty special, as we were the first ones on the street to own a TV.

It took Dad two days to set up the television in the den. He struggled with the "rabbit ears" antenna, dangling it just right in order to get the test pattern to come in clearly. It was well worth his effort: We spent the weekend indoors watching all the grainy programs while Mom organized her coronation party.

On the morning of June 2, the day of the coronation, Dad was not happy. Mom, convinced that the TV room was too small to accommodate all the people she expected, insisted that the TV be placed on the sideboard in the dining room. Moving the TV, struggling with the pattern and knowing that he would have to repeat the procedure and move it back into the TV room after the coronation program made for a very frustrated person. Not a man to swear, I won't mention what words quietly escaped under his breath.

Mom spent her morning in a kitchen that smelled of minced ham, celery and eggs as she made large platters of sandwiches. The crusts she'd cut off the bread ended up being our lunch, as there was enough of the filling left on them to satisfy our hunger. I brought the completed sandwich platters down to the cold storage in the basement and lingered as I secretly ate one of each kind.

After lunch, we placed all the chairs we had in the house in rows throughout the living and dining rooms. As the afternoon progressed, Mom's anxiety became more evident. She talked too fast, kept running up and down the stairs to put things away, fluffed up all the pillows, put out extra ashtrays and barked orders at my sisters and me. We could hardly wait for the guests to arrive.

Her stress was understandable. Since we owned the only television on our block, Mom had sent out an open invitation to the neighbours on our street. She had no idea how many would show up. What would happen if everyone came? Or worse, if no one came? I kept thinking of the delicious sandwiches downstairs and hoped for the latter.

As broadcast time approached, a stream of neighbours marched into the house and filled the chairs; many were left standing. Like the ringing of a bell, at the sound of the national anthem, everyone became quiet and stood up. Dad, a member of the RCMP, almost saluted. From then on, people talked in whispers, entranced with the wonder of watching the solemn ceremony being beamed into our living room.

An hour after the program began, Mom had not moved from her chair, mesmerized by the sights and sounds on the television.

"Mom! Aren't you going to serve the sandwiches?" I asked.

"You do it," she answered. I fetched the sandwiches from the basement, my sister Elaine got the cheese platter and we served them to our guests.

By the time the coronation party was over, Mom was all smiles at the success of her get-together and all the sandwiches were gone. God save the Queen! The only thing left to do was move the television back into the TV room, but that job would have to wait for tomorrow. Why ruin a good day?

*—by **Louise Szabo**, Nepean, Ontario*

Achieving Their Goal

By working as a team, this determined prairie family made their hockey dreams come true

The dream of six aspiring hockey players began on our farm in Grassy Lake, Alberta. Their ultimate goal was to become a renowned hockey family, enjoying the winter sport they cherished. In 1937, making a living on a dry land farm made it difficult to feed ten children, never mind outfitting six sons with hockey equipment. I had six brothers and three sisters; I was the youngest, and not yet old enough to play.

With our meagre living conditions, my brothers knew they could not afford the necessary hockey equipment, so they talked our mother into making it on her Singer sewing machine. Using her creativity and sewing skills, she fashioned elbow and shin pads, hockey pants, gloves and a set of goalie pads, all out of canvas. She then stuffed the protective pads with straw and Eaton's catalogues.

With such a large family to care for, the only time Mom had to sew was after bedtime, usually well past midnight. Imagine how difficult it must have been, sewing this hockey equipment by the light of a coal oil lamp; who knows how many needles she must have broken sewing through canvas and padding. After Mom completed her work, my six brothers—Rex, Lloyd, Pat, Bert, Jerry and Jack—pooled their money together and bought Toronto Maple Leaf sweaters from the Eaton's catalogue.

Due to the limited number of hockey rinks in the small Alberta towns of Grassy Lake, Burdett and Bow Island, my brothers, along with our dad, decided to make their own hockey rink on a coulee on our farm. Using horsepower and a slip scraper, they levelled the earth for a rink. They then hauled water from a free-flowing artesian well, three miles away, using a wooden-wheeled water tank. It took eight trips to make a single sheet of ice.

In those years, temperatures on the Prairies could drop as low as –40°F, but the boys persevered and hauled water over a number of days. If a warm southern Alberta chinook blew in, the process would have to be started all over again.

Once the rink was built, the boys realized they needed a shack to change in. With Dad's help, they found an abandoned 15-by-20-foot shack and, after lifting it onto skids, they used horses to haul it rinkside. Overcoming all odds, the Knibbs family began to realize their hockey dream; my three sisters, our mom and I became the fan base.

It didn't take long for word of the coulee rink to spread to nearby communities. The Knibbs "Leaf" hockey team began challenging other teams from surrounding towns to games, with hockey players arriving by horse-drawn sleigh, car or on horseback. Every weekend, the sound of clashing hockey sticks and bodies echoed through the hills, while cheering fans surrounded the rink.

The Knibbs "Leaf" team lineup was determined by their abilities. Jack, the sixth son, was in goal and Rex, the eldest, and Jerry, the fifth born, manned the defence. The forward line consisted of Lloyd, Pat and Bert, sons number two, three and four respectively. Our father, Jack, was the referee for the weekend hockey games, but showed no favouritism towards his sons. He taught us the values of determination, sportsmanship and honesty. When a penalty needed to be called, Dad did it immediately and never hesitated to send one of his own sons to the penalty box.

Unfortunately, the Knibbs family coulee hockey dream only lasted for two years, from 1937 to 1939, due to the onset of the Second World War. Rex, Lloyd and Pat were drafted into the army in 1940 and sent overseas. By the grace of God, all three returned home safely.

Although the hockey dream had ended for the older Knibbs brothers, Bert was selected to play for the Lethbridge Maple Leafs hockey team, which represented Canada in the 1949-1950 World Hockey Amateur Championships in Paris. The team came home victorious after winning the trophy and, thanks to Bert's success, the Knibbs family fully realized their hockey dream.

Bert became an inspiration to many of his nephews and other young players in southern Alberta. Throughout his life, he coached many of the youths in the town of Bow Island, where he lived. One young player named Troy Loney, who Bert mentored, was later drafted into the National Hockey League.

Throughout the years, our six brothers were an inspiration to my sisters and me. I was only three years old back in 1937, but the memories of those days and our family's coulee hockey team are an important part of my past. The lessons learned remain with me to this day.

*—by **Bill L. Knibbs**, Medicine Hat, Alberta*

The Georgetown Boys

A proud Armenian immigrant gives back to the country that welcomed him as part of "Canada's Noble Experiment"

From a humble orphan's beginnings to an outspoken public figure, my father, Albert Papazian, served his country well. Born in Aintab, Turkey, in 1911, Dad would have been around five during the dire Armenian genocide that occurred from 1915 to 1917.

Along with his mother, brother and sister, he escaped to Aleppo, Syria, after his father died during the First World War—presumably as a result of the genocide, although Dad never confirmed that. Fatherless, the family roamed the Middle East for about three years. My dad said, "As a boy, I remember being hungry and cold a lot of the time, wandering from one place to another, scrounging crumbs here and there and sleeping wherever we could find shelter."

In 1921, his poor mother, who died a year later, surrendered her children to an orphanage in Lebanon. Dad was only ten at the time. Five years later, Dad and his brother were sent to Canada. Fortunately for them, they were selected to be part of an experiment in refugee support. "Canada's Noble Experiment," as it was called, was the first humanitarian act on an international scale by our country.

An article in the Toronto *Globe* on February 28, 1923, titled "Shall We Let Them Die?" enlightened Canadians to the plight of the many Armenians in Aleppo, Syria. It described how the Armenian Relief Association planned to bring about 100 boys, mostly teenagers, to a farm in Georgetown, Ontario. The first group of 50 arrived in Georgetown on July 1, 1923.

The Toronto *Globe* continued its effort to encourage and publicize Canadian efforts in support of the Armenian refugee cause. In an item dated April 18, 1923, under the title "Little Armenians Will Be Welcome to Home in Canada," it gave the little town of St. Marys, Ontario, due credit for its campaign to raise funds. In another article on April 23, Woodstock and Oxford County came in for praise for having pledged the sum of $4,000 in aid.

Dad arrived in Georgetown in 1926 at the age of 15; by 1927, a total of 100 Armenian orphans had arrived there. Dad spent only about a month at the Georgetown orphanage before being indentured to a Dunnville, Ontario, farmer. He put himself through high school by taking night classes while working full time.

At 27, he entered the Ontario Agricultural College in Guelph, one of the few Georgetown boys to receive any post-secondary education, and graduated in 1942 with a Bachelor of Science degree in agriculture. After marrying Molly Gilmore, an Irish immigrant, he bought a farm in Winona and they continued to work it till 1990.

In the 1970s, Dad organized reunions for the Georgetown boys at the farm in Georgetown. The farmhouse is still there, in Cedarvale Park, now designated as an Ontario Heritage Site.

"I have always felt the need to make a contribution to the country that accepted me when I was in need," Dad said after accepting the Stoney Creek Chamber of Commerce's Citizen of the Year Award in 1980. That sense of service to Canada drove Dad to hold office as a Stoney Creek councillor between 1973 and 1980 and to help found the Georgetown Armenian Boys Association. He also helped found the Saltfleet Growers Co-operative and the Winona Peach Festival, a centennial project started in 1967 that is still held today. Dad passed away at the age of 79 in 1990 and is still missed.

*—by **Ed Papazian**, Kanata, Ontario*

Family Ties

Four generations of Bourassas gather every spring to share love and laughter

My maternal grandparents, Leo and Marie Bourassa, called Plamondon, Alberta, home all their lives. They married in 1946 and raised a family of nine. As the children left home, married and started families of their own, the need to enjoy time all together prompted the first Bourassa family reunion back in the early 1980s. Every year since, our family has reunited on the long weekend in May.

At first, we'd gather at my grandparents' cabin at Bayview Beach on the shore of Lac la Biche; later we moved the reunion across the bay to a rental facility with a baseball diamond, campfire area, kitchen hall and a few cabins.

The families would pack up food, toys for the kids, trailers, quads and, of course, winter gear, just in case! It wouldn't be a May long weekend if not for a little snow—or at least the fear of it!

One of our favourite traditions during the weekend is our annual entertainment night. Over the years, family members have performed skits from TV shows such as *Gilligan's Island,* and movies such as *The Sound of Music,* as well as magic acts and even ninja fight scenes. We've also recited poems and written original lyrics to the tunes of popular songs. One year, our "older" uncles dressed up and attempted a hip-hop number! We laugh and cry our way through all these acts.

I think one thing that makes our reunions so special is that our family makes the effort to come together from near and far. What started out as a group of about 15 has grown every year—through births and weddings—and now numbers from 50 to 80 people. What began as a small family tradition is now an annual event that brings together four generations.

Food is a big component for such a large family. Each of the nine siblings and their families are responsible for one meal during the weekend. This process includes buying, prepping, cooking, serving and cleanup. Grandma kept track of who did what meal every year so that breakfasts, lunches and suppers were divided equally. This works wonderfully, as once you've done your meal, you can sit back and relax for the rest of the weekend.

In the evenings, through wind, rain, sleet or snow, we sit around the campfire wearing layers of clothing or wrapped in blankets. Bags of chips, nuts and chocolates get passed around. Sometimes we sing, other times we debate, but mostly we share stories.

During the day, our time is spent playing everything from football and baseball to running relay races. Saturday is typically reserved for riding our ATVs over muddy trails.

Sunday afternoon is spent playing bingo, called out by Grandma. The great-grandchildren, including my own kids, love to participate. There are always prizes for the winners.

My grandfather died some time ago and, sadly, we recently had our first May reunion without my grandma, as she has passed away now too. It's important that we continue this family tradition and pass it on to our kids and their kids to come. When Grandma passed away, the first thing my kids asked was whether we'd still all get together over the May long weekend. Of course, the answer was yes, because—thanks to my grandparents—we have learned that staying connected is what's important.

*—by **Adrienne Ulliac**, Whitecourt, Alberta*

A-Camping We Will Go

Despite having five kids and little money, family vacations were wonderful, thanks to Dad's can-do attitude

When I was growing up, my parents, Clarke and Gwen Kennedy, took my siblings and me on many camping trips. At first, it was in borrowed hardtop trailers that my father, an Ontario Provincial Police officer, had helped various friends to build. Having five children in our family meant that we needed a trailer large enough to accommodate all of us and we didn't have a lot of money.

Then, one time while travelling through Sault Ste. Marie, Ontario, my father spotted an American-made tent trailer and decided that he could build one like it himself. He took several pictures of it and worked for hours in the garage, using plywood and thin-wall conduit for the tent frame. Measurements were sent to a place in Quebec and the resulting heavy-duty blue canvas fit perfectly over the top. The tent trailer was basically a box with a tent on top; the lid of the box opened out on each end to provide beds and the tent fit over top of all of it. Large enough to handle our family, it measured 16 feet from end to end when fully opened. The box itself was eight feet in length and seven feet wide.

It wasn't a luxury trailer: There was no bathroom or kitchen, and we had to rough it and head down the road to use the outhouse. But it was comfortable, providing a double bed for my parents at one end with another double bed at the other end for two of us girls. Inside the box part of the trailer, a board was laid across the countertops and this provided another bed for two more girls, while my brother slept on a cot on the floor.

Dad built a camp kitchen, which held our dishes and a two-burner gas stove. This was packed into the tent trailer once it was closed up. We only had a problem once, when the gas stove was not turned off completely and started to smoulder in the closed-up tent trailer! Fortunately, it was discovered early and put out.

Each of us had our own jobs to do when setting up or packing up the tent trailer. My dad took pride in the fact that it could be put up or taken down within ten minutes when we were all doing our part.

As we would be setting up, Mom would be preparing meals for us in the camp kitchen. It must have been a challenge for her, especially dealing with bugs and working in the rain at times.

One of the most ambitious trips I remember taking was in 1963. We left Englehart, Ontario, and travelled across Canada, heading to the West Coast and northern British Columbia—a long trip to make with five children. The tent trailer was set up and taken down many times on that trip and declared a success. In 1968, we pulled it from Burk's Falls, Ontario, all the way to the East Coast. We used that tent trailer for ten years, travelling around Ontario and Quebec; it provided many memories for all of us.

These days, as my husband and I travel in our 27-foot luxury trailer, I often think of that homemade trailer and how it provided us with so much fun and gave us the opportunity to see so much of Canada as a family. And it was all because one man decided to build his own tent trailer, allowing his family to experience the wonders of this land. I credit those trips with giving me the love of camping and travelling that I still have today.

*—by **Betty Moore**, West Guilford, Ontario*

Macaroni Sundays

For this 1950s family, there was nothing better than Dad's mac 'n' cheese served in front of the TV

It was the 1950s. Television was still in its infancy and sitting around the living room watching TV as a family actually brought people together—unlike today's technological world of personal devices.

Dad would prepare a Sunday dinner casserole that was a scrumptious, flavourful mix of elbow macaroni, stewed tomatoes, tomato sauce and aged cheddar cheese. And there were no store-bought tomatoes for us; Mom had grown them in our large vegetable garden, then spent painstaking hours simmering, peeling and canning them in Mason jars to store in the root cellar.

"Bill, what are you doing with my canned tomatoes?" my mother shrieked.

"They'll add flavour to the macaroni casserole. What are you saving them for?" he said with a wink. It was true. Rows of canned peaches, pears and tomatoes lined the shelves in the coolest and driest part of our basement, being saved for a rainy day.

Dad had special touches when cooking, such as adding an egg and some milk to our mashed potatoes as he whipped them into a bowl of fluffy deliciousness. As the eldest child in his family, Dad was no stranger to cooking. At age 12, he'd been expected to have dinner on the table when his parents arrived home from their gruelling factory jobs. Dad had learned to make apple pie, beef stew, poached eggs and the pièce de résistance—roast beef with roasted potatoes and Yorkshire pudding.

With my parents sharing the cooking, we were in many ways quite modern for the '50s. My mother re-entered the workforce when my younger sister started school, making me responsible for dinner at age 12 as well. This interfered with watching *Dick Clark's American Bandstand* and learning the latest dances. Once, while watching a dance contest, I saw flames leaping from the frying pan. I rushed in to save the day just in time. After that I learned to stay close to whatever I was cooking. I would get dinner started by setting the table, peeling the potatoes and chopping the vegetables. Dad would arrive home from work and give me pointers, teaching me how to cook.

Dad, of medium height and wearing his flannel shirt and cotton pants held up by suspenders, would peer out from his dark-rimmed glasses at the pots and frying pans, making adjustments, frying or simmering. He had big blue eyes, an open smile and a kind heart. To a girl like me, who did not take naturally to domesticity, he was patient and kind and never scolded (unlike my mother). Though we worked as a team, I left the real cooking to him. He knew his way around a kitchen and took pride in his fast and easy macaroni and cheese that we fussy eaters simply devoured.

Completing the casserole, Dad would pop it in the oven to merge the flavours. The cheddar made a crunchy, gooey top crust. Then we all gathered in front of the box to watch a much-anticipated movie—*Tarzan*. The TV station ran this type of action adventure film every Sunday. There was no question that it was family-friendly fare with Cheeta, the precocious chimp, adding humour with his zany antics and Boy (Tarzan's adopted son), played by Johnny Sheffield, rounding out the jungle family. Though many actors played the Edgar Rice Burroughs hero, truly it was Olympic gold medal swimmer Johnny Weissmuller who was the quintessential ape-man.

Each film had swimming sequences and battles with crocodiles, but the greatest battle Tarzan fought was with encroaching Europeans trying to ruin the harmony of the jungle by capturing wildlife illegally or harassing local tribes. Each film had Tarzan emitting his distinctive yodelling yell as he swung through the vines on a rescue mission. *Tarzan's New York Adventure* (1942) was my favourite, with Tarzan looking uncomfortable in a suit and then discovering the "hotel waterfalls" (really a shower) and standing under it wearing his suit. Soft-spoken Jane was there to bridge the gap.

During commercial breaks, we'd all dash to the kitchen to fill our plates as Dad served us. Breaking through the crusty cheese topping, with the aroma of tomatoes escaping, Dad spooned the gooey mixture onto our plates. We'd place our dinner plates on the coffee table or on special TV trays—metal trays with legs—so our knees fit nicely underneath. Imagine creating furniture for this purpose!

Dessert was served as we segued into *Walt Disney's Wonderful World of Color*. Earlier in the afternoon, Mom had cut up bananas and oranges into a large glass bowl. Typical kids, we craved sweets such as ice cream, chocolate chip cookies or butter tarts. Luckily for us, Mom limited sugar consumption. I can thank her today for my love of fruit and my trim waistline.

The crowning glory of Sunday night television was *The Ed Sullivan Show.* This strange, wizened, stone-faced emcee, a former New York entertainment columnist, had an eye for talent. His was the longest-running variety show in the history of television. To appear on his show was a hallmark of success. If you could sit through the plate spinners, juggling acts and smarmy crooners, you could see "live and on our stage" the greats of rock 'n' roll: Elvis Presley, The Beatles, The Doors and the Rolling Stones. Ed was the first host to break racial barriers and have African-American greats like Harry Belafonte and Nat King Cole perform.

When Elvis performed "Hound Dog" in 1956 with his gyrations, the teenage girls in the audience screamed and swooned. My three-year-old sister Wendy mimicked them, squealing and hurling her little body against the back of the soft sofa in mock faint. My parents got more laughs out of her that night than the stand-up comedians.

When I think of comfort food, it takes me back to those early times with my nuclear family. Fare such as grilled cheese sandwiches, hot chocolate and especially the macaroni and cheese, lovingly prepared by my dad.

*—by **Gail M. Murray**, Scarborough, Ontario*

When We Were Young

Looking back with fondness to a simpler time

I grew up with a baker's dozen siblings: I was the ninth child of 14. Although large families were common in our hamlet in Cape Breton, 14 children was on the high side of average.

Unfortunately, good living, fresh air and hard work weren't enough to save our father, any more than positive thoughts and novenas were. He succumbed to cancer at the age of 52, leaving my mother a young widow with many mouths to feed and never enough money.

While Mama perfected the craft of making meals out of practically nothing, we had chores to do and we did them obediently so as to get back to our games—games that were created on the spot, as toys were not a part of our lives. Everyone had a voice or an idea; whether the age was three or three times three, every opinion was heard. In retrospect, I realize how much respect we had for one another. The only hurtful remark ever used was to call someone a slink, whatever that meant in those days.

Having a full complement of playmates, we didn't need to go looking for an extra body to make up a team. Since our school system didn't have kindergarten, we were six or seven years old before any formal education took over. In the meantime, we had the whole outdoors as our playground, where we regularly created "bet you can't" games that kept us busy and out of trouble.

Resembling scarecrows with our flapping arms, we attempted the perfect balance needed to walk the fences that surrounded our property: rounded poles about six inches in diameter that required total concentration and held no mercy for a stumbler. Anyone trying to make the walker laugh and lose his or her balance would, at the very least, lose a turn.

Kicking our height while the broom was held at the proper level required balance and speed. These evening games were perfected in the big kitchen while Mama knitted and the little ones lay on the floor fashioning rustic houses out of kindling wood. We continually challenged ourselves. For one, climbing the almost vertical bank to reach the house instead of walking the few extra steps to the lane was a daily event. This involved taking a brisk run, then leaping at the precise moment to clear the ditch before climbing the rest of the way.

We walked to and from school at a marathon pace. As the distance was approximately a mile and a half each way, some of us got our time down to 15 minutes while carrying at least two books, scribblers, our lunch and whatever else was needed. Riding a bike backward was another one—was the genesis of Cirque du Soleil born in Mabou, Nova Scotia?

Comparing and measuring arm muscles doesn't usually favour the girls, but my sisters didn't disappoint. In fact, one was a definite threat that kept the boys "pumping iron."

We learned to fashion a seat out of two sets of hands that could transport the injured or tired. Riding horses and even cows, once, required extreme bravery, as one of the horses had a "no riding" attitude and meant it, while another was a racehorse. Was it bravery or innocence that propelled us towards possible danger?

One brother was interested in fishing and was accompanied by his sister on an outing. All was quiet as he tempted the trout while his sister watched closely, leaning on a branch jutting out over the water. Just as the fish were closing in for their treat, the branch gave way, taking her into the brook with it. Soaked and blubbering, she knew it was best to keep her distance as she sloshed home behind him.

Jumping off the Bailey bridge into the water some 20-odd feet below was a kind of initiation for the newbie, while "old hands" continued to take the plunge. Even an uncle would occasionally take the leap, to the delight of his young relatives. Summertime Sundays were usually spent waving at passing cars and checking for "foreign" licence plates. We would have been useful to the tourist board, as we knew which states provided the most visitors to our province.

Looking back, I realize we mastered whatever we attempted, as we all had the same determination to climb the hill, jump over the bank or kick the broom. We used our imaginations to our advantage without knowing, at the time, that we were teaching ourselves coordination, concentration and the appreciation of the joy of companionship.

What we didn't know about organized play, we knew about fun—and, of course, who had the biggest muscles.

*—by **Anne Megahy**, Toronto, Ontario*

Frying Up a Feast

There's something fishy going on in New Brunswick!

There is an East Coast tradition that continues generation after generation. If you were to visit any given house in New Brunswick during the winter months, I'm sure you would find someone cooking smelts for one of the many "smelt fries" happening around the Miramichi River.

Smelt fishing begins January 1 and is open until March 31. These small fish typically range in size from about seven to nine inches in length. It seems the smaller ones—five to six inches in length—are considered the most delicate and tasty. They are also the ones my husband Ray prefers!

It isn't uncommon to see a dozen shanties or huts out on the ice. The shanties are often heated with a small woodstove or propane heater; inside, you will find a hole in the ice through which they fish for smelts. Serious smelt fishermen set nets in which the smelts are caught and then sold to waiting customers all over New Brunswick. Here in the province, ice fishing happens not only along the Miramichi River but also in other areas as well. It is quite common to see people parked along the roadside with a "Smelts for Sale" sign leaning up against their vehicle.

Although I don't eat smelts myself, I remember my dad looking forward to the smelt season, knowing he would be able to acquire and enjoy one of his favourite treats.

Ray also gets anxious when smelt season rolls around. He will usually dump about ten pounds of smelts into the sink and carefully clean and behead the fish in preparation for our annual smelt fry!

The next step is to roll them in flour and sprinkle them with salt and pepper. Because the rest of the family isn't fond of the smell of the fish cooking in my kitchen, his orders are to take them out to the garage, where a roaring fire is burning in the woodstove. There, they are then fried in olive oil until they are a crispy golden brown.

Besides Ray, others anxious for the big fish fry include my son-in-law David, my daughter-in-law Kari and my 11-year-old grandson Jantzen, who smothers his smelts in tangy vinegar. New to the smelt family-cookout since last winter is my five-year-old grandson Rylan, who has developed a liking for the tiny fish.

Utensils and plates are carried out to the garage along with fresh rolls and vinegar, where they are welcomed by those ready to feast on this Miramichi delicacy. Through the years, smelt fries have been a popular happening here in this city. Local radio stations advertise events, some of which are held in church basements, halls and other favourite establishments. I have no doubt this tradition will continue for as long as these tiny fish are found in our rivers.

—by ***Linda Sweeney****, Miramichi, New Brunswick*

Remembering Gram

A granddaughter's loving tribute to her grandmother

Gram's deep Irish roots were nourished in the Roman Catholic faith. When sharing stories about her life, you became aware of the major impact the church had on it. The very fabric of her being was interwoven through the church's rituals and belief systems. Rather than creating burning questions that begged answers, it shrouded her in a blanket of comfort that was impermeable to doubt. She had a great acceptance of things.

Gram, who was born Francis Penelope McAleer but always went by "Penzie," had little time to discuss "what ifs." Her tidy remarks typically shut down the conversation with, "No sense growling about it." This wasn't barked at you but rather shared in a tone that indicated it wasn't worthy of discussion.

Gram was the height of discretion. She had little interest in gossip and downplayed family drama. As events would unfold, you got a sense that it wasn't news to her. If you asked her why she didn't say something, she'd brush it off with, "It wasn't my secret to tell."

She always seemed content. I never knew her to be impatient. I remember there was lots of chaos around in summertime with family and friends from away coming to stay and people randomly dropping in unannounced. There were kids of all ages running in and out of the house, generally followed by a slamming door. When I asked Gram if she found it irritating to be converged on with so much commotion, she claimed she didn't. "I can't believe how fast it's over and then everyone is gone," she said.

Gram loved to read. If a book didn't grab her attention early on, she would put it aside and try another. She had no desire to force herself to read something that didn't spark her interest. I sent her a book once about a person who claimed she'd had an after-death experience. I found the book quite interesting and wondered what Gram's impression would be. Her profound opinion was, "Ah—she just had a dream." It made me giggle. She enjoyed the book *Angela's Ashes.* When the sequel *'Tis* came out, Gram told me she started it but found there was "too much language" in it. "I'll wait for Florence (one of her daughters) to read it and she can tell me what it was about."

Gram kept a journal even before it was cool. My impression was that it was a log of factual information rather than her thoughts and feelings. She didn't wear her heart on her sleeve. She was pragmatic—not cold, just matter-of-fact. Gram had a great memory. I'm not sure the journal helped to cement her memories, but she was the family resource to confer with over a lost one, whether it be someone's name or when they "came home." These oral investigations often led to revisiting the time in question and learning more about the event.

Gram had no desire to travel. As her ancestors were from Ireland, I asked her if she ever wanted to go there. "Not really." She wasn't interested in going too far away. Gram's standing travel plan was going to town on Thursdays for groceries and other incidentals. This was the bulk of her highway gallivanting. Although she wasn't a world traveller, she was tuned in and well informed of current events happening around the world. I guess you could say she was a globally enlightened homebody.

She had an interest in cameras and kept a treasure trove of old pictures. She could tell you who was in the photo, the date and what was happening at the time. Her daughter Ann created a lovely scrapbook of Gram's memories all chronologically laid out. Many of us have spent time flipping through it getting glimpses of the past. I marvel at the stoic poses, compared to today's pictures of people doing things that in time may become an embarrassment recorded for a lifetime.

The house she lived in had been my grandfather's childhood home. When she married him, they lived with his parents and worked the farm. She raised her children there, including my dad. Although her home was clean and tidy, the décor was slow to evolve. Her motto was if it still works, why replace it? She was happy with the status quo.

Gram did like to be turned out well, though. In her bedroom upstairs in the old house were a number of shoes lined up neatly against the wall, so she could carefully select the correct shade to go with her equally hand-picked outfit. She seemed to like tan, taupe, off-white, white and ecru flats. Lavender and mauve were favourite colours for clothing, which she wore well. Not everybody can wear that colour, but she could. Heading out to church or into town, she'd be properly pulled together with a little cardigan on. I can see still see her purse draped over her forearm.

A staple in Gram's pantry were her homemade biscuits—little, dense, doughy concoctions baked until a lovely brown crust appeared. They went well with a cup of tea. I once asked her for the recipe. She wrinkled her nose and gave a brief summary without exact measurements. "Oh, I don't know—some flour and salt." Had I attempted to make them given her minimal directions, I'm sure they would have flopped. She wasn't coveting a private recipe; preparing them was just so second nature she would have really had to think about it.

Gram passed away several years ago. I was fortunate to attend her funeral at St. Anne's Church in Hope River. The day was a fiercely cold one, but it was clear and sunny. We gathered in the church for the Mass that would usher Gram into heaven. Not long into it, the power failed. People curiously looked around. As the weather was calm, it was a mystery why the power failed. The Mass carried on in a peaceful silence that embraced us. I wish I could remember who said, "Gram came in without electricity, and now she's going out without it."

Following the funeral, I walked through her old farmhouse. She hadn't lived there for a couple of years due to failing health and I was warned it wouldn't be how I remembered it. The warning could not keep me away from the place where I had such wonderful memories. I needed to feel her and knew for sure if there was a fragment of Gram left on this plane, it would be there.

Seeing the deserted house was like viewing an abandoned soul. What was left of Gram's meagre belongings was strewn about in rubble. The wallpaper clinging to the walls was water-stained and curled. Dirty curtains tethered to rods hung at angles. I found myself walking in measured steps, as I wasn't completely convinced the floor would support my weight. As I gauged my movements, my eyes would land on something that would take me back to a moment in time. The thing that most impacted me was the smell—a distinct smell that has not been replicated anywhere else in my life. They say the olfactory sense may be directly related to memory. I think that's true. The smell brought me back to all of the visits in my childhood that I had in that humble house. But the most poetic part of the visit was seeing Gram's little Canadian flag, with its bright red leaf peeking at me through the dreary rubble. A bright spot on a grey canvas—the essence of Gram.

*—by **Donna McAleer Smith**, Bowmanville, Ontario*

Natural Beauty

Appreciating life's little joys on a peaceful winter day

The first snowfall of the new year dumped 20 centimetres of snow in the Ottawa area, transforming it into a picture-perfect winter wonderland. The sun was shining in all its splendour, and the temperature was a perfect –8°C. What a wonderful day to go on a cross-country ski outing.

I dusted off my skis and hit the trails in the nearby forest, a mere 15-minute walk from home. I am lucky to live so close to nature. Gliding into the forest on my skis, I met a group of ladies on snowshoes standing around chattering like magpies as they looked up at a tall spruce tree. One of the ladies held out her hand. It had birdseed in it. To the delight of her companions, a chickadee flew down and alighted on her open palm. What an amazing sight! I was surprised that birds in the wild would be this tame, but another surprise awaited me when one of the ladies whispered, "Look behind you. Did you know you were being followed?" I slowly turned my head to see three tawny deer coming out from behind a clump of trees. Without any fear, they moved closer, expecting to get their share of treats. People have been feeding them, and now these forest animals don't seem to be afraid of humans.

I exchanged a few more pleasantries with the ladies and, after wishing one another a nice day, I continued along the trail. I glided effortlessly in the tracks set by skiers who had broken the trail on the freshly fallen snow before me. Except for the sound of the swish of my skis on the clean, crisp snow, I was surrounded by peace and quiet. Taking a deep breath, I filled my lungs with fresh air and the subtle scent of pine trees, savouring the beautiful scenery around me. Now and then, when a gentle breeze blew them off the snow-laden tree branches, sparkling showers of snow crystals rained down on me like a blessing from above.

The harder I skied, the faster my heartbeat. Gliding on my skis to its rhythm was so liberating and invigorating. I began getting warm from the physical exertion in spite of the cool temperature around me. It was time to slow down, cool off and catch my breath. I shuffled forward and felt my heart rate decrease. Glancing back over my shoulder to see the tracks I'd just left, I continued moving forward at a more leisurely pace. It made me think of what I left behind, not just on the trail in the forest on this beautiful sunny morning in January but also on the trail of my life, at the beginning of a new year.

Life isn't always rosy and fair, but we do have a lot to be thankful for. We live in a country where we have freedom and peace, and where our quality of life is something too many of us take for granted. Many of us have our faith, friends and family, and the love and respect that bind us together.

I remember an old Chinese story from my childhood. It's about a wise old man who taught his children the importance of being part of a family. He handed each of his children a single stick and asked them to break it in two. The children had no trouble doing that. He then handed them a bunch of sticks that were tied together. "Now, break these," he said. None of the children were able to break the bunch of sticks, no matter how hard they tried. "This bunch of sticks is family; when you stick together, you are strong and nobody will be able to break you," he said.

By the time I reached the end of the ski trail, it was time to head home. I'd enjoyed a most satisfying workout in a glorious natural environment. It made me feel good about myself, about life and the world we live in. Life has its ups and downs and, every so often, the ups are hard to climb. We just have to keep moving forward, try to live life to the fullest and make the most of it. If you look around carefully, you can find moments of joy and serenity everywhere, and sometimes you'll find that the hardest climbs are often blessings in disguise. May you find peace, joy and happiness wherever you are.

*—by **Kim Han**, Kanata, Ontario*

Gone Fishing

One catch and she was hooked!

As a kid, I always knew what Friday meant. Although to many people it meant fish for supper, to me it meant fishing all weekend. As soon as I got home from school, we'd pack up the camper and head out to our favourite fishing spot. It was kind of boring for a 12-year-old, but that was how it was. I was too young to stay home alone and not old enough to appreciate "parent time."

Mom and I went along for the ride, but Dad really loved it. It was his joy, his thing. There would be no stopping for a stretch or goodies, as we had to get to camp before anyone else in order to get the best spot. Dad would be first out of the car, unhooking the camper and unloading the fishing gear. That done, he'd casually announce, "I'll go catch supper while you girls set the table and get the fire going."

We often didn't eat until 7 or 8 p.m., but we'd patiently nibble on something—Mom would sometimes have a glass of wine and some cheese and crackers. I preferred a big old chocolate bar, with chips and pop on the side.

Then came the weekend shortly after Dad had retired. Mom had been asked to work late, so best if we go ahead without her and she'd drive out the next day. Of course, we were disappointed, but we packed up a few cans of beans and hot dogs—the "just-in-case substitute dinner." I grabbed some books and a sweater for around the campfire. A few hours later, we pulled into camp and set up. Dad stood looking out at the lake, watching the sun shimmering on the water. He seemed unsure about what to do. Tentatively he asked, "I guess I'll go get us some supper. Do you want to come along?"

Usually this was my parents' thing, their Friday-night date; I'd stay back and watch the fire, but tonight was different. The fire could wait, the fish wouldn't and neither of us wanted to be alone. I picked up Mom's rod and a couple bottles of pop. We sauntered down the familiar path to the little rock overlooking a quiet dark pool—the special pool.

"This shouldn't take long." Dad had his stance set and waited quietly for the right fish to come along. I'd propped Mom's rod between my knees as I leaned against the tree reading my book. This was not exactly the position of someone expecting to catch a fish—but then it happened! The line started running out and the rod was jerking up and down like crazy. I had no clue what to do. I yelled for Dad, although he was only a few feet away. "Dad, help me, I'm going to lose our supper!" Calm as usual, Dad put down his rod and assured me that I would do just fine. "No, Dad, here—you do it. I really don't like to catch fish. I just wanted to be here while you caught the fish." Dad took the rod and in a minute had everything under control while I just sat and shook. I needed chips, lots of chips.

Then I heard the words I knew Mom loved to hear. It was Dad talking to the fish and persuading him to give up his wonderful life for a hot frying pan. "Come on, little fishy, it's getting kind of cold here and my daughter has run out of snacks. That's a good boy; oh, you want another run. Okay, that's fine—take your time. I can wait." My teeth had started to chatter, half from excitement and half from the cold water splashing around my feet. This rock was not big enough for this kind of action. Then Dad handed me back the rod, saying, "Here you are. This is your fish. You bring him in; he's ready now."

I was afraid I'd lose the fish and disappoint my dad, but I think that little fish knew it was his duty to be my first catch and basically he just gave in. I sort of dragged the slimy, dirt-covered fish up onto the bank. I saw the smile on Dad's face and the proud look in his eye as he pulled out the hook—he knew my limitations. Then it was time for Dad's famous punchline, "Do you know where you caught this fish?"

"Yeah, Dad, right here," I said, pulling my mouth open to one side, looking like a bug-eyed fish with a hook stuck in its mouth. We laughed all the way back to camp, where we saw Mom waiting for us. She called out, "Good for you guys! Where did you catch him?" All three of us did the bug-eyed, dead-fish look in honour of my first catch. To this day, fishing is okay in my book.

*—by **Judi Hannon**, Terrace, British Columbia*

Marrying the Farmer's Daughter

Embracing an unexpected move to a new way of life

Never in a million years did I think I'd be a farmer. Of course, growing up in the rural community of Little Britain, Ontario, I had friends who lived on farms and sometimes I'd stay for a few days, but seldom did it mean helping with the daily farming operation. It wasn't until I met and married a farmer's daughter that this story started to evolve.

My wife Sandra, her brother Gary and their parents, Lawrence and Dorothy Thurston, took a great interest in their family history and knew much about their roots. They could tell you who was related and married to whom, almost from the beginning. Four of the Thurston brothers who emigrated from Norfolk, England, in the mid-1830s settled in and around Dunsford, Ontario.

Sandra and I are now living on the land that was settled by Jonas Thurston, one of those brothers. Back then, in a log house located in a field east of our current home, 12 children were raised. When they were old enough, their father Jonas paid a schoolteacher to live with them and teach the children basic lessons. Although there is nothing left of that log house today, parts of the woodstove still remain in the fenceline.

Thomas, one of Jonas' sons, built the present house. Boasting 12 rooms, it must have looked like a mansion in those days! When Lawrence and Dorothy were married in 1945, they moved in with Lawrence's parents, Ezra and Aggie. The house was divided into two living areas. Lawrence and Ezra did mixed farming, including cattle, pigs, horses, chickens and sheep. Since two families now lived on the farm, more income was needed. After much thought and hard work, a dairy operation came to be.

They all lived under the same roof for 14 years, at which point Ezra and Aggie left the farm and built a new house in the village of

Dunsford. Between living together on the farm and spending a lot of time in their home in Dunsford, Sandra and Gary became very close to their grandparents.

The dairy operation continued until Lawrence and Dorothy decided the work had become too much for them and Lawrence went into beef production. He farmed until he was 81 years old. Time passed and the folks moved into a retirement home. A couple of years later, Dorothy passed away, leaving a heartbroken Lawrence to carry on. We made sure he got back to the farm often, and it was during this time we decided that things needed to be refurbished.

One day, Lawrence asked Sandra and me if we ever thought about moving to the farm, and that's when we began to consider doing just that. Lawrence passed away a few months later and, although he didn't know for certain we were going to do it, I am sure he suspected.

Many a good time has been had here. One very special occasion was a Thurston family reunion. The homestead—the only farm that remains in the original family from the time the deed was registered—was opened up to anybody who wanted to come. Relatives arrived from all over Ontario and some even flew in from Alberta. Birthdays and Christmases continue to fill this home with love and laughter. Sandra and I are retired now, a little too old for the rigours of full-fledged farming, but we keep chickens, sell eggs and hay, and enjoy watching the cattle grazing in the pasture.

The farm is maintained and the land is workable, so hopefully we will be here for many more years to come. I'm sure our family that have passed on are looking down, smiling at our attempts to keep it alive.

*—by **Kenneth Sornberger**, Dunsford, Ontario*

What Money Can't Buy

Focusing on the important things in life

I have three siblings: Adam, Kaitlynn and Tara. We were a blended family from the time I was very young, and that has added to our special relationship. Our parents, David and Cathy Broughton, were from a middle-class family and, with four children, often struggled financially. We always had enough money to get by and to have a good life, but like many parents, they often had to say no to extravagant items or trips in order to make ends meet. I want to tell you why that did not matter to us at all.

Growing up, my parents had debt; cars broke down and we didn't always get everything we wanted. But we did have a pool in our backyard—a one-time purchase—that we loved to swim in; my dad built us our own tree house and we adored climbing trees. We played in the snow in winter, built snow tunnels and buried hidden treasures. In summer, we loved going camping on weekends to new places or even just the local campground. We also took many trips to the beach and nature parks.

Later, in my teens, when we got our own "camp" in the small rural community of Cumberland Bay, New Brunswick, this love continued—it was our favourite place to be on weekends! For the past eight years, we have spent summers there. We have campfires, take walks, swim in the river and just spend time outside. Our camp is not fancy: We sleep in tent trailers, there's no electricity and we're surrounded by woods.

Another beauty of our camp is that we have so many people there all the time. Our grandparents come often; my siblings and I still go—we're all in our 20s now—as do our aunts and uncles, extended family and friends. It's been so nice having this wonderful spot to gather and stay connected in such a disconnected world. I can't stress enough how much I love this place and what it represents. For me, it's about family, togetherness and enjoying the simple, important things in life. Those values have stayed with me.

When I look back on why I love nature so much and why I consider it such a big part of my life, I think it has a lot to do with my parents' priorities. Maybe they thought it was important that we appreciate the simple things in life, or maybe they were unable to afford to take us on expensive vacations, but for whatever reason, I loved that we spent our time this way and still do. I believe my parents had a fundamental understanding of what was important.

No amount of money can replace having parents who love and respect each other as well as their children. Money can't buy quality time with parents who teach you about life; it can't unbreak a broken home or prevent it from being broken in the first place. Making your family a priority and focusing on low-cost activities that are going to instill good values in your kids is priceless. I now look forward to the day when I can provide those things for my own family.

*—by **Melanie Saulnier**, Fredericton, New Brunswick*

KINDNESS

From heartwarming gestures to saving lives, here are incredible stories about everyday Canadians who do good works—in their communities and around the world

The Wedding Dress

A girlhood promise kept and a lifelong friendship cemented

My teenage years were spent in Hamiota, Manitoba, where my father was a sergeant in the RCMP and the officer in charge of our area. On many Sundays after church, my friend Jean and I would walk along the railway tracks leading out of town. We picked pussy willows and wild roses, and enjoyed listening to the wild bird songs and the peacefulness of green fields stretching for miles. We talked about school, our families and, naturally, boys. We promised each other that the first one married would loan the other one her wedding dress.

Jean became a teacher and I joined the Canadian Women's Army Corps, training as a secretary and working as an army secretary for two years. Jean and I wrote to each other frequently. Jean married in 1946 just as Tom, my soldier boyfriend, returned from two years overseas in the tank corps. I went home with him to Maidstone, Saskatchewan, to meet his family, so I was sadly unable to attend Jean's wedding.

Tom and I moved to Vancouver, where he enrolled in forestry at the University of British Columbia. He lived at UBC's Veterans Fort Camp, while I lived at the YWCA and worked as a secretary at the Henry Birks store. Jean and I kept in touch through letters and phone calls.

Tom and I set our wedding date for September 10, 1947. Money was scarce, so we only invited our parents and a few friends who lived in Vancouver. I intended to wear a suit that I could use later for work.

A few weeks before the wedding, I received a parcel from Jean—her wedding dress, veil and long, lacy gloves. The dress fit perfectly! I felt like a princess as I walked down the aisle of Christ Church Cathedral on my father's arm. I hadn't told Tom about receiving it; his smile and the look in his eyes told me that I looked as beautiful as I felt.

Jean and I, now widows in our late 80s, have kept in close touch over the years through letters, calls and a few visits—friends for life.

*—by **Jean E. Hubbard**, West Vancouver, British Columbia*

Queen of May

How Miss Watson made a wise choice

Back in 1941, when I was attending school, we had a wonderful teacher named Miss Watson. Wanting to introduce some "English" customs to our group of students from various ethnic backgrounds, she taught us a maypole dance and invited our parents to attend. This is how I remember that great day.

I wondered who Miss Watson would pick to be the Queen of May. I'd heard that she would choose the prettiest girl who could also dance nicely. What an honour! Tomorrow Miss Watson would announce who would be queen!

That night, bathing in a square galvanized tub, lathering my long hair with care, I breathed in the scent of fresh flowers released from the shampoo. Mummy poured rinse water over my head as I crouched in the old tub. Water ran over my head, down my neck and trickled across my tummy like summer rain. With swift, strong fingers, Mummy braided my hair and helped me slide my nightie over my head. "May I practice my smile in the hand mirror, Mummy?" I asked wistfully. Hiding her own smile, Mummy passed me the mirror, knowing my secret longing to be chosen Queen of May. Finally, I settled into bed, almost feverish with anticipation. It took longer than usual for me to fall asleep.

The next day, I practiced dancing all the way to school, singing: "And who excels in dancing, must be the Queen of May!" Shaking my pigtails loose, I let my kinky red hair fall over my shoulders and down to my waist. At school, every eye fastened on the teacher. "Good morning, Miss Watson!" we chorused in unison. After mumbling the Lord's Prayer and saluting the flag, we sank into our seats.

"I have decided," announced Miss Watson, "to have Elizabeth be the Queen of May!"

Elizabeth! Stunned silence. All eyes turned to the back corner where Lizzy huddled at her desk. "But Miss Watson," protested Lizzy, I don't think I'm able..."

"Nonsense, Elizabeth," said Miss Watson firmly. "You are perfect for the part. And now we shall turn to arithmetic."

I worked on my assignment half-heartedly. Lizzy! Of all people. Miss Watson was the only one who called her Elizabeth. The kids all called her "poor Lizzy." And with good reason. She stood a head taller than everyone in class, and she had missed a lot of school, so she was hopelessly behind her former classmates. She studied earnestly with the little ones but didn't play with them at recess; she just stood forlornly by herself. I felt sorry for Lizzy. Stricken by polio at a young age, she was forced to wear a heavy boot and leg brace. Her spine was twisted and her gait halting. During inclement weather, she had to remain at home, as it was too far for her to travel on horseback.

I glanced behind me at Lizzy. Her troubled face was not pretty, I thought. How could Miss Watson be so blind? Lizzy's not beautiful and she can't even dance! "And who excels at dancing, must be the Queen of May," I sang with my classmates.

Finally, May Day arrived and it was marvellous. A shimmering sun shone on the tall flagpole adorned with colourful paper streamers hanging from a ring high in the air, transforming the schoolyard into a fairyland. Trees bursting into bloom perfumed the yard with a delicate scent. Everyone assembled on the grass, watching the maypole dancers. I held my streamer as I danced, ducking under and over the other streamers while singing the maypole song. By the time the song ended, all the streamers had been woven into a pattern—a kaleidoscope of colour around the pole. The dancers smiled with pride.

Presiding over it all sat Lizzy. A royal-purple robe hung from her shoulders and draped artistically over her feet, completely concealing the hated boot. A dazzling tinsel crown adorned her hair. Sitting proud and tall on her throne, she smiled down on her classmates. She was truly radiant! Now I saw the wisdom of Miss Watson's choice. Happiness had made Elizabeth beautiful.

*—by **Ardith Trudzik**, Edmonton, Alberta*

Water for Africa

A spark is lit and an entire community answers

While I was dressing to go out on New Year's Eve 2007, a TV commercial came on with John Lennon singing, "So this is Christmas, and what have you done? Another year over and a new one just begun." My response? I've done nothing! After celebrating for a few hours that night, I thought, I'll dig a well in Africa! How hard can that be?

When I investigated and discovered the cost, my New Year's resolution appeared to be going in the direction of most other New Year's resolutions. Then I attended a service for the week of prayer for Christian unity at our church. The speaker told a story of how, one day, an adult came across a boy throwing thousands of starfish back into the ocean, one by one. He asked the boy what difference he thought he could make. The little boy threw another starfish into the water and said, "I think it made a difference to that one."

We can't change the world, but we can do something—donate five cents, make a dozen cookies for someone who is sick, anything! My husband, Bob, and I walked out of church so fired up. I told Bob about the well that night and together we decided to raise as much money as possible in one year. It might not be enough to dig a well, but we were going to try our best.

We started small. When I wasn't working, I babysat two little girls and that money went into a teapot. One of our daughters lived at home at the time and paid a little board, which also went towards the well. I told myself I was working at it, but along came a story in an issue of *Reader's Digest* that slapped me on the side of the head: A Calgary family was volunteering around the world for a year. Their first stop was Kenya, Africa. This is what the mom wrote: "I'm no international aid worker, but having visited several schools, the thing that is needed most in Africa is water, followed by dormitories for girls."

Water makes a difference in Africa for many reasons, from thirst and health to crop irrigation and gardens that provide food and income. It's also the women who make the trek of miles, often several times a day, to supply the family with drinking water. Water is like the centre of a wheel and from the hub are spokes such as education, self-esteem, gender equality, longevity and hope.

For my birthday in March, I told my daughters about the well and asked for a donation from them instead of a gift. Together, we painted houses, cleaned farm machinery and vehicles, sold garden produce and scrap metal, had yard sales and rented out our cottage. If anyone in the neighbourhood was having company, they'd phone me and I'd deliver dessert, birthday cakes or whatever baked goods they liked for a fee. We even sold hot dogs outside the local grocery store. Finally, a church in Palmerston, Ontario donated four quilts for us to auction off.

Around the end of May 2007, with much trepidation, I put flyers in our neighbours' mailboxes that told them about my project and asked if they had empty liquor, wine or beer bottles and cans that they'd consider donating to the cause. All they had to do was tie the included ribbon to their mailboxes and I'd come by on Saturday. Every mailbox had a ribbon on it. Even friends who hadn't received flyers had procured their own ribbons. We received our first cash donations that day, too. Many said to come back again and they'd try to empty some more bottles!

Our pickup truck was stacked three cases deep when we pulled into the bottle depot. One man had to wait for my seven-year-old grandson, Reid, and me to unload. He asked Reid if he was getting the money. "No," Reid said, "Gramma is digging a well in Africa." The man—a perfect stranger—gave us his money, too.

People began telling their families, colleagues and sports teams about my well and we began getting phone calls: Can you make a pickup? We'd come home and there would be a stack of bottles outside the garage. After I took three loads to the depot in one week, they probably started to question my drinking habits! In the end, we received bottles from Tobermory to Chatham here in Ontario and cheques from New Westminster, British Columbia, to St. John's, Newfoundland and Labrador. We even received a cheque from the United States.

Over that summer, every time I was too tired or without another fundraising idea or the goal seemed impossible, something would happen. I had high hopes that my crops of strawberries, pumpkin and squash would bring in quite a bit of cash, but unfortunately we had an incredibly dry summer. I was feeling pretty disappointed until a little girl brought me a plastic baggie containing $1.22. She wanted kids to have water, too.

The night we reached our goal of $10,000 was at a neighbour's 60th birthday party. The invitations asked for donations to the well instead of gifts—everyone's invitation except Bob's and mine. Almost $400 came in and it seemed fitting to go over the top surrounded by the friends who had supported our fundraising all summer.

Our fundraising dollars went to WaterCan, a registered charity out of Ottawa. Their mission is simply, "Clean Water for All." Our first donation went to a primary school in Ethiopia with 730 students and eight classrooms. Girls had to bring water from an unsafe source several kilometres away; washroom facilities were minimal and students had to make do with the surrounding bushes. This lack of privacy especially discouraged young women from attending school. WaterCan built a well with a hand pump, latrines for both girls and boys, and taught basic hygiene, because if you've never had water, you don't waste it washing your hands.

Our other donations went to building rainwater catchment systems, storage tanks and washing stations at Trust Preparatory School in Kampala City, Uganda, and Ndatela Primary School in Tanzania. We also donated towards an extensive water project at Shadrack Kimalel Primary School in Nairobi, Kenya, the city my family visited on a great adventure in 2009. In an attempt to re-establish Uganda after its 20-year civil war, WaterCan dug 15 wells in the Kyenjojo District. We sent the funds for one of these wells and plan to finance others.

At the beginning of our efforts way back in 2007, it was all about the first $10,000. Looking back, the journey has been more meaningful than the goal. I didn't expect so many people to help! Most of us are not in a position to make a large donation to a development organization. But I've discovered that a ten-cent bottle can shape a miracle. One lady simply collected the pocket change from her family as they arrived on Christmas Day—and that $1.22 in the baggie remains one of the most memorable donations. In the words of my favourite hymn, "It only takes a spark to get a fire going." And that's exactly what happened.

*—by **Doddi Reid**, Palmerston, Ontario*

Vanquishing the Fort McMurray "Beast"

Wildfires took everything, but one woman finds joy again, thanks to an act of kindness from an unexpected source

In the spring of 2015, the community of Fort McMurray, Alberta, was evacuated and ravished by a raging wildfire. The day started like any other beautiful spring day in the remote northern town. As I left for work the morning of May 3, it was hot and sunny, with blue skies. By noon, the city was in flames. The winds had shifted, sending uncontrolled wildfires towards the city limits and forcing me and nearly 90,000 other Fort McMurray residents to flee for safety.

As the evacuation alert was issued, I raced home from work to gather as many personal items as I could. When I arrived, firefighters were already going door-to-door telling residents to evacuate. With just minutes to pack a few belongings, I left my home not knowing whether it was safe from the fires, or when I would be back.

As I slowly made my way south, I was horrified and saddened to see my city on fire. The abandoned vehicles, burning buildings, water-bombers, helicopters and remnants of burned trees were shocking. Thankfully, my husband and I had a safe place to go—my sister's in southern Alberta. Many of the city's evacuees ended up in shelters. Compared to many, we were the lucky ones. As it turned out, it was Canada's largest recorded evacuation due to a wildfire in our history.

In the days following the evacuation, I was glued to all the media coverage and reports. The devastation continued to spread across northern Alberta and into Saskatchewan for the next two months, consuming approximately 1.5 million acres in total. The support and generosity that poured in from all over the world was staggering. From donations of money, gas, water, food, shelter, clothing and so much more, everyone wanted to help. But it was one small gesture that helped my family get back to what was important.

Mine was one of hundreds of Fort McMurray families who lost everything that day. Most things we knew we could replace—beds, dishes, clothes. But in the chaos of evacuating, I left behind my craft supplies, quilts and sewing machine. Naturally, I was overwhelmed and distressed over being displaced; not knowing when I'd be able to quilt again made me even more upset. But while the fire stole my materials, it couldn't touch my love for quilting.

I knew I needed some sense of normalcy to get through the trying months ahead, which is what inspired me to contact the online company Craftsy. I had no clue where to start, so I used the "live chat" feature and was connected with a woman named Lizzy. After explaining my situation, I simply asked if the company would consider replacing or reselling me the quilting items I'd recently purchased at cost to help me return to my favourite hobby. Little did I know, Lizzy and Craftsy had something bigger in mind.

Just after I returned to Fort McMurray, about a month after the fires, Lizzy surprised me with the news that Craftsy was sending care packages with quilting supplies to help me rebuild my crafting studio. A few weeks later, I received two boxes packed full of everything from a rotary cutter, cutting mat and ruler to thread, ribbon and two quilting kits. The cherry on top was the Janome MC 8200 sewing machine—a top-of-the-line machine courtesy of Janome Canada. What more could I want? I had everything I needed to return to my hobby, and I was officially back in quilting heaven!

As I continued to adjust to the "new normal" waiting to rebuild our home, Craftsy's generosity left an indelible impact on my life, and it couldn't have come at a more meaningful time. After everything we had been through, Craftsy gave me a reason to laugh again. I look forward to creating new projects and many years of happiness ahead because of Craftsy's charitable spirit. I'm now using the machine to make one of the quilt kits. Every time I use it, see it or even talk about it, my heart swells with happiness. While my life rebuilds around me, quilting helps keep me smiling and focused on what's important. "The Beast" tried to take everything that day, but it can never take quilting away from me. I thank Craftsy and Janome for helping me get back to what I love.

—by ***Eldora Baillie****, Fort McMurray, Alberta*

Born to Help

Therapy dogs are a priceless community gift

An "old soul" with endless love to give—that is how I always described my beautiful golden retriever, Maya. Given her calm demeanour and loving personality, I'd always envisioned Maya as a therapy dog. At seven years of age, after a lengthy application process, she achieved this status with the St. John Ambulance Therapy Dog program. This program brings comfort, joy and companionship to many, including the sick, lonely or those residing in full-time care facilities.

Clients reap the therapeutic benefits of the unconditional love they receive from these amazing animals. Dogs are nonjudgemental, undeterred by human frailties and accepting of physical and mental illness. They have a calming influence, which is wonderful.

A regular visitation program can be implemented in many places, including long-term care facilities, palliative care, children's health centres, mental health care facilities, schools and more—basically any setting that would benefit from the unconditional love of a dog.

The residents of the facility where Maya and I visited weekly accepted and welcomed us with open arms. They looked forward to seeing Maya, a reminder of days gone by when they had pets of their own to love and cherish. Maya would proudly walk from one room to the next, tail wagging, always eager to greet the next person. Each resident she approached was more than willing to shower her with undivided attention and affection. In return, Maya's calming presence brought them undeniable happiness.

One resident in particular proudly displays Maya's picture in her room, beaming with joy during our visits. She would wait at the entrance to her room, exclaiming enthusiastically as we approached, "I've been waiting for you, Maya!"

During her first visit, Maya was interacting with a wheelchair-restricted resident who hadn't spoken for quite some time. Maya solemnly stood alongside the wheelchair. The woman's unsteady hand came to rest on Maya's head and I watched a smile slowly spread across her face and a light begin to shine in her eyes. I listened as she spoke for the first time in months; she said "Maya." I knew then that my precious golden retriever had truly found her calling in life.

At only eight years of age, unfortunately Maya was diagnosed with terminal leukemia. She fought a brief but extremely courageous battle, remaining stoic and giving of herself until the very end. Only days before her diagnosis, Maya was visiting students at our community college during exam week to help alleviate their stress.

Maya's role as a therapy dog may have been short-lived, but the impact she had on everyone she met was immeasurable. This is the truest testament to her legacy.

St. John Ambulance Therapy Dog volunteers and their pets continue to proudly serve communities throughout Canada. These individuals and their incredible dogs exemplify the priceless gift of volunteerism.

*—by **Janice Murphy**, Hamilton, Ontario*

A Lasting Legacy

A "champ" in every sense of the word, young Kamryn will always remember Canada's veterans

It might sound unusual for a six-year-old girl to lay a wreath at a Remembrance Day ceremony, but for our daughter, Kamryn, it's part of a legacy that goes back nearly 100 years.

When Kamryn was 11 months old, she was hospitalized with upper respiratory concerns. As a result of her illness, and a long-fought battle that saw her spending a week on life support, she had to undergo amputation surgery, losing both legs, her right hand and several fingers on her left hand. Our lives and Kamryn's were forever changed and the future was uncertain. We were left with so many unanswered questions and did not know where to turn.

While our daughter was in the hospital, a physiotherapist met with us and discussed Kamryn's future and provided hope about the many possibilities that would be available to her as an amputee. The most powerful words she said that day were, "One thing I can tell you is that Kamryn will walk. I don't know when, but she will." This is also when we first learned about The War Amps Child Amputee (CHAMP) Program. We were welcomed into The War Amps and they have become our extended family.

The War Amps was started by war-amputee veterans returning from the First World War. They later created the CHAMP Program to help child amputees. The War Amps has provided Kamryn with financial assistance for different artificial limbs, including those for walking and swimming, and a tumbling arm that she uses for gymnastics. We also get to attend CHAMP seminars, where we learn about the different types of artificial limbs and devices that are available, and how to deal with issues like teasing and bullying.

It has been a tradition for Kamryn to lay a wreath on behalf of The War Amps at our local Remembrance Day ceremony in Grande Prairie, Alberta, with Shannon Krasowski, a graduate of the CHAMP Program and a fellow leg amputee. Shannon has been able to explain the importance of honouring our veterans to Kamryn. She has shared personal stories of how she has met war-amputee veterans and heard their first-hand accounts of the devastation and destruction of war.

As a young Champ, Shannon was given a lion statue by a war-amputee veteran for her courage. Recently, she passed this statue down to Kamryn to recognize hers. Someday, Kamryn will pass it along to another young amputee who looks up to her.

We believe that laying a wreath is building the foundation for Kamryn to understand how much our war veterans gave up for our freedom and how the CHAMP Program would not exist if it was not for them. Kamryn shares a special bond with war-amputee veterans because she understands what it's like to be an amputee, and as our war veterans age, it is even more important for young people like her to pass on the Remembrance message to ensure that we never forget their sacrifices.

As Kamryn's parents, we cannot express enough how The War Amps has changed our lives. We will always be appreciative of the work of the war-amputee veterans and the legacy they have left for child amputees like Kamryn. It is for this reason that she lays a wreath every year in their honour and will do so for many years to come.

*—by **Dale and Allan Bond**, Grande Prairie, Alberta*

Saving Our Shorelines

A national effort to keep Canadian shores clean and safe for humans and animals alike

I discovered the true value of volunteering in environmental conservation while doing field research at a remote island in the Haida Gwaii region of British Columbia during the summer of 2001. As a research assistant for a local conservation society, I helped monitor the activity of cavity-nesting birds, participated in boat surveys of seabirds and visited gull colonies to count nests. It was an experience I will always remember: It's when I first realized how volunteering can benefit our natural world.

Now, years later, I manage the Vancouver Aquarium and the World Wildlife Fund's Great Canadian Shoreline Cleanup, a national initiative that engages volunteers across the country to clean up our shorelines. Presented by Loblaw Companies Limited, the program also collects vital data used to increase public awareness about the impacts of shoreline litter. Picking up trash might not sound glamorous, but it's meaningful work. At the end of the day, you know you've made a difference in your local community and on a national scale.

The results of a cleanup are dramatic. You don't tend to notice the impact you're having until the moment you're done: There's always an immediate sense of pride as you gaze upon a newly transformed shoreline. The Shoreline Cleanup shows change is possible through individual actions. It goes even further, though, highlighting how individual behaviour affects aquatic environments. With the help of more than 55,000 volunteers who participate in the program annually, thousands upon thousands of items have been removed from Canadian shorelines.

Perhaps the best part of working with the Shoreline Cleanup is the opportunity to speak with volunteers and share in their passion for community stewardship. One of my favourite stories is about a trio of siblings from Oakville, Ontario. Jack, Julie and Emma are active youth volunteers who are passionate about environmental and social issues.

They give back to their community through various social change projects and help protect the environment by organizing shoreline cleanups. They inspire members of their community to become active citizens and demonstrate how everyone, no matter what age, can make a difference.

Cleanup teams frequently tell me just how much fun they've had on the shorelines, and they love to report back on some of their unusual finds. If you can think of it, it's been found during a shoreline cleanup, including the proverbial kitchen sink. Some of the more unusual finds have included a wedding dress, a gold ring, Christmas decorations, false teeth, a lava lamp, clothing and even an Elvis costume! Yet after each cleanup, it isn't these strange and unusual items that remain in my mind—it is all the small bits of trash that may not be obvious at a quick glance.

It can be frustrating to see how much of our litter ends up on shorelines, especially when many items found are often recyclable or have reusable alternatives. Be they plastic bottle caps, cigarette butts, fragments of chip bags or a part of a plastic fork, these small pieces are everywhere: under benches, near curbs, along lakeside trails. They are difficult to clean up on a regular basis and are just one of the reasons why shoreline cleanups matter.

In a typical year, more than 57,000 Canadians volunteer to clean about 3,035 kilometres of shorelines—roughly the length of the St. Lawrence River. They collect more than 99,000 kilograms of litter, the approximate weight of 22 large school buses. If you think that amount of weight sounds staggering, from 1994 to 2017, the Shoreline Cleanup picked up approximately 1.2 million kilograms of shoreline litter—approximately 259 school buses' worth.

When the data comes in each year, I look forward to seeing what was found, but I'm also excited at the knowledge that, with every cleanup, volunteers from coast to coast are showing we can make a difference. If we refuse a straw, choose reusable alternatives to disposable items and look for creative ways to minimize waste, then less litter will find its way to our shorelines.

It's a terrific feeling to be part of a movement that works together for a common goal. We're working towards cleaner waterways for everyone, including the wildlife and people that depend on them.

—by ***Susan Debreceni****, Toronto, Ontario*

Curling for a Cure

For the past 20 years, the "Hope Classic" has been raising funds to fight breast cancer—and raising community spirit, too!

Diane calls down the sheet to Sydney, "Nice shot, Syd!" who just smiles, waves to her skip and steps to the side to await her next throw. As she waits, she watches as women are yelling encouragement to their brushers on the other sheets. They are all smiling and laughing. The sound of brooms against the ice and rocks crashing together in the house are mixed with the heavy bass rhythm from the DJ in the dining area. Despite the friendly on-ice competition and fun-loving nature present in the club, everyone is here for a very serious cause.

Diane and Sydney are two of more than 250 women from across northwestern Ontario who gathered together at the Fort William Curling Club on a cold, snowy weekend in Thunder Bay at the Bearskin Airlines Hope Classic to raise money to fight breast cancer. Recently, they marked the 21st year of not only raising money but also providing the women in attendance with a relaxed, fun and supportive environment to share laughter, stories and tears. For all those involved, the event is about renewing long-lasting friendships or creating new ones, all while supporting one another in the fight against breast cancer.

The idea for the event began when Linda Buchan, who had undergone breast cancer treatment, was approached about starting a women's bonspiel to raise money for the Breast Cancer Support Group. Linda contacted Cliff Friesen, the co-owner of Bearskin Airlines, about supporting the idea. Cliff, whose daughter had also just undergone breast cancer surgery and treatment, was very supportive, enabling the first annual Bearskin Airlines Hope Classic to take place at the Fort William Curling Club in 1997.

Linda passed away in December of 2002, just before the seventh annual Hope Classic event, and although it was extremely difficult for the organizing committee, they all agreed to carry on with Linda's dream. The event has grown into one of the most popular women's bonspiels in Thunder Bay, and now Sydney—Linda's granddaughter—along with the organizing committee and women from across northwestern Ontario, continue to make a difference and honour Linda's memory.

As she comes into the club, Sydney walks into a sea of pink. Pink wigs, signs, decorations and clothing are everywhere. This event is special because you don't have to be an experienced curler to participate. This is only Sydney's third year as a participant. Sure, there are teams that have been curling for years, but the majority of women come to support the cause, not to compete. Everyone is invited to participate; experience is not required. Someone will help you out, or, in some cases, help you up. Participants come to support their family, friends and communities. All of the money raised at the "Hope" stays in Thunder Bay to support the specialized care at the Thunder Bay Regional Health Sciences Centre.

Since that first event more than two decades ago, the women participants continue to be supported by friends, relatives, acquaintances and businesses in their effort to raise money. The women, and all those who support them, are passionate about it because so many of them know someone—a friend or family member—who has been affected by breast cancer. That's why the women of northwestern Ontario plan to continue to gather at the Fort William Curling Club on the first weekend of every February, to support one another and the fight against breast cancer. The generosity of their various communities never fails to amaze and inspire. In the space of 20 years, the Hope Classic has raised $2.87 million, ensuring that women in northwestern Ontario have access to exceptional screening, assessment and support services close to home and family.

Planning is well under way to ensure that the annual event continues the tradition of fun and support for all those in attendance. Each year's goal is to reunite with friends, share some inspiring stories and hopefully raise enough money to help all those touched by breast cancer.

—by ***Jayson Childs****, Thunder Bay, Ontario*

Helping Blanding's Turtles

Volunteers donate their time to keep this endangered species safe

For three summers, I had the opportunity to work as a "species at risk" researcher at both Kejimkujik National Park and National Historic Site, and the Mersey Tobeatic Research Institute in Nova Scotia. Through this work, I was introduced to a species of turtle that would gain a very special place in my heart, the Blanding's turtle.

Blanding's turtles are an endangered species in Nova Scotia, and therefore have extensive conservation efforts focused on them. One of these efforts is the protection of their nests each June, which I have been lucky enough to help out with for the last four nesting seasons. Nest protection occurs in all three of the known Blanding's turtle populations—Kejimkujik National Park, McGowan Lake and Pleasant River—and wouldn't be possible without many incredible volunteers.

It all begins around 7 p.m. each night, when the blackflies and mosquitoes start buzzing around and the heat of the day slowly begins to cool. This is when I head to the campground in "Keji" to meet up with the rest of the volunteers, who spend their evenings monitoring beaches and roads for nesting turtles.

Most of the nesting turtles we know about are found on the cobble beaches of Kejimkujik Lake, but many also find the shoulder of roads desirable. Thankfully, the volunteers are there to make sure cars slow down. Reduced speed limit signs are put up and speed bumps are installed in one area.

My favourite places to monitor for turtles are the beach sites. There is nothing to complain about when you get to be outside on a nice summer evening, walking along a beach at sunset while listening to frogs and birds. Even the bugs can't ruin the night. Every so often we stop, grab our binoculars and scan the beach for turtles up ahead. Too often, there are turtle rocks, which, as their name implies, are rocks that look like turtles—they fool me every time!

Sometimes, however, those "rocks" begin to move and you realize it's an actual turtle! That's when I get a little excited, as it means we might get to fulfill our purpose. Sometimes, a turtle will just be wandering along the beach; other times, it's already digging a hole. If it's in the process of digging, we slowly and quietly sneak up to it for a closer look.

If the turtle becomes startled, it might disappear into the water and not return that night, but if it's committed to nesting, it isn't easily disturbed. At this point, we are able to see how far along the turtle is in the nesting process. If the hole is fairly deep, there is a good possibility the turtle will lay her eggs in it. When the turtle sticks her neck way out then pulls it all the way back into her shell, you know the laying process is about to begin. As her head goes in, an egg comes out!

Approximately ten to 14 eggs later, she begins to bury the nest and conceal it. Concealing is a lengthy process in which the turtle moves rocks and dirt around to make it look as though the nest area never existed. It can take hours for a Blanding's turtle to finish concealing. By the time it's done, you would never be able to find the nest unless you had the smelling ability of a raccoon. The amazing part is that the turtle conceals the nest without ever looking at it! She uses her back feet to dig the hole and cover up the nest, and then just walks away back to the water.

Although Blanding's turtles are the main focus of the nest protection program, occasionally we encounter a snapping turtle nest. Since these turtles are also a species at risk in Nova Scotia, we try to protect them as well. I'll often see one along the roadway or in the middle of the road, in which case I stop my car to carry it across. It's important to always move turtles across the road in the direction they were going and not move them somewhere far away. They know where they're heading!

Snappers are one of my favourite turtles, mostly because they look like little dinosaurs that survived extinction. I remember one day, a couple of volunteers and I stood by a snapper on the side of the road while she laid 41 eggs! When she was done, we put a nest cage over it to keep the eggs safe from predators.

In fall, all the nests that were protected in spring are monitored for hatchlings that have crawled out of the nest. They begin hatching in mid-September into early October, depending on the weather conditions over the summer. If it is a hotter summer and the eggs get a chance to incubate better, hatchlings may start arriving as early as the end of August.

Anyone who has ever seen a baby turtle will understand why this is a very cool thing to be a part of. It's always exciting when you get to look into the nest cage and see a hatchling that you helped give a chance at survival! It makes all the nights of fighting off blackflies and staying up until 1 a.m. worth it.

Before we let the hatchlings out of the nests, we take their measurements and give them an ID code. Sometimes, though, the hatchlings find a gap through the nest cages and escape before we can tag them. The hatchlings are released just outside the nest cage and they go wherever they need to. Not all hatchlings head straight to water; many of them go up into the woods or into a nearby bog. We try not to interfere with their natural instincts.

I'm proud to be a part of the Blanding's turtle nest protection program in Nova Scotia, and to have had the opportunity to meet the amazing volunteers who contribute hours of their time to helping turtles. In a world where many animals need our help more than ever, we could use more people like them!

*—by **Wesley Pitts**, Hantsport, Nova Scotia*

Volunteer Veterinary Team

Helping animals, their people and the community

As I looked across the large gymnasium where we had set up our temporary, MASH-style animal health care clinic in Burns Lake, British Columbia, I saw the lineup of people with their pets constantly increasing. We were in for a busy day.

I was lucky enough to be part of the Canadian Animal Assistance Team (CAAT), a volunteer veterinary team that travels to communities to provide veterinary services for low-income families. I was well aware of the fact that animal overpopulation and disease issues are common concerns where veterinary care is not routinely available, which has a devastating effect on animal welfare. I was there to be part of the solution.

As I looked at the line of people and pets, I noticed an older lady with her tiny white dog in her arms. She held him close and was patiently waiting her turn. When I spoke to her, she told me his name was Peanut and he was there for his vaccination. I examined him and discovered he had a condition where one of his testicles had not descended (cryptorchidism). I explained to her that there are definite health risks with this condition and they can be quite serious. She was nervous about the surgery, but after reassuring her we would do all we could to ensure his safety, she looked at me with trusting eyes and carefully handed him over. I took him into my arms with great care and looked into her eyes to let her know I understood how important he was to her.

After a successful surgery, he was moved into our recovery area. I called his owner over and set up a chair for her to be able to sit with him. She was so relieved and delighted to have her little friend back in her arms. She snuggled him into a blanket to keep him warm and talked to him. She and her whole family stayed with him for the rest of the afternoon until he was ready to go home.

The next day, as we prepared for another long day of seeing medical and surgical patients, I saw the same woman patiently standing in line again, but without Peanut. I immediately went over to ask if he was all right. Her face opened up into a big smile. She said he was doing well and she was extremely happy she had brought him to us. She knew he was going to be healthier because of the care he had received. She told me she was waiting in line to be able to properly thank us.

The night before, once they had returned home, her daughter had explained to her that the entire team of people from CAAT were volunteering their time, had paid their own way to the community and did fundraising to be able to provide the services. She and her family sat around the dinner table and decided they would all contribute what they could. She had come to bring a donation to our organization. I was speechless.

Watching that family leave, so happy because we were able to provide what was needed for their little dog, I couldn't help but smile. I became involved in this volunteer organization to contribute to the welfare of animals. Moments like that, however, prove to me that helping the animals, helping the people and helping the community as a whole are all undeniably intertwined.

On our last day, as we packed up our hospital supplies and equipment and left the gymnasium, it looked like we had never been there. However, I knew that out in the village it would be evident for a long time. The impoundment rate at the local pound has decreased by 75 percent and the local rescue group's intake has decreased by 50 percent since we started our annual clinics in Burns Lake. The local animal welfare groups also continue working to maintain what we started, using the teaching aides we provide during the educational programs we offer while the clinic is open.

The majority of our work is in British Columbia's First Nations communities, though we've been to communities in the Northwest Territories, Nunavut and the Yukon, as well as in other countries. CAAT was first founded in 2005 as a disaster-relief team that went to help the animals displaced by Hurricane Katrina in Louisiana.

I was sad to leave the wonderful community of Burns Lake, but there are countless others in need. I have no doubt that, in every place, I will meet people just like Peanut's owner, who love their pets, want to help their pets and just need the opportunity to be able to do so.

*—by **Chris Robinson**, Cambridge, Ontario*

Sewing With Pride North of 60

A community program has participants "dreaming big dreams"

You can compare the wildflowers of the Canadian Arctic in spring and summer to the ladies and youth of the sewing program in Gamètì, Northwest Territories. To give you some perspective, Gamètì is accessible only by small aircraft most of the year. In winter, the ice road enables people to drive out for about six weeks a year, heading about five hours south to Yellowknife. At 64 degrees north, Gamètì is a Tlicho (pronounced Klee-cho) Dene community with a population of about 275.

In 2015, I joined my husband, Mike Westley, here. He is the community adult educator, and he wanted to share my love of sewing and quilting with the community. Thanks to funding from Dominion Diamond Corporation; Municipal and Community Affairs; Education, Culture and Employment (ECE); and support from the community senior administrative officer, Judal Dominicata, and Chief David Wedawin and his council, I was able to buy fabric and sewing machines to get started.

Before I knew it, I had a full house plus a waiting list! Participants who knew how to sew already mostly used hand-cranked sewing machines and other retro equipment. I couldn't wait for all the ladies to use modern sewing machines! Before long, there was a magnificent bloom of pillowcases, bags, wall hangings, table runners and other attractive projects being produced. Sewing gifts for the elders is part of the program, too, and we had a wonderful time delivering them.

With generous support from our backers, we were able to expand the program. Now, we not only have classes for more ladies (ages 24 to 72) but also for school youth age ten and up as well. In all, roughly 15 percent of the community is now sewing!

This year, the ladies took on the monumental task of making their very own bed quilts—queen and king-sized! With patterns chosen and fabric selected, the sewing started in earnest with classes on days, evenings and weekends. Once the quilt tops were completed, and with the help of Air Tindi (our local airline), they were flown to Yellowknife. There, the wonderful staff at North of 60 Quilting Services were able to complete the quilts on a long-arm quilt machine, and then the quilts were flown back again. The end result was a beautiful garden of quilts in an array of colours, just like the Arctic landscape. We held an open house so the ladies could share their work with the community.

We even have a message board set up in the classroom, so participants can express how they feel. One of my favourite comments is, "I'm dreaming big dreams for my sewing." What is truly inspiring to me is the self-confidence and raised self-esteem that comes from learning something new.

So, every winter, like the wildflowers under the snow, beneath the majesty and splendour of the Arctic aurora, on a cold winter's night and with the stars twinkling way up high, we'll all be snug and cozy under our quilts made with dedication and love.

*—by **Lynn Turcotte**, Gamètì, Northwest Territories*

Paddling With Purpose

More than 1,000 kilometres travelled in memory of friends lost to cancer

It happened almost a decade ago, but I still remember the great feeling of excitement as my friend Tom Wilson and I loaded our kayaks onto the freight train at Sudbury Junction station. We were heading out on a paddle to raise cancer awareness in memory of my good friend Max Welton and Tom's friend Renee Kitely, who succumbed to the disease at the young age of 18.

Tom and I would paddle 1,030 kilometres, starting from the Jackfish River north of Lake Nipigon and across the lake to the Nipigon River. This is where I received most of my blisters. We would then shoreline Lake Superior down to Batchawana Bay.

The train ride was more than 13 hours, plus we spent two hours getting our gear to the river, where we were greeted by a bald eagle and a flock of white pelicans.

As we paddled Lake Nipigon, I could not help but think how my friend Max would have appreciated the sheer beauty of the eastern shore of the Nipigon River. Max was diagnosed with pancreatic cancer at 47 years old and passed away only four months later. He was a great friend.

We had three weeks to complete our route, so we paddled anywhere from eight to 16½ hours a day. We had four windbound days and many broken-up days of paddling. Once on the Nipigon River, we had three hydroelectric dams to portage, the longest portage being four kilometres.

This wasn't a sightseeing trip, but we did take in as much scenery as possible while concentrating on the waves and weather changes that could come upon us quite suddenly.

You quickly develop respect for a large body of water such as Lake Superior. You do not conquer her; she lets you ride her waves and tells you when it's time to get off.

We passed many picturesque locales, such as Rossport and Terrace Bay. After stopping for supplies in Marathon, we continued on to

Pic River, where we were treated to a beautiful sunset as we pitched our tents for the night.

I wish I could have shared this experience with so many people. It was humbling to say the least, riding in six-foot to eight-foot waves and counting seven strokes to a wake at times. We spent almost three full weeks getting to Batchawana Bay due to the strong headwinds and were pleased to realize we had met our goal in only 19 days.

It's hard to describe such a trip in such a beautiful part of Canada, other than to say it was awesome beyond belief. Our story was printed in the local newspaper to encourage people to donate to the Canadian Cancer Society. This trip was not only dedicated to my good friend Max and Tom's friend Renee but to all cancer victims and survivors everywhere. This was for all of you.

*—by **Scott Prevost**, Elliot Lake, Ontario*

From Milk Bags to Bed Mats

Thanks to a dedicated group of volunteers, orphans in Haiti are sleeping a bit easier

Every Tuesday morning for two hours, more than a dozen people from Essex County meet in the basement of St. Andrews Anglican Church in Harrow, Ontario, to turn plastic milk bags into sleeping mats for Haiti, a country devastated by earthquakes and hurricanes. Plastic bags are excellent for making mats and other useful items: The plastic doesn't rot; it's easy to wash; it breathes; and insects can't breed in it.

After we flatten the milk bags, we staple 15 of them together at the bottom. My husband, Prosper, puts two piles in a hinged wooden frame and uses an X-acto knife to cut the bags, following the slits in the frame, resulting in inch-wide plastic strips. We sort the loops by colour for fun and to make each mat individual. We join the loops and roll them into a ball. Volunteers then crochet the strips into school bags, pillow covers, large mats for sleeping on, or smaller ones to sit on. Many of us do some of this work at home. If anyone donates money, we buy school supplies.

Our project started in May 2011 when Kathy Harnadek read an article about people making similar mats. She invited my six-year-old granddaughter Chianna and me to go with her to Essex, where we watched people cutting bags, joining loops and crocheting or weaving mats.

Next, we began collecting milk bags. At first, we took them to Essex for cutting and came home with the loops. When a group in Kingsville stopped making mats, they lent us their cutting frame and we began to cut the bags ourselves. Since then, we have acquired four more frames, which we use and also lend to other groups.

We collect the milk bags from schools, restaurants, churches, seniors' residences and grocery stores, as well as businesses in Harrow and neighbouring towns. We have also received thousands of milk bags that have never been used. These bags are harder to cut, but the loops are smoother and easier to crochet.

Someone said that it takes 600 bags to make a mat, but I've read different totals. Each bag has some loss at the top and bottom, and occasionally bags get torn. We use the waste to finish the pillows. Full Circle, our local thrift store, gives us anything they can't sell and which they think the Haitians can use. Those items and our finished products are sent to Ground Effects in Windsor, where the owner, Jim Scott, takes everything to Haiti and personally distributes them to a selection of orphanages there.

When we first started, Jim spoke at our church and showed slides of his work in Haiti. He left, taking what we had collected so far. He also went away with six boxes of used French books, donated by the Essex County Library, as the people of Haiti speak either French or Creole.

We used to take everything to Ground Effects ourselves, but now we gather so much so fast that Jim has to send a truck. So far, we have sent 379 sleeping mats, 118 small mats, 108 school bags and 60 pillows. We have also donated school supplies, clothing, shoes, bed linens, toys and kitchen supplies.

Volunteers in Blenheim, Ontario, who had been weaving mats, gave us a loom and we gave them a cutter. They bring their mats to us and we send them on to Ground Effects.

Several years ago, we held an Elder College course for seniors. Jim gave a talk and slide show. Then Kathy, Prosper, Veronica Jamieson and I explained what we do with the milk bags.

We love this voluntary activity and have become a close group. Once a month we have pizza and twice a year we have a potluck lunch or eat out at a restaurant. Thanks to the wonderful people in our group and those who give us milk bags and other items, our pile of supplies for Haiti continues to grow. We are keeping thousands of plastic milk bags out of the landfill sites and helping people who need help. The most satisfying part is that we know our mats are actually getting to Haiti.

*—by **Esther Meerschaut**, Harrow, Ontario*

From Rescue to Rescuer

This pup knows how to give back from the heart

One November our lives changed forever, thanks to an addition to our family that became a true blessing. Our daughter, Stacey, came upon a dog tied to a tree on a property where, as it turned out, the owners had departed for parts unknown. Seeing this emaciated dog looking as if she hadn't a friend in the world, Stacey stopped her car to examine the situation.

She walked slowly over to the poor bedraggled hound, not knowing if she'd be set upon or worse. The dog peered cautiously at her, then stood up and marginally wagged her tail. She didn't pounce or bark but stood quietly, waiting for some sign of friendship. As Stacey reached out a hand, the dog slunk down low and cowered. Her pitiful expression spoke volumes and Stacey was deeply moved.

Returning to her car, she sped home for food and water; her return was greeted with more wagging of the tail. When she deposited a dish of food and another of water nearby, the dog waited, glancing longingly at the offerings, obviously taught to seek permission.

Stacey prompted the dog to eat and she did so, delicately and daintily. The water got the most attention and that was when Stacey noticed there were no dishes whatsoever in the vicinity of where the dog was tied. Not only abandoned, she'd been left to slowly starve.

Once the local SPCA was notified and had seized the dog, she was then examined by a local vet and pronounced quite ill from malnutrition. Stacey already had two dogs and a rescued cat, but our dog had died of cancer several years previously, so Stacey felt it was safe to offer our home as a refuge of love and care.

We adopted the dog, weighing just 35 pounds, and named her Keli Ann. She is loving but very quiet, cautious to the point of constant trepidation and still dainty in her eating habits.

She was eight months old when she came to us. Likely never having been played with, she does not even understand the concept of chasing a ball. She loves to swim, but she'll assume a submissive position if anyone tries to throw her a stick. Through all of this and owing to her kind nature, we discovered that Keli Ann loves babies. Any and all babies draw her immediate attention. She will sniff them from head to toe without once touching them directly with her wet, cold nose. She rarely barks, but when she does it certifies that she's part beagle, along with the obvious Nova Scotia duck tolling retriever.

We registered Keli Ann with the St. John Ambulance Therapy Dog Program the following year. Since that time, she and I regularly visit our local regional hospital, plus a nearby seniors' residence. Her calm manner is greeted with smiles and exclamations of warm welcome wherever we go, and she relishes the attention of the staff as well as the patients and visitors.

She is one of several dogs to visit South Shore Regional Hospital in Bridgewater, Nova Scotia, and the program allows our community to interact positively with those involved in health care. The tensions of the day seem to disappear when there's a bit of attention from a dog with a wagging tail.

Keli Ann is excited each and every time her Therapy Dog scarf and identification tags are put on. She also seems to stand a bit taller as she prances about on her rounds, hearing a lot of, "Hi, Keli girl, how's the pretty dog today?" and "Hey, Keli, come on over here and say hello." She'll put her front paws up on a patient's bed so she can be reached and seems to understand she's needed when she's encouraged to remain by someone's side just a little bit longer.

We may bemoan her early beginnings, but we are thankful for what we have today—a dog with the biggest heart in the world, who now weighs in at more than 65 pounds. She is ten years old and counting, and sleeps a bit more each day, but her enthusiasm and trust in people never wanes and the value of the service she provides is undeniable. She asks for nothing but a gentle word and a pat on her head and in return, she gives from her heart.

*—by **Beverlee Brown**, Bridgewater, Nova Scotia*

Flying High on Knowledge

Volunteers with more than 700 years of combined military service share their expertise with students

Retired now, I was a teacher with the Annapolis Valley Regional School Board in Nova Scotia for 35 years. For the last decade or so, I have been privileged to be a participant—first as a teacher and now as a volunteer—in a flight education program at the Greenwood Military Aviation Museum (GMAM) at the RCAF base in the small town of Greenwood, Nova Scotia.

Here in the Annapolis Valley, we are an hour or two away from the city and some of its learning opportunities, such as museums. It is not always possible to get our students to these locations. The GMAM has provided local schools with access to learning experiences in technology, flight and history, especially through its wonderful flight education program.

The program is piloted by Lloyd Graham, a retired air force navigator. It all began with a conversation I had with Lloyd back in 2003, in which I expressed what a shame it was that a wonderful resource like the museum was not being utilized by our schools, especially since flight education was part of the Grade 6 curriculum in Nova Scotia.

Within days, Lloyd came to my school to pick up a copy of the province's department of education curriculum guide. With a team of aircrew volunteers, Lloyd created a flight education program that could be given through the museum and was positively received by the school board. This was an ambitious mission and one into which Lloyd and a team of museum volunteers put many hours.

The program is successful thanks to the exceptional commitment of some 23 volunteer instructors who are mainly retired air force aircrew, along with a few active-duty air and ground crew, as well as civilian personnel. All of these volunteers bring a wide range of expertise to the program in such areas as long-range patrol, fighter and helicopter operations, theory of flight, the Cold War era, search and rescue, and aircraft design, to name a few. In a typical year, volunteers have a combined total of 721.5 years of military service and more than 150,000 flying hours.

The flight education program runs from January to April. Each instructor makes a commitment of about 35 hours per session and, after a dozen years, more than 5,000 students, teachers and chaperones from 14 different schools have participated. Groups of students are guided through six stations where they spend 20 minutes engaged in every aspect of flight education—and it all runs with military precision. Once back in the classroom, students are asked to reflect on their museum experience and write letters to the instructors.

It is not only a wonderful opportunity for students to experience flight education and history from those who lived it but also an occasion to interact with our veterans, ask questions and hear their stories. Now that I'm retired, I get to hang out with these exceptional people on flight education days. I have an even greater respect for the instructors and the time they spend with the students. I now realize what a commitment of time it really is. I also enjoy seeing how much fun they have.

—by ***Connie Weinberg****, Aylesford, Nova Scotia*

Making a Difference

Volunteering in Swaziland was life-affirming

"Where are you going? Switzerland?" asked my good friend Dan. "No," I corrected him, "Swaziland!" Two years ago, I decided to follow up on a dream I had when I was a young woman. I had always wanted to volunteer in a developing country, but life got in the way—a career as a journalist, boyfriends, marriage. Now in my middle years, I thought it was a good time to fulfill that early vision. My supportive husband, Stephen didn't mind me taking off for a year, my communications consulting work in Toronto would be there when I returned and my health was good.

While searching for options on the Internet, I found Crossroads International, a Canadian not-for-profit volunteer organization that has been around for more than 50 years. They were looking for a communications officer for a one-year posting with the Swaziland Action Group Against Abuse (SWAGAA), a Crossroads partner organization that specializes in preventing gender-based violence. After a few interviews, Crossroads called with the good news. I got the position.

I had to look at a map to find out where Swaziland was. It's a hilly country just over half the size of Vancouver Island, wedged between South Africa and Mozambique. I learned that it's an absolute monarchy, has the highest HIV/AIDS prevalence in the world and most of the population of 1.3 million people live on less than $2 a day.

When I arrived, the Crossroads liaison officer took me to my new home in the town of Manzini, population 70,000. The bungalow was neat and beautifully furnished and the rent was reasonable (paid out of my living allowance from Crossroads). It was an easy walk to my office, but I was told not to linger outside after dark, since it wasn't safe. That meant hustling home, since the sun went down at 6 p.m. I never encountered any problems, as I stuck to this advice religiously.

Luckily, there were excellent markets. Swaziland gets much of its fruit and vegetables from South Africa and I enjoyed delicious meals. Sometimes, I tucked into a Swazi staple called pap, ground maize that resembles grits. This was often paired with chakalaka, a spicy tomato/bean/veggie relish and barbecued meat—goat, beef or chicken.

My new job focused on advocating for gender justice and liaising with media. Reporters were constantly looking for a response from SWAGAA on stories of horrendous abuse; one in three Swazi girls is sexually abused before they turn 18. I was also in charge of creating educational materials; I wrote press releases, organized presentations, updated social media and oversaw a weekly radio show (in SiSwati, the national Swazi language). My favourite task was speaking about self-esteem to members of SWAGAA's Girls Empowerment Clubs.

It was hard at first. I groped along trying to figure out the phone system, make sense of purchase requisition forms and learn a few words of SiSwati. *"Sawubona,"* I'd say, greeting my colleagues every morning. When it came to saying thank you, *"ngiyabonga,"* I'd inevitably get tongue-tied and use the greeting instead.

Most nights I was too exhausted to do anything but fall into bed after dinner. On weekends, with a couple of fellow volunteers, we'd check out Swazi events such as the annual Umhlanga ceremony, or Reed Dance, where 10,000 young women wearing beads, sashes and the traditional short skirt (*isigege* and *izinculuba*) bring reeds to the Queen Mother to rebuild her compound, then dance before her son, King Mswati III. He now has 15 wives and picks a new one at the event.

By Christmas I was ready for a break. Stephen came over from Canada, and we took off to Kruger National Park in South Africa to track wildlife. Driving through the massive park (the size of the Netherlands), we encountered zebras, antelope, buffalo and rhinos. It was thrilling to hear hippos quarrelling at night and watch protective mama elephants and their babies during the day. A highlight was the night safari, where we encountered a pride of around 20 lions.

The real adventure, however, was back in Swaziland. Before the end of my mandate, the Children's Protection and Welfare Bill passed into law and the Sexual Offences and Domestic Violence Bill was waiting to be signed by the King. With these in place, eventually the country will have a fighting chance to deter perpetrators of gender-based violence with stiffer sentencing.

Back in Canada, I realized my work was a life-affirming experience. I feel I really helped make a difference and impacted positive change. Would I do it again? In a heartbeat!

*—by **Maureen Littlejohn**, Toronto, Ontario*

Northern Manitoba Matters

Reclaiming traditional food skills up north

In the fading sunlight of a northern Manitoba evening, all dressed up in a tuxedo, Winston stands proudly in the most unlikely of locations: a chicken coop. He has many reasons to be proud this evening, not the least of which is the reason for his outfit—a party celebrating his 50th wedding anniversary. At the moment, however, he's celebrating a different 50: the number of chickens he's been raising for the past six weeks.

Thanks to his hard work, his chickens are happy, healthy and on their way to becoming a nutritious northern food source. His coop, built with the help of a few friends, is jokingly described by visitors as "the Ritz hotel for chickens"—comfortable, clean and spacious, with a pretty view of the lake.

Winston, who describes himself as an outdoorsman, is an experienced hunter, trapper and fisherman, but he has never raised his own meat before. That didn't stop him from jumping in and committing to spending three months of his summer raising chickens.

He's not alone, either: There are eight other families alongside him who, together, are raising a total of 450 chickens. They call themselves the Cross Lake Chicken Club and they're the reason I find myself in Cross Lake on this summer evening. I work at Food Matters Manitoba, a registered charity that partners with northerners, newcomers, farmers and families to harvest, prepare and share good food. My job is to support food projects happening in communities around Manitoba's north.

Residents of northern Manitoba face alarmingly high food prices. In some communities, a four-litre jug of milk can cost almost $15, while a 4.5-kilogram bag of potatoes could be $33. With such prices, and with many northerners surviving on quite low incomes, it's easy to understand why families struggle to eat fresh, nutritious foods and face the subsequent health consequences.

Across the north, however, residents are working for change by reclaiming traditional food skills, building gardens and greenhouses, raising livestock and reaping the benefits.

Up north, these kinds of projects aren't as straightforward as in the south, and that's where Food Matters Manitoba comes in. We help farmers, gardeners, hunters and others fund their projects, source materials and connect them with people who have the knowledge they need to succeed.

Though the learning curve is steep, the Chicken Club has risen to the challenge. In the true spirit of northern innovation, they are often trying new things or repurposing old ones to improve their systems. As the birds get big enough to slaughter, they will be shared with friends, family and elders, and the whole community will get a taste of the chicken raisers' efforts.

And so, every morning and evening, Winston visits his birds to replenish their feed and water supplies, make sure the pen is intact and safe, and cleans the coop out as needed. Sure, they're cute and fun, but they're also food, and he looks forward to the day when he'll be putting them on the table for his family.

*—by **Anna Levin**, Winnipeg, Manitoba*

PrimRose Donkey Sanctuary

Volunteering at this "forever home" for elderly, neglected or abused donkeys is hard but uplifting work

From the cozy comfort of my SUV, I peer out at the grey, drizzly day and sigh. Before me, the undulating vista of the Northumberland hills disappears into a shroud of murky cloud, and I wonder what happened to the day's sunny forecast. Just ahead, I can make out the 150-year-old barn of the PrimRose Donkey Sanctuary, surrounded by the peaceful, drifting shapes of donkeys, their long ears fluting skyward.

It's Monday morning in Roseneath, Ontario, and I'm about to start my day as a "newbie" volunteer, helping to make the sanctuary's denizens—which in addition to donkeys also include an assortment of mules, goats, sheep and pigs—comfortable and happy.

Swaddled in a raincoat and boots, I wave hello to Sheila Burns, the sanctuary's founder and director; she's chatting with volunteers by the barn and sorting out the day's activities. I soon discover there's a mountain of work to be done: Besides cleaning the barn and manger, bales of straw and hay need to be delivered to stalls and paddocks, animals must be moved to various stalls for the vet and farrier, and twice-daily feed rations must be specially measured and mixed with meds and vitamins for some of the sanctuary's residents. While a volunteer crew is busy erecting a protective wall to keep out the damp wind, all activity is intensely scrutinized by several wary-eyed barn cats.

Grabbing a rake and wheelbarrow, I get to work helping two other volunteers with mucking-out. Despite the chilly air, it doesn't take long to work up a sweat. We dig through our chores with easy banter while a few shaggy donkeys watch us thoughtfully. It's a bit of a job squeezing by a "pace" or group of donkeys with a wheelbarrow full of poop and dirty straw, but I soon learn that with donkeys one has to be patient. Not really the stubborn creatures often depicted, they just insist on doing things their own way—in donkey time. "Walk on," I gently urge Sarah Rose, a lovely chocolate jennet. After thinking this over for a few minutes, she finally budges.

Throughout the day, I hear of the animals' varied histories; many, like Joey, suffered their fair share of abuse and neglect. Others are here because their owners, for various reasons, were no longer able to care for them. PrimRose, the sanctuary's namesake, is now in her 40s. The first donkey to arrive in 1994, PrimRose carted people around Toronto's Black Creek Pioneer Village for many years and was later transferred to numerous homes before finding her "forever home" here at the sanctuary.

By late afternoon, we are soggy, sweaty and pleasantly tired. We've just served up the last donkey dinners, the buckets are brimming with clean water, and the sweet smell of fresh hay permeates the barn. I'm dying for a hot bath and a glass of Merlot, but before I go, I steal a few moments with Patsy.

Having suffered loss of vision due to a previous eye infection, Patsy still gets around with a little help from her seeing-eye donkey, Jonathon Cupcake. As Jonathon stands guard, I speak to Patsy gently and stroke the inside of her incredibly soft ears. She presses her head into my chest and nuzzles my jacket, my chin, my nose and I feel her warm breath seep deep into my heart. Forget slogging poop and getting grubby and all of the sore, aching muscles: In this moment, I learn what it means to be snuggled by a donkey, and it makes all the hard work so worthwhile!

*—by **Janette Slack**, Cobourg, Ontario*

Lessons Learned in Ethiopia

Teaching English was the main objective, but learning was a two-way street

In the summer of 2015, Debra Boos, Diane and Madeline Martel, my eldest daughter Kaila Keutzer and I were members of a Canadian teaching team that made the long journey to Ethiopia to teach English for a three-week period in the Karayu community of Dhebiti. There were 75 students in the "English Language Boot Camp" created by ANSO Collectives and Educational Support Society based in Grande Prairie, Alberta, and the Gudina Tumsa Foundation in Ethiopia.

From the moment we arrived in Ethiopia, we felt welcomed and cherished. We resided at the school site for the full three weeks, except for a few trips to Metehara, the local market, Awash Park and the sugar cane fields. The accommodations were very basic, with intermittent running water and sporadic electricity. The weather was extremely hot, with many days over 40°C. We only had cellphone service if we walked up the mountain behind the school. Internet access was nonexistent.

Our school day ran from 8 a.m. to 12:30 p.m., then a break; classes resumed from 3 p.m. to 5 p.m. Our primary focus was teaching English, because at the high school level the students have to write national exams in English in all subject areas. If they are not successful, their academic career is over; for female students, this means the onset of marriage and child-rearing. Where we were, girls are married as young as 14 unless they go to school. Education is literally their way out of the poverty cycle in which they've grown up. If the students are successful, they will continue on to university. The government initially pays for their education, but the students have to reimburse the government once they have finished their degree.

The students have a very clear understanding of the value of education and the importance of learning English. They are amazingly dedicated and focused on their education. Not only were they committed to their education but they were also committed to pleasing us. They were kind and thoughtful. Not once did I carry my supplies to the classrooms; I could take only a couple of steps before one of the students would whisk in and take things out of my hands, saying, "I will help you, Brenda!" If we teachers and staff members went for a walk, in no time the students would fall into stride with us, asking, "Where you going? We come too!" Whenever we met up with the local people, the students seemed proud to introduce us and communicate for us. We would be invited into their humble homes. Their loving demeanour made us all feel like we were part of the community.

During break time at school, the students would gather around us, asking questions, wanting to learn more about Canada and our way of life. In the classroom, they were eager to learn. They would copy down everything, whether they were asked to or not. They yearned to share their answers with you. "All correct?" they would ask. They were eager to learn the language and were not afraid to laugh at themselves when they made a mistake. "That is a mosquito," one student said, pointing to a church during one of our walks. "Do you mean a mosque?" I asked. "Oh yes, a mosque, a mosque, not a mosquito—buzzzzz!" Laughter ensued. We had so many charming moments like that—memories we will hold on to for the rest of our lives.

Although I have been teaching for 26 years, my experience in Ethiopia provided me with many teaching "firsts." I have never had my students evacuate the classroom to dispense with a poisonous snake before! Nor have I ever had a goat wander in during the middle of a lesson before. I have never been so limited in resources—a cement classroom, desks and a dusty old chalkboard were all I had—yet so empowered by my ability to teach creatively and to have such a positive impact on my students' learning. I have never developed such a strong bond with my students in such a short period of time. This bond, at times, could seem overwhelming. The last day was very difficult—students and staff alike were shedding tears and sharing many hugs.

The students prepared a performance for us on the final evening. The girls dressed in traditional clothing and sang a beautiful song, which roughly translated said: "If it was near to us, we would come and visit you again and again and again, but Canada is so far away. What shall I do? The pain is in saying goodbye." We were all feeling that pain. These students have so little, and yet they gave so much. It was truly a humbling and life-enriching experience.

*—by **Brenda Keay**, Coldstream, British Columbia*

Racing for a Cure

Experience life in the fast lane and contribute to a great cause!

In 2012, we held the first Racing for a Cure event in Edmonton. The event brings together exotic car owners and enthusiasts who want to help give back to the community and the general public who want to help raise money for children's charities. Since its humble beginnings—the first year with nine cars on the racetrack—Racing for a Cure has evolved into a world-class event attracting more than 60 exotic and super exotic cars and thousands of attendees each year.

To date, Racing for a Cure has raised more than $1 million for children's causes. This amazing charity provides support and programs to children with cancer and their families in Alberta and the Northwest Territories. Their mission is to identify and meet the needs of children with cancer and their families, from the time of diagnosis throughout treatment and beyond, right through to support, clinical programs and research.

Racing for a Cure offers the thrill-seeker a chance to ride shotgun in an exotic car on a closed race course with a trained driver at the wheel. These high-octane machines reach breathtaking speeds as they manoeuvre a 2.7-kilometre technical road course featuring high-speed chicanes, banked corners and full-out straights.

The inspiration for our event came from the desire for auto enthusiasts to give back to the community. A group of exotic car owners and friends came together to develop Racing for a Cure into an epic interaction between some of the most exclusive exotic automobiles on the planet and the heartwarming stories of the mighty kids living with life-threatening cancers.

This incredible event features some of the rarest Ferraris, Maseratis, Lamborghinis, Ford GT40s, Aston Martins, Porsches and McLarens from around the province of Alberta and elsewhere. In past seasons, we have featured one of the world's fastest Ferraris—a custom pearl yellow Ferrari ZXX Evo, boasting 900 horsepower and a top speed of 400 kilometres an hour. This one-of-a-kind supercar, valued at $3.4 million, is in great company beside an equally stunning street-legal orange Maserati MC12 Corsa, worth $3 million. Several other very rare exotic cars have made dreams come true at Racing for a Cure, including a $1.6 million Rosso Corsa Ferrari F40 LM, a $2 million custom-ordered electric-blue McLaren P1 and a variety of modified and unique Lamborghini Aventadors. No wonder Racing for a Cure is now one of the premier gatherings of exotic cars in the world.

Exotic car owners/drivers are required to complete a full-day race certification at the track before taking willing passengers out for an adrenaline-pumping, heart-pounding thrill ride that they will remember for a lifetime.

Racing for a Cure starts the day by giving rides to the VIP children who have been affected by cancer and their families. For many of our drivers, this is the most rewarding and best part of their weekend experience.

After the VIPs have had their thrills on the track, the event then opens to the public for the day. For a donation of $50, the public can experience a ride in an exotic car valued at $250,000 to $500,000. For a donation of $350, they can ride in a super exotic valued at $650,000 to $3.4 million.

Designed to be a family fun day, there's excitement on and off the track. For the little ones, there is a kids' zone with bouncy castles, balloon animals, face painters and magicians. Trackside has a Show and Shine, showcasing everything from custom vintage hot rods to modern exotics. Families are encouraged to come and spend the day enjoying the sights and sounds as the exotic cars tear up the track.

The day wraps up with an incredible gala event, featuring dinner, live and silent auctions, and great entertainment. Some of our live auction items in previous years have included a trip for two on a private jet to the famous Barrett Jackson car auction, and also a trip for four to the 100th running of the Indy 500 in Indianapolis as VIPs with team Schmidt Peterson, which fetched an astonishing $70,000.

Fortunate to have found a measure of success as the owner and designer of Venus Eye Design, I have been privileged to spearhead the event in recent years and have been involved with Racing for a Cure since day one. It takes many corporate sponsors and dedicated volunteers to put this event together. Each year everyone works hard to ensure that a great time will be had by all and, more importantly, many courageous kids with cancer will receive tremendous support.

*—by **Mike Christiansen**, Edmonton, Alberta*

Turning Dining Out Into Helping Out

Two young Canadians create an easy way to give back

Growing up, my cousin Andrew Hall and I never liked to eat our vegetables—especially Brussels sprouts! It was Thanksgiving 1996 and we were eight years old. We had, of course, eaten our turkey, mashed potatoes, stuffing and gravy. All that was left were the Brussels sprouts, and we each had a pile of them.

"Eat your food! Starving kids in Africa would love to have it," Nan would say as we pushed our food around our plates. Being eight years old, we thought of a plan that would help the kids and get us out of eating our veggies: We would put the extra food in an envelope and mail it over to Africa to help kids there. To our dismay, Nan wasn't impressed and, as you can imagine, the night ended with us finishing our vegetables.

A lot older and marginally wiser, Andrew and I now see why our plan of mailing extra food from Canada to Africa won't work, but that hasn't stopped us from trying to solve the issue of hunger!

In 2013, we started Mealshare, a nonprofit that partners with restaurants to provide meals to people in need, both locally and abroad. Here's how it works. At our partner restaurants, our logo is placed next to some of their menu items. When one of the "Mealshare items" is ordered, the customer gets their meal as usual, but a meal is also provided to someone in need—it's a "buy one, give one" model!

Restaurants pay a portion of their proceeds from each Mealshare item sold to our nonprofit, which allows us to donate funds to a partner charity that will provide a meal. Mealshare works with local and international charities, ensuring support raised through Mealshare helps Canadians, as well as people in developing countries where hunger is often a major issue.

We began Mealshare with four restaurants and have been excited to see it grow. We now have 65 partner restaurants across Western Canada and customers have shared more than 60,000 meals through Mealshare. In the near future, we hope to have 100 partner restaurants across all of Canada.

Restaurants appreciate Mealshare because it's so easy for them to participate. One restaurant owner from British Columbia said, "From our perspective, it's kind of a no-brainer. It's a feel-good thing and, for the people dining, it means they are giving back as well. What the heck; everyone wants to feel good and to help people out."

Andrew and I have been so excited to see how much support there is for Mealshare. We find that almost everyone wants to share with those less fortunate, but so often life can be too busy to find the time. Mealshare helps with that, because it doesn't take any extra effort on the part of the customer. They just find a partner restaurant and enjoy a meal with their family or friends. At the end of the day, if Mealshare makes it a bit easier for Canadians to share with those in need, we think we've done our job—and no international shipping of Brussels sprouts required!

*—by **Jeremy Bryant**, Edmonton, Alberta*

Generosity in Motion

A community pitches in to keep its historic movie theatre alive

In 1917, the Rumford family of Forest, Ontario, bought a building in the centre of downtown Forest and began showing motion pictures. They operated the Kineto Theatre for 60 years, until they sold it to the Kiwanis Club of Forest.

My first time at the Forest Kineto Theatre—more than 50 years ago—was as a wide-eyed youngster watching *Black Beauty* with my big sister. My friends and I watched our fair share of movies there during our formative years. In case you're wondering, "Kineto" is short for "Kinetoscope," which was the early type of projection system used.

I recall when the Kiwanis Club of Forest bought the Kineto from the Rumford family; my wife and I went to see *Coal Miner's Daughter*. It was packed, and we had to sit in different rows, but the Kiwanis did their best to keep us close. Since the Kiwanis Club took over the Kineto in 1977, new seats have been installed twice, and the heating and air-conditioning systems have been upgraded.

In 1985, I joined the Kiwanis and have been active in promoting the Kiwanis' Kineto Theatre ever since. At that point, the Kineto still had 1940s-era carbon arc projectors. Movies arrived on 20-minute reels and were very flammable. Once a movie started, the licensed projectionist could not leave the projection booth. The club was struggling with a heavy mortgage back then, and individual members signed bank notes to keep the theatre going. We saw the potential of property ownership and held on until we were able to do away with the mortgage, thanks to financial assistance from the community via raffles and donations. What a relief that was to the club! From there, we've never looked back.

When a theatre in nearby Sarnia closed its doors, we jumped at the chance to purchase their xenon lamphouses. Instead of using both, we kept one for parts and installed a system so that when movies arrived, they were spliced onto one large reel that operated much like an eight-track. Next was the installation of a Dolby 5.1 surround sound system, courtesy of volunteers with electrical and technical skills.

In September 2011, our movie booking manager came to us with some sobering news: 35-mm prints were becoming hard to acquire because of the introduction of digital equipment. Well, obstacles like this had never stopped the club or the community before. So, we began a campaign that November and soon had local service, social, sports and fraternal groups donating four-figure dollar amounts. Many local residents donated large sums as well. Thanks to all the support from many people in the town and surrounding area, large and small anonymous donations, grants from the Forest Community Foundation and the Ontario Trillium Foundation, the Kiwanis Kineto Theatre was able to present its first digital movie in April 2012.

The Kiwanis Club of Forest threw a gala evening to honour significant contributors, and an open house was held where every member of the community was thanked for their help.

The theatre now has a new, up-to-date marquee, and we have also installed a chair lift, courtesy of a long-time member, to allow access to our basement meeting room—a room dug out and constructed by the club members. During all these upgrades, we have tried to maintain the historical aspects of the building along with its movie heritage, which is proudly displayed in our second-floor Kineto Museum.

In recent years, we have partnered with other local organizations to offer a number of community-oriented festivals, including the Lambton Film & Food Festival, held annually in downtown Forest on the last weekend in May, plus the Forest Film Festival, held during the fall and winter months, and the fall Forest Concert Series. These have met with great success.

In addition to the ongoing operation of the Kiwanis Kineto Theatre four nights a week, our 40-member club also sponsors an annual Santa Claus parade, a bike safety rodeo, a community kite festival, a babysitting course for teens, scholarship and citizenship awards in local schools, and a birthday greetings program for Forest's seniors, in which local seniors receive either a birthday cake or theatre passes. Pancake breakfasts, bingos and other fundraisers help us provide these services to the community.

*—by **Ward Burr**, Forest, Ontario*

Give Me Shelter

One community member makes a noticeable difference

Community mailboxes are springing up all over Canada as door-to-door mail delivery goes the way of milk delivery. But it seems that once they are set up, nobody takes care of them. Some are vandalized, and others quickly become covered in dust and mud. While they are often a focal point for neighbourhoods, people seldom linger —especially when the weather is poor.

"I thought the mailboxes were neglected," says John Mosiuk, a semi-retired resident of Cedar-by-the-Sea, a community just south of Nanaimo, British Columbia. "So I decided to do something about it." John drew up plans for a shelter that would cover not only the mailboxes but also provide a cover for the community newspaper boxes, as well as provide a bulletin board for neighbourhood announcements. Canada Post was then contacted for permission to build the structure.

As every project needs funding, the neighbourhood's Block Watch captain, George Creek, contacted the 39 households that use the boxes to show them the plan and ask for support. Thirty-seven households agreed to donate $20 to the project's material costs. Wood was purchased from a nearby cedar mill. Other materials were donated by neighbours, and local building supply stores donated supplies or provided them at a discount.

Over the course of a week, posts were set in concrete, and John precut and stained all the components, and then hauled them in his trailer to the construction site. There, he, George and a third neighbour, Paul Panchuk, assembled the structure.

What has the response been like? People love it! They can now open their mailboxes while protected from the persistent rain and their newspapers remain dry, even on the most blustery days. People using the boxes appreciate the shelter and the fact that it improves the look of the neighbourhood.

It's fitting, then, that the first notices to be pinned to the bulletin board were cards of appreciation from pleased neighbours. Even the mailman likes it! Now, he can sort mail out of the way of the rain and snow—heck, he even kicked in the last $20 to help cover the material costs!

Creating the shelter was an easy and beneficial project that brought our neighbourhood together, and word of it seems to be getting around. Not long ago, several cars were seen pausing near the shelter, their occupants snapping photos. A couple of folks even brought measuring tapes and took measurements. We are situated in an out-of-the-way rural area, so I suspect they made a special effort to visit the shelter.

*—by **David Hill-Turner**, Nanaimo, British Columbia*

Moulding Young Minds

Fifteen years of working with teens keeps this volunteer young

My past few years of volunteering came about because I am a man who knows how to knit. It all began during World War II, when the frequent German air raid attacks over London, England, sent all us junior school children scurrying into "blast-proof" brick shelters around the edge of the school playground. There, in very dim light—one small light bulb about every 50 feet—we sat on benches, busy learning to knit small squares of all colours and types of yarn for some unfortunate grown-ups to sew into patchwork blankets. I never got to see a finished product, but I suspect it was full of holes long before the moths got at it.

Fast-forward to more recent times—the year 2000, shortly after I retired from civil engineering—and now the setting is a Toronto school, the York Mills Collegiate Institute. A family friend, Madge, was helping the home economics—a.k.a. family studies—teacher show teenagers how to knit. "No way," said the few boys in the class, "boys don't knit!" "That's where you're wrong," replied Madge. Next day, I was dragged, kicking and screaming, into the class. It was the first time I'd been in a high school classroom in more than 40 years!

After a few hours explaining about needles and stitches, how to cast on, pick up dropped stitches and properly terminate the whole operation without simply pulling the needles out, the boy knitters were quite proud of their efforts, especially when they realized knit and purl were the only two basic stitches to remember. My teaching reputation climbed quite high as a result—so high that I was then asked if I could help the teacher in the tech shop on a trial basis.

Fifteen years later, I am still volunteering five half or full days each week. Fridays I sometimes stay home, explaining to the students that that's my laundry day. My expertise is largely in woodworking, although I can teach the rudiments of metalwork as well. The workshop is quite large, and most of the classes are full, with 22 kids per class. We teach the course to Grades 10 through 12; it includes written studies, computer drafting, welding, and hands-on woodworking and lathe projects. Typical projects for the higher grades include Muskoka chairs (single and double, for adults or toddlers), bookshelves, tables of all sizes, desks, chests, lizard cages (two so far!), benches, baseball bats, inlay work, rocking horses and so forth. Junior grades might create bread or cheese boards, picture frames, jewelry boxes, model cars or trucks, bird feeders and such like.

The students can take home what they build; if they don't want to keep their creations, staff members are always happy to be offered our surplus output. At the end of term, when Ma or Pa drive to the school to take home their child's project, it's gratifying to see big smiles, and hear comments like, "I can't believe you made that—it's great!"

Working every day in a noisy, dusty workshop full of 60-plus teenagers can become tiresome. Perhaps the hardest part is answering all the questions, ranging from "Where's the sandpaper?" and "What's the difference between a centimetre and an inch?" to "I've glued this in the wrong place; how do I get it apart?" Common complaints like "I don't know what to build" and "I have to go to the washroom" aren't much fun either. Nevertheless, I believe that working with young people and being part of their environment every day keeps me feeling young—although some mornings I wish I could just stay in bed.

Recently, I switched back to family studies, which is mainly about nutrition (dull stuff); parenting (how did Adam and Eve manage without this course!); and cooking (good fun). Alas, it seems that not many students are helping in the kitchen; some are at a loss to open a can.

I enjoy working with teenagers, but I feel sorry for them to some extent. The family is not the stable unit it once was. In this troubled world, who knows what future these kids will need to face? Many of them spend one week with their mother and the following week with their father. I hope we can encourage them to make this old world of ours a better place for us all—and, who knows, maybe I helped a little.

A final word about that knitting class: I did a little research and found out that knitting was once primarily a man's task. I read that Arab nations were great knitters centuries ago: Men could be seen busily knitting while dashing across the desert on their camels!

*—by **John C. Hudspith**, Toronto, Ontario*

VALOUR

True stories that commemorate the sacrifices of our brave men and women in uniform

Battle of Vimy Ridge

Winston Pearson, a veteran of the Great War, recounted his ordeal during the Battle of Vimy Ridge to his son, Bob Pearson. This is Winston's story

The Canadian infantry was reorganized during the harsh winter of 1916-1917. Each platoon was to consist of four sections: Lewis machine gun, bomber, rifle grenade and rifle. At almost seven kilometres in length, Vimy Ridge was the keystone in the German defence of much of the Western Front. At the southern end, it rose gradually to the crest, which the Germans occupied. At the northern end, the slope was much steeper and terminated in a hill with steep sides, known as the Pimple. Having the crest in their possession gave the Germans several advantages. They had good observation of our area and also all the water drained towards us, so that much of the time our trenches were almost impassable. The ground sloped down rapidly on the German side of the ridge and they could actually bring supplies almost to their front line by train.

The subsoil of Vimy Ridge was a soft limestone, known to us as chalk. This was ideal for tunnelling and excavating areas for housing troops and storing supplies. Both sides made good use of this feature. There were many coal mines operating just north of the ridge, in the Lens area, a very short distance from the front line. Both sides needed coal desperately and there seemed to be an unspoken agreement that coal mines were not to be shelled.

The Allies had been unsuccessful in previous attempts to take the ridge from the Germans. The French suffered 140,000 casualties in several attempts, and 46,000 Frenchman were buried in shallow graves where they fell on our side of the ridge. Some graves were so close together that you could jump from one to the other. A number of Imperial Scottish divisions also made a determined attack on the left of the ridge that resulted in 17,000 dead.

I enlisted in the army in 1915 at the age of 16 and was wounded in France at 17—although my official age was listed as 19. I spent the winter of 1916-17 in the Vimy Ridge sector and took part in the attack on April 9, in which we captured the ridge from the Germans.

We spent most of our spare time that winter putting the trenches in decent shape, building plank roads and narrow-gauge railroads that would be run by mule power, making and stocking well-concealed supply depots, and helping the engineers with tunnelling. Most important of all was the moving in of a tremendous amount of artillery: When lined up, there would be a gun in place every seven yards.

During the winter, our observers made note of German artillery positions and other key points. Our guns were trained on them, but we left them unharmed. A few days prior to the main attack, our "heavies" went into action, estimating that they could put 70 percent of the German artillery out of commission and destroy much of their defences. If the enemy positions had been worked over during the winter, the German artillery would have been moved to new positions that we may not have spotted. I saw our heavies completely flatten a village in two hours.

We were taken off the line for two weeks and practiced in a specially prepared location, where tape was laid out on the ground to represent a life-size model of the area we were to attack.

Zero hour was set for 5:30 a.m. on the morning of Monday, April 9. We were sent up to the front line on Thursday night, for 24 hours. The trenches were in terrible condition; we were waist-deep in mud and water. Wanting us to be reasonably fit for the attack, we came out Friday night, arriving at some artillery dugouts on Saturday morning. We spent Saturday getting some rest and making sure our guns, rifles and ammunition were in first-class condition.

Easter Sunday was a beautiful day and we made good use of it. We sat around soaking up the sun, allowing it to dry our clothes and warm our bones. At dusk on Sunday evening, we began to move up to our jump-off position. Arriving at about 2 a.m., I was in the first wave of the attack into "no man's land"—the area between enemy lines—and another in our front-line trenches.

Shortly before zero hour, our sergeant came around with a very welcome shot of rum. He offered me a second, as I was on the end of the line, but I refused, as I wanted to keep a clear head. Little did we know that a mere two hours later, we'd both be badly wounded by machine-gun fire and trying to make our way to the rear in search of a first-aid post.

When zero hour struck, every piece of artillery seemed to go off at once. No one single explosion could be heard—it was just one continuous roar. The enemy resistance was not too serious, except for their machine guns, which caused many casualties, especially in the early part of the attack. The surprise and speed of our attack threw the enemy off balance and many were captured before they could even get out of their shelters. The number of German prisoners captured equalled our casualties. Our 1st Division, on the right of the corps, captured all objectives on schedule. The 4th Division, on the left, had some trouble but eventually got their attack going again and captured all their objectives as well. The weather had changed and a cold wind was blowing snow and fog around, making visibility poor.

About half an hour after the attack began, I was hit by a machine-gun bullet. At first, it felt as though a mule had kicked me; it almost knocked me off my feet. A few seconds later, the pain set in. It was as if I were being repeatedly jabbed with a red-hot poker. I was loaded down with my regular equipment as well as extra ammunition, emergency rations and Mills bombs (hand grenades). All this weight on my shoulder became almost unbearable. I was fortunate to get help loosening and removing all of my gear. With my right arm supporting my left, the pain subsided somewhat.

The bullet had entered my left arm just below the shoulder joint. It made a very small hole where it entered but then hit a bone, breaking it into many pieces. The bullet also shattered, tearing a great hole in the back of my shoulder. It must have bled plenty, but of course I couldn't see it—I later discovered my clothes were stuck to me from shoulder to foot.

I dropped into a shell hole to get my bearings. A soldier who'd had his leg blown off occupied it. He was hollering for the stretcher-bearers, but had little chance of them appearing. The machine guns had taken a heavy toll in this vicinity and the first-aid men had more wounded than they could possibly handle.

Shortly after, my sergeant, Spike Kemp, dropped in beside me. He had a bullet through his side and was having difficulty using his left leg. We decided to try and reach a first-aid post on our own. We tried following a trench, but the mud was too deep for him to navigate. By standing on one leg, supporting my arm on my other leg, I was able to give him some help, but this was too slow going. We followed signs to a first-aid post, only to discover it had been moved. We tried to use a tunnel, but signallers were busy stringing wires and wouldn't let us in.

The snow squalls had stopped and we were able to see the ruined towers of Mont-Saint Éloi, a familiar landmark. We went overland, and about two hours after I'd been hit, we finally found a first-aid station, where I received medical attention. I was amazed that I hadn't bled to death, but have since discovered that unless a major artery has been hit, even the most severe bleeding will eventually stop. I was deemed to be a "stretcher case," while Spike was a "walking case." That was the last I saw of him, although I learned that he reported back to the unit in France some months later.

We were four stretchers loaded onto a special car to be shoved along a light railroad by German prisoners. At first, I was a little afraid of them, but they seemed to have had all the fight knocked out of them. In some places, there were as many as 100 prisoners escorted by only two of our men with no trouble. The rest of the day was spent making our way to the casualty clearing station—the nearest advanced hospital to the action. At times I travelled as a stretcher case, but when that seemed too slow, I joined the walking wounded (more than 10,000 Canadians were killed or wounded at the Battle of Vimy Ridge).

The hospital was made up of two tents. One was for triage, while the other was an operating room. It looked like a slaughterhouse, as there was no time to clean up between surgeries. I lay down on a stretcher and the next thing I knew I'd been operated on and was on a hospital train headed for the base. After a couple of days there, where I almost lost my arm due to infection, I was rushed across the Channel and was lucky enough to be treated at an English civilian hospital, where, thanks to expert and dedicated care, the infection cleared up and today I have reasonably good use of my arm.

—As told to ***Bob Pearson****, Strathroy, Ontario*

Lessons My Father Taught Me

For this devoted daughter, writing about her dad's life is a labour of love

Dad had three brothers serving overseas in World War I. Two had already been injured and his cousin, Blair Fraser, was killed after less than a week at the front. Dad was determined not to be cannon fodder, but he felt duty bound to serve. He used his smarts and enrolled in radio college to study to become a telegraph operator. He learned signalling such as Morse code and semaphore. As a child, I can remember him tapping out Morse code, and when my brother, David, was learning signalling in the Scouts, Dad demonstrated his expertise at semaphore with tea towels serving as flags.

Dad never talked about war—although he served in two of them—except to say, "It was a waste." He finished his fourth form in Gore Bay, Ontario, but he waited until the summer crops of 1917 were harvested before activating his plan. He moved from Manitoulin to Toronto and enrolled in college but needed to earn his way financially. I do not know all the jobs he did, but he worked as a waiter at Bowles Lunch restaurant on King Street East; the building is still there.

His address on his enlistment papers was a boarding house. He often joked about his adept boarding-house reach. His enlistment papers also showed that he weighed 122 pounds and stood five feet six inches tall. An illness six years earlier—a ruptured appendix—had stunted his growth. He often remarked on his short legs: A mere 29 inches. He used to say that if his legs were in proportion to his trunk, he'd be a tall man.

By October 22, 1917, he was assigned to the Toronto Signal Training Depot. From there, he went to Ottawa. More than once, I remember him remarking that Ottawa was the coldest place he had ever been. He was billeted at Lansdowne Park and slept in the open-air stadium in December. They were given one wool blanket as cover and three eight-inch boards on which to sleep. It was cold—very cold. It was no wonder, then, that later in life he hated to be cold. At least he only had to stay in Ottawa for a week.

From Ottawa, his corps went by train to Saint John, New Brunswick. They boarded their ship, the SS *Grampian,* and sailed to Halifax to join a convoy to cross the Atlantic. The *Grampian* arrived in Halifax three days after the Halifax explosion. After revisiting Halifax in 1980, Dad shared with us the devastation that he saw the first time he arrived.

The SS *Grampian* set sail for England on December 21, 1917. Dad told us about crossing the Atlantic in rough seas; he claimed he did not get seasick, but most did. He recalled spending Christmas at sea; Christmas dinner was a rotten egg and a bit of fish. A vivid memory, to be sure, but a related story puts the trip and him into perspective. The boys at his table had collected a Christmas tip for the busboy, who was a young civilian from the Caribbean. Later they found out that the ship's chief steward had taken the tip for his own. According to Dad, "We boys fixed him!" He never did say what that entailed, but I remember the sense of justice in his voice when he recounted that tale.

Dad arrived in England on New Year's Eve 1917. Later he learned that until that convoy arrived laden with foodstuffs and new recruits, only a five-day food supply remained for all of England. I could only imagine that he wished to be back in Gore Bay, warm and well fed.

Dad did not talk much about what he did in the war. He did tell me about learning to ride horses and admitted he was thrown from a horse; whether that caused the facial swelling or the sprained ankle in his army medical record, I don't know. Dad was assigned to the Canadian Engineers Training Depot 14th R.D. in Seaford, East Sussex, on January 1, 1918, the day after he arrived in England.

The good news was that the war ended before Dad had to go to the front. The radio college had been a good plan. Dad's medical examination prior to leaving Great Britain at Kinmel Park camp in Wales showed him in good health: He had grown to five foot seven and now weighed 150 pounds. His return ship was not named in his military records. But he always noted that his return just after Christmas in 1918 was on a better ship with better food. He also recalled that the camaraderie aboard the ship was not the same. The boys who had sailed with him from Halifax were gone. The men who sailed home in 1919 had changed in many different ways.

—by ***Marion Fraser****, Toronto, Ontario*

Dodging Death

Luckily, rumours of her grandfather's death were greatly exaggerated!

While serving in France during the First World War, my grandfather Harry Thompson MacKenzie was reported to be killed in action. Luckily, his death was reported in error. I was a year old when he actually passed away in May 1952, but his wife Dot, my grandmother, kept his memory vividly alive. Photographs and stories were abundant.

Harry was away at war from 1915 to 1918, so my grandparents' romance took place via letters. Dot moved from Nova Scotia to Saskatchewan in 1917 to teach and didn't return until a month before their wedding in 1921. Harry was 19 years old when he enlisted in the army in February 1915. He was with the 6th Canadian Mounted Rifles when he arrived in France that November and was soon promoted to sergeant major, serving there until August 9, 1918—the date he was wounded, and the date he supposedly had been killed.

The family, having been notified of Harry's death, mourned for three weeks until they received a letter from Harry dated after his supposed death. The official letter from the Minister of Militia and Defence in Ottawa, rectifying the error, was dated September 27, 1918, seven weeks after he was wounded; who knows when the letter would have reached Nova Scotia.

Regarding his incorrectly reported death, my grandfather wrote, "For three weeks my relatives believed me dead, memorial services were held for me, flags were lowered, and it was not until they received a letter from me, dated three days after my supposed death, that they began to check up with authorities to find out if I really was still alive. The news that I was only wounded and not dead was soon substantiated in official circles and the period of mourning for my death ended abruptly."

The mix-up was due to an error in the translation of the coded cable. The cable stated that he had been admitted to a hospital in Abbeville, France, with gunshot wounds to the knee—not that he'd been killed.

An entry Harry made in his diary on August 19, 1918, reads: "Doc tells me that I came within an eighth of an inch of losing my leg."

A few years afterwards, my grandfather was reunited with fellow veteran Harry Guy Ruffee, who had grown up with my grandfather in Bridgetown, Nova Scotia. He had also been incorrectly reported as killed! "Mourned As Dead, Vets Meet Again," read the newspaper headline, and beneath that, "Nominated Today for the Mark Twain Death Greatly Exaggerated Society." My grandfather relished the commonality with Twain and bragged that he was a member of the Mark Twain Society.

After World War I, Harry was in the Canadian Armed Forces Reserves. In 1942, while living in Toronto, he joined the army again at the age of 47. He was more than pleased when assigned the position of district salvage and disposal officer for military district No. 6 in Nova Scotia. He was promoted to captain and served in the Royal Canadian Ordnance Corps, with headquarters in Halifax and Debert, Nova Scotia.

Several years later, while visiting Montreal, Harry died suddenly of a heart attack. My mother was pregnant with my brother, who was born five days after my grandfather's death. Mom and Dad named him Harry Thompson MacKenzie.

My grandfather rests at Riverside Cemetery in Bridgetown. The military headstone, discoloured with time, is a slab of rough-edged stone, nestled flat on the ground. The raised lettering on the smooth surface proudly displays an etched cross, below which reads: Harry T. MacKenzie, Captain, RCOC, 22 May 1952—age 57.

*—by **Catherine MacKenzie**, Fall River, Nova Scotia*

Noble Steeds

Canada sent tens of thousands of horses into battle, but only a select few returned

When I was a boy, my father always told me fascinating stories about events in history and, as a result, I developed a lifelong interest in the subject. In 2014, I happened upon a story that really caught my attention.

I was doing public relations for the Royal Canadian Air Force Association's #427 London Wing in London, Ontario, when I first heard about the Sir Arthur Currie Memorial Project, a cornerstone of which is a life-size sculpture of the World War I general, created by Canadian artist Adrienne Alison. I contacted an organizing committee member, John Sargeant of London, Ontario, for more details. In our conversation, John mentioned that Sir Arthur Currie's warhorse, named Brock, was buried on Currie's brother's farm just outside of Strathroy, Ontario. He had also heard of another warhorse buried in eastern Canada, but he couldn't recall the location or the horse's name.

That chat with John prompted a childhood memory. As a young boy, I would join my father, Don Martin Sr., on drives out to the Knowlton, Quebec, area to visit my grandmother. On the way, we would pass by Lt.-Col. George Harold Baker's summer residence at Baker Pond near Knowlton, and I recalled my father saying that Col. Baker's warhorse was buried there. After some research, I was pleased to discover that my father was correct—Col. Baker's horse, Morning Glory, was indeed buried there.

Colonel Baker, the only member of Parliament to serve overseas during the First World War, sent Morning Glory to France in 1915. They were separated for most of the war, with Morning Glory serving as a mount for a battalion commander. Colonel Baker visited his horse for the last time a month before being killed in 1916 during the Battle of Ypres. In 1918, his friend Brig.-Gen. Dennis Draper brought Morning Glory home to the Draper farm in Sutton Junction, Quebec, where the horse lived until 1936, passing away at age 26.

Few warhorses were as lucky as Morning Glory. Canada shipped more than 130,000 horses overseas to fight with Canadian, French and British forces on the front lines, along with mules and donkeys. At least a quarter of these heroic horses died every year in battle; more succumbed to disease and starvation. There is a bond that develops between a soldier and his horse, and so I find it unfortunate that it was only officers who had the privilege of having their horses shipped home. The other surviving warhorses were either slaughtered for meat or sold to farmers as workhorses.

I was also amazed to find out that these two horses, Brock and Morning Glory, were among the very few—only about 60 in total—who returned home to Canada after the Great War. It has been said by people wiser than me that we would never have won the Great War without horses—they kept everything moving. I believe this to be true.

*—by **Don Martin Jr.**, Melbourne, Ontario*

Camp X

A remote facility on the shores of Lake Ontario was home to Canada's top-secret spy school

A top-secret Second World War spy training school was unofficially known as "Camp X." It was established December 6, 1941, in Whitby, Ontario, through a cooperative effort between the British Security Coordination (BSC) and the Canadian government. The BSC's chief, Sir William Stephenson, was a Canadian from Winnipeg and a close confidant of the British prime minister, Sir Winston Churchill, who had instructed him to create "the clenched fist that would provide the knockout blow" to the Axis powers. One of Stephenson's successes was Camp X.

The camp was designed for the sole purpose of linking Britain and the United States. Until the direct attack on Pearl Harbor, which took place on December 7, 1941, the United States was forbidden by Congress to get involved with the war. How timely that Camp X should open the day before that attack by the Japanese.

The camp's location was chosen with a great deal of thought: a remote site on the shores of Lake Ontario, yet only 30 miles straight across the lake from the United States. It was ideal for bouncing radio signals from Europe and South America, and of course, between London and the BSC headquarters in New York.

The choice of site also placed the camp only five miles from Defence Industries Ltd. (DIL), currently the town of Ajax. At that time, DIL was the largest armaments manufacturing facility in the Commonwealth. Other points of strategic significance in the camp's locale include the situation of the German prisoner of war camp in Bowmanville, and the position of the mainline Canadian National Railway, which went through the top part of Camp X.

The commanding officers of the camp soon realized the impact and importance of Camp X. Requests for more agents and different training programs were coming in daily from London and New York. Not only were they faced with training agents who were going to go behind enemy lines on specialized missions but now they had been requested to train agents' instructors as well. These would be recruited primarily from the United States for the Office of Strategic Services (OSS) and for the Federal Bureau of Investigation (FBI). Soon there were trainers training trainers for new camps that would be set up in the United States.

To ease the demand for experienced trainers, a very successful program of weekend courses for OSS executives was established. The psychological aspect of the training was most critical. Equally as crucial as the agent's training in silent killing and unarmed combat was the development of his ability to quickly and accurately assess the suitability of a potential "partisan." He had to be able to recognize a would-be recruit by being alert at all times and in any situation. He was trained to listen for a comment about the government, the Nazis or how the war was progressing, and to subsequently engage the individual in conversation, perhaps offer him a drink or buy him a meal. In this manner, he could further identify the individual's philosophy and thoughts about the war.

Paramount among the objectives set for the operation, including the training of Allied agents for the entire catalogue of espionage activities (sabotage, subversion, deception, intelligence and other special means), was the necessity to establish a major communications link between North and South America and European operations of the Special Operations Executive (SOE). Code-named Hydra, the resulting shortwave radio and telecommunications centre was the most powerful of its type. Largely created by a few gifted Canadian radio amateurs, Hydra played a magnificent role in the tactical and strategic Allied radio networks.

When you step back and look at the 1940 big picture, you can see exactly why Canada was so important to the SOE as a base for their agents. If the agents were to be recruited in Canada, why not train them there? Soon the BSC had large populations of French Canadians, Yugoslavs, Italians, Hungarians, Romanians, Chinese and Japanese at their disposal and in a concentrated geographical area. It was easier to send a few instructors over to Canada than it was to send 500 or 600 potential agents to Britain, only to find that they were not secret agent material.

The agents who trained at Camp X would have no idea as to their future mission behind enemy lines, nor, for that matter, would the instructors or the camp commandant. Camp X's sole purpose was to develop and train agents in every aspect of silent killing, sabotage, partisan work, recruitment methods for the resistance movement, demolition, map reading, weaponry and Morse code.

It was not until the agent completed the ten-week course that the instructors and commanding officers would assess each individual for his particular expertise and subsequently advise the SOE in London of their recommendations. For example, one agent might excel in the demolition field, while another might be better at wireless telegraph work. Upon their arrival in Britain, the agents would be reassessed and would be assigned to a finishing school where their expertise would be further refined. Once this task was completed, another branch of the SOE would take over and develop a mission best suited for each individual agent.

There were many inexplicable events that occurred at Camp X, including some strange and disturbing deaths. One involved 29-year-old political warfare instructor Kenneth Wilson, who was sent to Toronto and told to register at The Royal York Hotel, where on the morning of June 18, 1942, a staff car from Camp X would drive him to a secret location. This same staff car would return him to the hotel at the end of the day. He spent long hours at the camp training agents, and that evening, he returned to the hotel. After dinner, he retired to his room and, exhausted, was soon asleep.

Early the next morning, he telephoned the assistant manager and asked if there was a doctor in the hotel. He was told that there was no doctor present, but one could be sent for very quickly. He then said not to bother because he thought he was feeling a little better. At about 9:30 a.m., he again telephoned and asked for a doctor, who was immediately requested. The doctor stayed with him for about an hour. By this time, he appeared to have recovered completely, so the doctor left. Meanwhile, an assistant had gone down to the hotel to stay with Wilson, and at about 11:15 a.m. he suddenly became much worse. Medical assistance was called immediately, but before the doctors could arrive, Wilson died. At age 29, the brilliant BSC executive had died from sudden heart failure, leaving behind a wife and an 18-month-old daughter. Was he poisoned? Was he murdered by German Abwehr agents operating in Toronto?

Another incident involved one of the most talented silent killers in the world, the great William Fairbairn. Fairbairn was 59 when he was sent to Camp X to train men 30 years his junior. One night, after he retired early, a fire broke out in the mess, just down the hall from the room where Fairbairn was staying. Guards were quickly at his window, where flames were now climbing the wall. Two of the guards managed to pull Fairbairn through the window. Within five minutes, the entire building was razed to the ground. Could this possibly have been a coincidence, the fire happening on the same night he was staying there? Or was there a more cynical explanation?

The strange occurrences continued. Another odd death involved 25-year-old Howard Benjamin Burgess. He was excited about his new position as chief instructor in Canada when he arrived in late May 1942. On June 3, the young, healthy Burgess suddenly dropped to the ground, unconscious, while on camp property. Everyone was in shock. The camp doctor was immediately summoned. Doctor Millman quickly placed the now-bleeding Burgess into the back of his car and raced him to hospital. A guard was posted outside of Burgess's room and told that no one was to enter the room other than Dr. Millman and the head nurse, who had now been sworn to secrecy under the Official Secrets Act. Three days later, Burgess succumbed to the mysterious illness. The official cause of death was a cerebral hemorrhage.

Years later, while writing my book *Inside Camp X*, I decided to investigate this strange death of someone who appeared to be in excellent health. Exhaustive research found some very disturbing facts. The official records on file at Camp X did not agree with the official cause of death. The death certificate and burial permit showed the cause of death as acute glomerulonephritis—a severe kidney disease. I took a copy of the death certificate to a doctor who advised that a person succumbing to such a disease would have been very sick, weak and emaciated—hardly the strong, healthy man that was Howard Burgess. I was also able to track down the then-retired head nurse, who confided that the injury was caused by a gunshot wound to the right temple.

There were other mysterious deaths at Camp X as well—proving that fact really can be stranger than fiction.

*—by **Lynn Philip Hodgson**, Port Perry, Ontario*

Legendary Flying Goose

The Grumman G-21 Goose aircraft has been part of Canadian history for more than 70 years

In 1936, the Grumman Aircraft Engineering Corporation in the United States was commissioned to design and build a roomy, luxurious, amphibious flying boat to transport wealthy businessmen in the Long Island, New York, area. They required a twin-engine, eight-seat plane with a customized interior and retractable landing gear that could operate in the air and on water. Having experience building planes and parts for the United States Navy, Leroy Grumman used this technology to design the Grumman G-21A. The first "Goose" came off the assembly line in 1937.

The aircraft was soon adopted by the United States Coast Guard and, during World War II, a total of 31 aircraft also served with the Royal Canadian Air Force (RCAF). The RCAF used the Goose for transport, reconnaissance, rescue and training operations. Britain's Royal Air Force also used the G-21 for air-sea rescue duties. In keeping with their tradition of naming aircrafts, it was the RAF who originally bestowed the name "Goose" on this plane. Postwar, the Grumman Goose was in demand by commercial operators worldwide and was used by nine civil operators, including Canada.

I have had the privilege of flying in a Goose a number of times as a passenger with Pacific Coastal Airlines. Every time is a new adventure, beginning with climbing aboard the aircraft and experiencing the sounds and vibrations of the big 450-horsepower engines to watching the pilot manoeuvre levers on both the ceiling and floor of the cockpit. But my biggest thrill was landing on the ocean amid choppy seas and windy downdrafts. The Goose seemed to barely clear the treetops on its approach to the bay, crosswinds forcing it to bounce up and down, which left my stomach in my chest. As the belly of the plane touched the surface of the bay, the spray of water covered my window for a few seconds, obscuring my view. The aircraft slowed down instantly then tipped to one side, dipping one wing tip into the water as we approached the dock. Suddenly, I noticed flames coming out of one of the engines. The pilot assured me there was nothing to worry about, that it was actually quite common! What a ride—it certainly got my adrenaline pumping.

I can almost imagine what it must have been like to be in the cockpit during World War II when there were 14 Grumman Goose aircraft patrolling British Columbia's west coast between 1940 and 1956. Fellow G-21 aficionado Juergen Puetter owns one of the last planes built and is on the fly with his Grumman Goose, exploring some of the last true remaining frontiers of North America. His Goose affords him the opportunity to land in secluded bays, lakes and lagoons along British Columbia's rugged coast. This enables him to launch a small watercraft to go ashore and explore remote, white sandy beaches, hike old trails, view grizzlies in the wild or discover the ultimate fishing hole.

Pacific Coastal Airlines in Vancouver owns a large fleet of G-21s. As far as I know, the planes are currently grounded due to a lack of key components, but the airline is working to get them back in the air. This workhorse of a plane has been a lifeline for remote villages and communities, logging camps and sports fishing lodges along the West Coast for a quarter of a century; it has also played an important role in aviation history and hopefully will never be forgotten.

*—by **Gordon Baron**, Dawson's Landing, British Columbia*

Making a Connection

Tracing the history of a meaningful photo helped bring it to life

I keep an old black-and-white photo on my desk for a reason. I have a number of pictures of my father, but I chose this one because whenever I look at it, I think about so many things. My dad, Lt. John Horsburgh, is in the centre of the photo; on the left is Sgt. Clifford Hebner and on the right is CSM Cormack. Studying the photo, I wonder why the jeep is partially hidden in the haystack and why Sgt. Hebner has a dent in his helmet. I also notice how CSM Cormack appears to be sleeping with a pipe in his mouth while holding a rifle with a bayonet at the end of it. Most of all, though, I wonder what these three individuals are thinking about. To me, the picture conveys so much more than simply portraying my dad and two Royal Canadian engineering corps comrades sitting on a trunk behind a haystack.

Taken in early August 1944, the image shows them in relaxed poses that I sense must belie what they had just been through: D-Day, with its horrendous death toll, destruction and utter chaos; the breakout from Juno Beach with the fierce fighting, unimaginable bombing and shelling; and examples of bravery and evil that showcased the best and worst of war. On the back of the picture my dad wrote: "The day after the start of the big push for Falaise."

Earlier, in July, Clifford Hebner had won the Military Medal for outstanding leadership under fire south of Caen. Caen was also the location where my father won the Military Cross on July 18, 1944, as a result of his actions in conducting a thorough reconnaissance of the River Orne while under fire from the Germans. The reconnaissance facilitated the building of a bridge, which enabled more than 100 tanks to cross the Orne in the next 24 hours en route to Falaise.

On the back of the picture, written in brackets beside Sgt. Hebner's name, is "since killed." While my dad lived to see the end of the war, Sgt. Hebner died less than two months after this picture was taken. Tragically, he was killed in Belgium on October 5, 1944, while trying to defuse a German land mine. He is buried in a cemetery near

Antwerp, Belgium. He was only 32 years old and was married, but as far as I can determine, he did not have any children. I couldn't help but want to know more about Sgt. Hebner. If I was able to locate a member or members of his family, I figured they might appreciate having a copy of this photo. I wondered if anyone from Sgt. Hebner's family has had the opportunity to honour his sacrifice by visiting his grave in Belgium.

As I thought about the picture some more, I also wondered how Sgt. Hebner's death affected my dad. I suspect that military censorship was such that my dad was limited in what he could say about his comrade's death. I am sure the words "since killed" did not even begin to convey the sense of loss and sadness my father must have felt when he gazed at this picture and wrote his comments on the back.

Sadly, after my father had successfully dodged death in northwest Europe, he was killed seven years later in a float plane crash while serving his province as the senior hydraulics engineer in 1952. Sgt. Hebner, my father and CSM Cormack were examples of men who lived Albert Schweitzer's dictum that "you who will be truly happy are those who will have sought for and found a way to serve." This picture makes me think about the concept of service, about how important it is to have a belief in this simple yet profound concept and that through service, we can make a difference in the lives of others. There is no doubt this photo speaks to me in a very personal and profound way.

I decided to undertake a search for information about Sgt. Hebner and CSM Cormack. After months of getting nowhere, someone finally responded positively to one of my inquiries. The response came from a most unlikely source. My wife and I attended a Winnipeg Fringe Festival play titled *Jake's Gift*. It's a heartwarming, award-winning play about a World War II veteran who travels back to Juno Beach to visit the gravesite of his older brother. It turns out that the name of the brother buried at Juno Beach is Chester Hebner. On the off chance there was some connection between this name and the Clifford Hebner I had been searching for, I sent an email to the play's website, including the picture of my father and his two comrades.

I immediately got a response from Julia Mackey, who wrote and plays all the characters in *Jake's Gift*. Julia emailed me back, stating that she had written the play as a result of seeing Chester Hebner's gravesite at Juno Beach. Julia had the information about the Hebner family I sought. We arranged to meet Julia and her husband Dirk for lunch, where Julia showed me another picture of Clifford and his friend

CSM Cormack taken during World War II. Most important to me, however, she showed me a photo of Clifford's younger sister and her husband visiting Clifford's gravesite in Belgium. At its core, *Jake's Gift* is a play about the importance of remembering. I had been looking at a picture taken almost 70 years ago, some four years before I was born, wanting to know and understand this picture on a deeper level. What a gift it was to meet Julia and Dirk, who were able to bring this very meaningful and unique picture to life.

Remembering has to do with the past; it involves thinking about people and events that were important to us. I also believe, however, that the importance of remembering has to do with the future in terms of how it shapes our lives, clarifies our values and fundamentally helps us determine who we are and who we want to be as we move forward in life. I am very thankful for a photo, a play and two individuals, Julia and Dirk, who have helped me to remember.

—by ***Mac Horsburgh****, Winnipeg, Manitoba*

Canada's Dambusters

One fateful spring night in 1943, a crew of brave airmen embarked on a secret mission

When I saw how innocent people were being shot to death by the German military—for no good reason—I said to myself, "We have to win this war at all costs!" That was also how my friend Fred Sutherland saw his role in World War II as a front gunner in a Lancaster bomber, one of several tasked with destroying Germany's Eder Dam on the night of May 16 through 17, 1943.

In a private ceremony held on November 30, 2013, Fred's contribution to the war effort was recognized when members of the No. 703 Wing Royal Canadian Air Force Association presented him with a lifetime membership and citation acknowledging his bravery.

A longtime resident of Rocky Mountain House, Alberta, Fred was born February 26, 1923, in that province's town of Peace River. He enlisted in the air force when he was 18 years of age. Little did the new recruit realize what lay ahead. He would soon be drawn into one of the most intense battles in World War II—the renowned Dambuster raids.

Fred joined a close-knit crew of seven dedicated airmen and flew 25 bombing missions before his team was assigned to the secret operation. "We were called in one day and invited to join a newly formed squadron—No. 617—under Wing Commander Gibson," Fred said, adding, "Our crew, under pilot Les Knight, was chosen because we had an excellent bombing record. If we joined the squadron as a crew, we could stay together. And since we liked each other and performed well as a team, we wanted to stay together."

The airmen had no idea what their secret mission was until the actual day of the raid. "During the briefing, you could feel the tension in the air," Fred remembers. The idea of skipping a bouncing bomb over water to break a dam seemed absurd. As the crew's engineer, Ray Grayston, put it, "It horrified us to think they'd put this great lump of metal, like a cricket pitch roller, underneath a Lancaster. It interfered with the handling of the aircraft."

Yet the airmen had no choice. Gibson's orders were clear: "If you don't do it tonight, you're going back tomorrow night." With pilot Les Knight in control, the crew, including Fred, took off from Scampton airbase at 10 p.m. They were part of the first wave of nine aircraft. Although others tried and failed, it was Knight's crew who successfully bounced their bomb against the Eder Dam to score a hit. Fred saw a gaping hole in the dam and marvelled at "the unbelievable force of water coming out and how high the water was." The collapse of the Eder Dam temporarily crippled Germany's economy, so the men under Knight's command were elated. On returning to base, however, they discovered that a large number of the airmen on that particular mission had been killed: It turned out to be a very sad day after all.

A similar raid on Germany's Dortmund-Ems Canal—a strategically important waterway—in September 1943 resulted in disaster. As usual, Les Knight was at the controls with Fred manning the forward gun. Blinded by fog, the low flying Lancaster hit a treetop. Although Knight was able to pull the damaged craft up, he ordered Fred and six others to jump. Knight, who bravely stayed with his plane, was killed in the crash. The rest of the crew landed in German-occupied Holland unhurt but surrounded by danger on all sides. On landing, Fred quickly hid his parachute and began a treacherous journey through enemy-occupied territory.

Years later, when serving with British Columbia Forestry, Fred survived a second plane crash. Experiencing two plane crashes in a single lifetime is remarkable, yet Fred remains hale and hearty. He is also one of the last three Dambusters in the world today. No doubt about it, Fred Sutherland is a genuine Canadian World War II hero.

*—by **Annette Gray**, Markerville, Alberta*

The Forgotten Ones

Recognizing the terrible ordeal suffered by Canadian POWs during the building of the "death railway"

By definition, the word pilgrimage can mean "a journey to a special or unusual place." My husband Roger and I decided to embark on a long-awaited pilgrimage to Kanchanaburi, Thailand, to visit the infamous Thailand-Burma Railway, better known as the "death railway."

We were inspired to do this by a remarkable 96-year-old man named Jack Jennings, my second cousin, who still lives in Devon, England. Jack was captured during World War II in 1942, when Allied forces in Singapore surrendered to the Japanese. After many months as a POW in Changi, Jack was one of thousands of Allied servicemen transported, in horrific conditions, to Thailand to labour on the construction of the railroad. After reading Jack's memoirs, we were so in awe of his story that we decided to do a pilgrimage to retrace some of his footsteps. The timing could not have been better, as 2015 marked the 70th anniversary of the end of World War II and so it was an especially well-timed and poignant journey.

We began our pilgrimage in Singapore, as this was where Jack began his years as a POW. We visited several historic sites, the first being the Adam Park estate where Jack's 1st Battalion, the Cambridgeshire Regiment, took its last stand against the Japanese before the British troops—including Jack's battalion—surrendered. We also visited the Changi area, where Jack was held captive, and Kranji War Memorial, where many of Jack's comrades were laid to rest.

From Singapore, we flew to Bangkok and headed northwest to Kanchanaburi to retrace his steps on the railway, with the guidance of the staff at the Thailand-Burma Railway Centre.

First, we undertook an upcountry pilgrimage, following parts of the original railway bed, north to the Thailand-Burma (now Myanmar) border at the Three Pagodas Pass. We paid our respects at the Chungkai and Kanchanaburi war cemeteries. We also visited the site called Hellfire Pass and walked across the Wang Pho viaduct bridge, both built by POWs under inhumane conditions with incredible suffering and loss of life. We rode the railway on the still-existing track from Kanchanaburi to Nam Tok and then took a long-tailed boat ride on the famous river. All the while, we were thinking of the men, who, 70 years ago, "gave their tomorrow for our today."

Our pilgrimage led us to the conclusion that the POWs who built the infamous railway are often the forgotten ones. It seems the survivors of this brutal 3 ½ years of captivity are forgotten men, because the fall of Singapore is viewed by many as the greatest military disaster of the British Empire. Subsequently, it seems the men who survived this terrible ordeal receive very little recognition for their horrific experience, even to this day. Something else to consider is the fact that few people even know that Canadians were POWs on the infamous railway, as they were serving with British regiments and are counted in with the British statistics.

Does the name Norman Maurice Dorval mean anything to most Canadians? He was a Canadian from Dawson, Yukon, serving in England with the East Surrey Regiment, who was executed at Tha Makhan POW camp after a failed escape. Do we know about James McCracken of the Royal Artillery from Keswick, Ontario, who died of beriberi while a POW at Kanchanaburi? And what about Roy M. Borthwick of the RCAF from Vancouver, who was one of several airmen who helped destroy three spans of the main bridge in June 1945? These were just three of our forgotten ones. (Thanks to the initiative of Bob Hemphill of British Columbia, a plaque recognizing Borthwick's contributions was unveiled in 2016 at the Thailand-Burma Railway Centre giving him the recognition he so deserves.)

We would wholeheartedly encourage all Canadians interested in World War II history to explore the railway story with the help of the amazing staff at the Thailand-Burma Railway Centre in Kanchanaburi. They organize personal tours or pilgrimages with leading experts on the railway. Advance research from their extensive records can be conducted for any family connected to POWs so they can follow in their footsteps and visit precise locations.

Every November, we hear the words, "lest we forget," and yet there are Canadians buried in Thailand who are almost forgotten. We must remember that there is a corner in some foreign land that will be forever Canada.

*—by **Christine Cameron Emmett**, Brighton, Ontario*

Canadian Kangaroos

Paying tribute to some unsung heroes

Nicknamed the "Kangaroos," they were officially called the 1st Canadian Armoured Carrier Regiment. This Second World War regiment was composed of two fighting squadrons of personnel carriers. One squadron, each with 53 carriers, could lift an entire infantry battalion into battle. My father, Arnold Frederick Hare, was a proud Kangaroo.

The Kangaroos were so named because their primary function was to safely transport army personnel to their front-line objectives throughout Holland and into Germany in the steel belly of a tank chassis—the same way a mother kangaroo protects and carries her young within her pouch.

They made military history, being the first heavy-armoured personnel carriers ever commissioned, the development of which was a guarded secret at the time. Many of the soldiers selected were farm boys and mechanics who had the necessary skills to traverse difficult terrain and maintain their tanks.

They carried men and supplies to the front lines and brought back the wounded, often at great risk. Their efforts substantially reduced casualties. While working through long days and often terrifying nights, they formed incredibly close bonds and a deep loyalty to one another. They also developed a fondness for their specially altered tanks, often naming them after sweethearts or mothers back home.

My father told some harrowing stories of near misses and lost comrades. Even though we children pestered him for more of what we thought were incredibly romantic and death-defying stories, he would grow quiet and tell us that war was truly terrible, and not to be glorified. He'd gone overseas an immature, inexperienced farm boy, eager to get into the thick of things, but returned a seasoned and more sombre man.

The Kangaroos achieved many firsts, including becoming the only regiment to be formed, battle-tested and decommissioned on foreign soil. After the war, members were sent home to their far-flung hometowns in Canada, without fanfare or recognition for their courage and service.

Over 70 years after the war, the surviving Kangaroos still meet for a reunion in Toronto every November. Originally more than 500 strong, they are now few in numbers but still proud, patriotic and more than willing to share their stories, particularly the ones that demonstrate their spirit of camaraderie and shared humour. Many say it was the hijinks and laughter they shared in the midst of chaos and fear that got them through. Before they are all gone, it's time to recognize their quiet heroism and sacrifice.

*—by **Colleen O'Hare**, Parry Sound, Ontario*

Lone Rider

Motorcycle dispatch riders were relied upon to get key information where it was needed, without being intercepted

I was 19 years old when I enlisted for duty in the Second World War. I ended up in the Royal Armoured Corps, 5th Division, as a motorcycle dispatch rider with a small group referred to as the Divisional Maintenance Area—or short form—DMA.

After completing my basic training at Fort William, now Thunder Bay, I arrived at Camp Borden in March 1943 for more training before being sent overseas. One day, as I was watching tank drivers and mechanics changing the tracks of their tanks in the mud, and truck drivers struggling with their big vehicles under the same conditions, I noticed the ease with which the fellows in the motorcycle training group were able to clean up and maintain their machines. I decided then and there that I wanted to be a motorcycle dispatch rider—even though I had never ridden a motorcycle in my life.

Being a dispatch rider was a whole lot different, I think, than any other job in the army. First of all, you had to be content to be on your own, because you ended up being alone quite a lot of the time. And I know it was the only job in the Armoured Corps that was strictly voluntary. You volunteered to ride that motorcycle and, at any time you felt that you didn't want to ride it any more, you could say "I don't want to do this," and they'd find another job for you, in a tank or something like that.

Our trainer at Camp Borden had been a motorcycle stunt rider at fairs and carnivals before the war. He gave us lots of helpful tips about riding and instructions on how to crash a motorcycle and be able to walk away in one piece. We were taught how to stay alive and I paid a lot of attention so that I could do precisely that.

Riding dispatch was an exciting period in my life. Most of my time overseas was spent in Italy, from November 1943 until March 1945. We ended up in Holland and we were still there on May 8—VE-Day. I look back and I think of the tremendous responsibility that they gave this 19- or 20-year-old kid. I just accepted it and then went out to do what had to be done. A big part of my job was delivering important messages that were too risky to be sent by radio or by telephone because the Germans could tap in and listen to what was being said. We also did some convoy work; sometimes, you'd have a truckload of supplies to deliver or maybe a few tanks. The people in charge would say, "Take this from point A to point B," and they'd give you a map and away you'd go.

I got to meet some wonderful people and had some great experiences in Italy. The Italians and the Germans had been in an alliance for a time. But when we first arrived, the Italians had just surrendered to the Allies, not wanting to participate in Mr. Hitler's war anymore. So, we ended up fighting only the Germans. The gratitude that the Italians showed us often made for some wonderful friendships that a lot of the guys built up while we were there.

My job was such that I was never really engaged in the actual fighting, but I was constantly delivering messages pretty close to it and had my share of near misses. Sometimes, I'd be in a position where I'd have to find a foxhole and hunker down for a while. But, generally, I spent my war years riding my motorcycle—and fighting the elements.

*—by **Harry Watts**, Kitchener, Ontario*

Uncle Wilfred Remembered

Childhood memories of a favourite uncle are rekindled by a visit to his World War II gravesite in Belgium

In September 1944, my uncle Wilfred Atwood of Oak Park, Nova Scotia was killed during the Second World War in the Battle of the Scheldt, when the Algonquin Regiment and others were attempting to cross the Leopold Canal in Belgium.

Since I was only seven years old at the time, the impact of the news did not hit me as hard as it did my older brothers. As I became older, I began to realize the loss that my family and I had experienced. Uncle Wilfred was single and, living right next door, my brothers and I were treated like his own.

I have so many fond memories of Uncle Wilfred. One incident that stands out for me was the time he took me to his parents' home and he and I picked wild strawberries behind their house. When we took the berries inside, my grandmother served them up with sugar and cream; the two of us sat at the table and enjoyed the treat, and especially each other's company. We enjoyed many such moments.

Unlike today, when soldiers who lose their lives in battle are usually brought home for burial, Uncle Wilfred was buried in Belgium. Thanks to the Internet, I was able to see the place where he was buried, as well as read his name and related details on his tombstone. But it had always been a dream of mine to visit his grave and see where he spent his final days.

That dream became reality in May 2008, when my daughter Lois and her husband Stoy took me on a trip to Belgium. Via the Internet once again, I was able to contact Iris Van Landschoot, who gave me quite a bit of helpful information; when we arrived in Brussels, I called her and she and her husband Daniël became our guides.

We visited Adegem War Cemetery, where Uncle Wilfred and many other soldiers were buried, and we walked along the Leopold Canal, where the World War II crossing had been attempted. There was a building across the canal where marks of the fighting were still visible on the walls. A local historian came by and gave us additional facts about that particular area and details about the battle and some of those who were killed.

While overseas, we were also able to visit the Canadian War Museum, which was built as a tribute to the Canadians who liberated the Flemish people from Nazi domination. Thanks to Lois and Stoy, as well as to both Iris and her husband for adding so much to our visit, it was indeed the trip of a lifetime and one that I will always treasure.

—by ***Miriam (Atwood) Thompson**, Pugwash, Nova Scotia*

Accentuate the Positive

A daughter marvels at the resilience and determination of her mother—a Canadian war bride

When Mother sent me the faded blue airmail letter, dated August 15, 1946, it looked just like so many of the other letters she'd received from England when I was a child.

I didn't pay much attention at first, but I unfolded it one evening and realized it was written not to my mother, but rather by my mother to her new sister-in-law, Pearl, in Canada whom she hadn't yet met. It is a simple letter, from one woman to another—a bit tentative, a bit formal, as it is when a new relationship is just beginning. Aunt Pearl had saved it all these years and finally returned it to my mother to pass on to me, knowing I would treasure it. This is what the letter said:

> *Dear Pearl,*
>
> *It was very kind of you to write to me and send congratulations on the new baby, and very many thanks for same. I've only recently come out of hospital and am now staying with my stepsister in Surrey for a rest. After being in hospital for six weeks I feel a bit weak, but I shall soon get well again, as I'm fairly tough. My baby is very sweet and is really very good. The death of my mother upset me terribly, as she was really all I had. She was looking forward to seeing the baby and looking after me, too, but I suppose it just wasn't to be. There must be a purpose in these things I'm sure, although it's difficult to find at times. I've no idea when I can get out to Harold, but it will be as soon as I can. I have so much to settle up here now, and in any case, the immigration department states a child has to be several months old before they can be transported. As I'm now staying not far from London, I shall go and make inquiries. Naturally I miss Harold—it seems a very long time ago since he went back and much has happened since. I'm anxious for him to see his daughter, too, but eventually the time will come along and we shall all be together again. Once again, many thanks for letter and card. I hope you are all keeping well, and shall look forward to seeing you sometime in the future.*

Sincerely yours, Evelyn

My mother, Evelyn, had met my father, Harold Bennell, in London, where she worked as a nurse and he was a member of the Canadian Army. They were married in August 1945 and I was born in July 1946. However, my father had already been sent back to Canada, discharged from the army, and had found a job in Toronto. The original plan was that my mother would join him in Toronto at the earliest opportunity, but with the death of her mother, which postponed the trip, and my birth, which postponed it further, some months elapsed between my father's departure and my mother's opportunity to leave England.

Instructions eventually came to prepare to sail in early December 1946, on the SS *Empire Brent*. My mother was then living in her mother's home in Southsea, on the south coast of England. She was instructed to report to a hostel at the west end of London. The following morning, she and a crowd of other war brides, many also with children, boarded a train to Liverpool. Mother later commented, "It was a long journey to Liverpool, as the railways were still on a wartime footing. There was no conveniences for babies and little children. However, we had just been through six years of war, and we had become adept at making do."

Mother and 12 other war brides shared a cabin on the upper deck with their children. Once they fed and settled the children, they introduced themselves over a cup of tea, talking about people they were leaving behind and what lay ahead. Less than 12 hours later, the *Empire Brent* started for sea but collided with a cattle scow before she got out of the River Mersey. Repairing the hole would require several days' work, so all the war brides and children made the return journey to London and the hostel. Once there, they were besieged by the press. Mother then stayed with her sister until time for the second departure.

The journey was unpleasant, with high gales and bitter cold. After eight days, they reached Halifax, where the army was out full force to help with children and luggage. After going through customs, they boarded a train. Mother, however, had not been feeling well during the sea voyage, but had put it down to stress and the nasty weather. She began to feel worse on the train, and a doctor's examination resulted in a diagnosis of appendicitis. The doctor arranged for her to be transferred to the nearest hospital in Rimouski, Quebec, promising that my father would be notified.

As mother was worrying about this turn of events, the train stopped. All around were fields and snow. The doctor then came with the news that there was a fire on the line ahead, which would cause some delay.

He had arranged for a freight car to be sent on a branch line. It would be heated and a doctor would come with it and escort her to Rimouski. But just as she was ready to transfer to the car, the train started moving again and shortly arrived at Rimouski, where an ambulance was waiting in a driving snowstorm.

Mother was admitted to hospital, the doctors removed her appendix and she spent nearly two weeks in the hospital for rest and recuperation. The Red Cross visited, a kind nurse supplied her with magazines, and the Roman Catholic priest visited daily with news of me in the nursery. On Christmas Day, several of the nuns came to visit. Despite the language barrier, there was warmth and laughter. Mother later wrote to me, "I am not of the Roman Catholic faith, and I do not remember being asked about my religion. We were strangers from a train, mother and daughter needing help, and far from home, and they gave us the best of attention and loving care, and I have been forever grateful."

Finally, the Red Cross put mother and me on a train to Montreal, and then from Montreal to Toronto, where my father met us on New Year's Day 1947, nearly six months after I had been born. Upon his arrival in Canada, he had found a job, purchased a house and a car, and made preparations for his new family. He had put up a Christmas tree with a stuffed panda bear under it for me and kept it until we arrived. It had been a worrisome period for him, as he was the recipient of numerous telegraphs that read, "Delayed..." with a new estimated arrival date.

Looking back, the simplicity and ordinariness of Mother's letter is quite startling. Her attitude that nothing was going to get in the way of her plans to come to Canada is implicit. While she could not have known of the various events that would occur during the long journey, that attitude carried her through a lot: a near shipwreck; a nasty ocean voyage; an appendicitis attack under adverse conditions; surgery in a foreign country; and over six months of delays—all with a baby and on her own. She'd set her heart on a future in a new land with her husband and family, and nothing was going to deter her.

I still marvel at the sheer strength of will it took to overcome the obstacles she faced. She told me once that a number of the young women who were on the ship during the collision changed their minds and remained in England. She, however, never had second thoughts. I remember her remarking that she believed the secret of life had to do with keeping a positive attitude.

In her 90s, macular degeneration caused her severe vision loss, but she went line dancing three times a week, participated in an art class, joined a book discussion club and walked every day. Once, when I called her on the phone, she gently told me that she would call me back later, as she wanted to be sure not to miss the landing of the Mars Pathfinder on TV. "Just think, dear," she said, "I'm in my 90s and at last I'm going to find out what Mars is like." In a future era, she'd have emigrated there, too.

*—by Expat Canadian **Irene Martin**, now residing in Skamokawa, Washington*

Tales From the Sea

Memories of adventure, danger and intrigue serving aboard the HMCS *Cayuga* during the Korean War

I was born in Rapid City, Manitoba, in December 1930 and joined the Royal Canadian Navy in 1948 at the age of 18. While serving aboard the HMCS *Ontario,* the Korean War began and there was a call for volunteers to serve in Korea. I transferred to the HMCS *Cayuga* and together with the *Athabaskan* and the *Sioux,* we sailed for Korea on July 5, 1950. The following are some of the memories I have of my two tours of duty patrolling Korea's west coast at the beginning of the Korean War.

One time, while fuelling up on the atoll of Guam, Leading Seaman George Johnson rescued a dog that was part of a litter being drowned. Captain Brock allowed the dog to be kept onboard provided she was trained. We named the dog Alice and she served onboard the ship for two tours of duty; she was a great mascot that greatly raised the morale of the crew.

Our first United Nations (UN) patrol was escorting a troop ship to the port of Pusan while North Korean troops were within 25 miles of port. On our next mission, we became the first Canadian ship to fire in anger since the Second World War, bombarding the city of Yosu.

The *Cayuga,* along with a great number of UN ships, took part in the Inchon invasion on September 15, 1950. This resulted in a rapid advance by Allied troops up to the Yalu River. On October 16, 1950, we were leading the HMS *Kenya* north of Inchon when we had a very narrow escape: We discovered we were in a minefield. We immediately ordered the *Kenya* to turn to starboard, but we had to proceed, as our forward momentum had us in the minefield already. At one point, we heard metal scraping on metal as we made contact with one of the mines, but it must have been a dud, as we escaped unharmed.

Along with the *Athabaskan* and the *Sioux,* while heading to Hong Kong in November of 1950, we ran into a fierce Typhoon Clara in the Formosa Strait. A crewman from the *Athabaskan* was swept overboard. We turned to pick him up but missed. The *Athabaskan* also turned, and, through skilful handling, the ship managed to head straight to him—two sailors at the rail grabbed the swimmer just as the wave crested. After Ordinary Seaman Elvidge was safely back on board and dried off, he said, "Now I know there is a God." That night, about 2 a.m., *Cayuga* was hit by a rogue wave. The helmsman swung the wheel to starboard to head the ship into the wave to prevent a rollover. We rolled 52 degrees—no Tribal-class destroyer had ever exceeded that degree of roll. Slowly, the ship returned to an upright position—a frightening experience for all aboard.

On one mission, we spent 54 straight days at sea, escorting aircraft carriers that were supplying guerrilla bases on offshore islands behind enemy lines, bombarding shore installations and assisting guerrilla operations raiding enemy-held islands. We had enemy artillery fire directed at us a number of times. Fortunately, they missed but did come very close.

During our second tour, while assisting on a guerrilla raid, three South Korean marines were badly wounded by the enemy. They were brought back to the ship, where our surgeon, Dr. Cyr, operated on them, saving their lives. A reporter wrote a story about this incident and it became national news back home in Canada. Apparently, the mother of the real Dr. Cyr, who was practicing in New Brunswick, contacted Ottawa and suggested there was an imposter aboard. Captain Plomer summoned the doctor to his cabin, where he eventually admitted that his name was actually Ferdinand Demara. He was shipped back to Ottawa and discharged from the navy. Hollywood later made a movie about him, called *The Great Impostor,* starring Tony Curtis.

At a naval reunion in 1979 in Victoria, we were able to meet Ferdinand Demara again. He told us that he was now a doctor of divinity working in a hospital in Anaheim, California. Over the years, his exploits led to charges of fraud, forgery, embezzlement, theft and vagary. Personally, I found him to be a good, down-to-earth man who was well liked by the crew.

*—by **Leonard "Scotty" Wells**, Scarborough, Ontario*

Izzy's Story

The legacy of a Canadian soldier and the power of love

We mostly think of our soldiers as being tough, dedicated, and highly trained to serve and fight for peace to protect Canada, and to help protect all the innocent victims of war around the world. Little do we know, think or hear about the humanitarian side of each and every soldier who puts his or her life on the line every day in the service of peace.

This is only one story of a Canadian unit—the 1 Combat Engineer Regiment (1CER)—which lost one of their own, MCpl. Mark (Izzy) Isfeld, on peacekeeping operations in Croatia in 1994.

In 1993, while on tour in Croatia with his regiment, MCpl. Isfeld drove into a village and noticed something on a pile of rubble by a destroyed house. Although it looked like a small child, it was actually a life-size doll. He took a photo and, on his next leave home to Courtney, British Columbia, he showed it to his parents, Brian and Carol Isfeld. Mark said, "Look, Mom: A little child has lost her doll and a doll her little child." Remembering his happy upbringing in Canada, he added, "These kids don't have a childhood."

Carol was moved by the photo and felt the need to do something to help her son cope with the daily challenges he faced on duty. Giving a gift of a doll to the children of war, to bring a little happiness into their lives, would also bring joy to Mark as he gave them out. So Carol began crocheting little dolls—girls with yellow pigtails and boys with blue berets. She sent them to her son and, as Mark gave out the dolls, he became known as the soldier who collected little smiles, little handshakes and little hearts.

Tragically, the following year, Mark was killed by an exploding land mine on June 21, 1994, in Croatia. After his death, Mark's troop named the doll after Izzy and continued giving out Izzy dolls to the children in his honour. Over the years, the Izzy doll has become a symbol of peace, showing the humanitarian side of all Canadian soldiers.

Nationwide, knitters and crocheters joined Carol's cause to bring smiles to the children of war. Their candid comments expressed the joy they felt in helping the children. Many of the elderly crafters had lived through wartime and the Great Depression. They said they knew what it was like to have nothing, and that creating an Izzy doll for a child who had nothing was something they just had to do.

To relieve suffering in the world, Vancouver resident and Canadian veteran Billy Willbond and his wife Lynne started ICROSS Canada (International Community for the Relief of Suffering and Starvation). Since its inception in 1998, ICROSS Canada has repurposed and distributed millions of dollars' worth of medical equipment to suffering Third World villages, sent medical aid and much more. Billy sought and received permission from Carol Isfeld to use the Izzy doll for, as Billy put it: "the poorest of the poor on the planet." Carol suggested the knitters and crocheters use darker colours for the skin tones, making the dolls more real for these children. It would be called the "Izzy African Comfort Doll" and even more crafters were excited to volunteer.

Although Billy's death in 2014 has left an unmistakable void, many veterans across Canada—including Maj.-Gen. Lewis MacKenzie (Retired), the patron of ICROSS Canada—continue to collect used hospital equipment, Izzy dolls, African comfort dolls, and medicines for shipment to Third World countries and countries needing assistance.

Much has happened in the years following Mark's death. More than 1.5 million Izzy dolls have brought comfort, peace and love not only to the innocent victims of war but also to children suffering globally because of natural disasters, starvation, displacement and trauma. Many Canadian charities, doctors, health care workers, students and others also take thousands of Izzy dolls with them each year to distribute to children in South America and Third World countries.

In 2007, following the death of Carol Isfeld, I became the "Izzy Doll Mama." I'm fortunate to be working in partnership with the Canadian Military Engineers, other Canadian Armed Forces personnel and, in particular, with former Canadian Military Engineer Association president Lt.-Col. Ken Holmes (Retired), who is my military adviser. As well as those mentioned above, the Isfeld family and the multi-talented singer, songwriter and author Phyllis Wheaton, whose book *In the Mood for Peace: The Story of the Izzy Doll* was published in 2011, have taught me the true meaning of "humanitarian." Here is a short excerpt from *In the Mood for Peace*:

"(1 Combat Engineer Regiment members)...were witness to Izzy's beaming smile while packing homemade knitted dolls in his uniform pockets—they even teased him about it in the beginning. But as they, too, began to give out dolls (following his death), they could attest to the joy of the children, hands outstretched to receive these gifts. It was a good feeling, a momentary pleasure that indeed lifted the spirits of the giver and receiver even in the midst of the most forsaken circumstances. It was at this point that Mark's troop named the dolls the Izzy doll, after their friend and brother. Carol said she was overjoyed at 1CER's benevolence that would ensure the children of war were not forgotten, and that her son would be remembered through this legacy project. It was at this moment that the Izzy doll began to take on its stature as a phenomenon—not yet in numbers, but in direction. No longer a mother and son project, the 1CER had given the Izzy doll wings that would take this homemade toy to the farthest reaches of the earth, cheering hundreds of thousands of children in the years to come."

The giving of time, talent and love that Canadians across the country have shown for the suffering children of the world through the Canadian Military Engineering Izzy Doll Project continues to be a journey of love.

*—by **Shirley O'Connell**, Perth, Ontario*

A Letter Home From Afghanistan

A military veteran who served in Afghanistan shares her thoughts and experiences

I was a 24-year-old private when I served with the Canadian Armed Forces in Afghanistan. Upon my return from that deployment in 2010, I wrote a letter to the students of Joseph Teres Elementary School in Winnipeg, which I attended as a child. The school wanted a story from an active soldier to present as part of its Remembrance Day service. I was honoured to provide my thoughts on the role of Canada's Armed Forces in general, as well as a description of my time in Afghanistan. Recently, my mom suggested that my letter from back then might be of interest to other Canadians, *Our Canada* readers in particular—so, here it is!

My name is Caitlin Yacucha and I am a soldier. My job is to set up and talk on radios and many other different pieces of technology. I have been in the military for five years and have travelled all over Canada.

The Canadian military has an important job in Canada. We provide aid for natural disasters, like the floods in Winnipeg or the ice storms in Quebec. It is important to us that Canadians understand what our mission is and that we have their support. That means a lot to soldiers, especially when they are far from home and their families.

I went to Afghanistan from November 2009 to September 2010. That's ten months, almost one year. When Canadian soldiers go overseas, we are trying to help people. In Afghanistan, we sought to achieve peace and stability. We try to help people and children by building schools, medical clinics and roads. We also help to train the Afghan army and police, so they can protect their own country.

I remember when I first arrived in Kandahar, Afghanistan, after more than 15 hours of flying, and it was cold outside! Even though it's in the desert, there is still winter. Although we didn't get any snow, it was always really dusty. There was a lot of sand everywhere. When summer came, it started getting hot. Sometimes the temperature was more than 60° Celsius outside! It was definitely a different world over there, and it made soldiers happy to receive letters or packages that had little pieces of home inside. Sometimes our families sent us games or candy!

I was in Afghanistan over Christmas and I had to work on Christmas morning. It was a great feeling coming in to work and seeing a whole pile of cards and letters from home. And they were from people we didn't even know! But those letters reminded us of home and that, even though we were far away, we hadn't been forgotten. We tried to make the best of it and we were lucky enough to have a Tim Hortons and a hockey rink in the main camp! We worked with lots of different nationalities too, such as Americans, the British and Australians. It was fun making friends with people from so many other countries.

It wasn't all fun, though. Afghanistan is a theatre of war and there were a lot of times that our camp was attacked by rockets that exploded within our fences. We could always hear guns firing and helicopters and fighter jets screaming through the sky. There were too many times that I stood on parade at the position of attention, my hand raised in salute as fallen soldiers were being carried into an airplane back to Canada or the United States while "Amazing Grace" played in the background.

Remembering the soldiers who fought and died in the world wars, other conflicts and during peacekeeping operations is very important. They helped define what Canada is today and that's something that we can all be proud of. We can learn a lot from the veterans of these tragedies. Who we must not forget is the new generation of veterans of Afghanistan. Their stories are just as important in the fabric of our nation's identity and it is our duty as Canadians to remember them and learn from them. There are stories that I will have in my mind for the rest of my life. I am proud to be a Canadian soldier and will continue to carry the torch passed on by those who have fallen before me. For I am a veteran and I will never forget.

—by Sgt. ***Caitlin Yacucha****, Winnipeg, Manitoba*

A Tribute to Our Vets on Remembrance Day

"Flags of Remembrance" raised simultaneously at sites across the country are a visual reminder of sacrifices made

As a proud Canadian, as well as the founder of Veteran Voices of Canada, which recently marked its tenth anniversary, I feel Canadians need to be visually reminded more often of what our servicemen and women have sacrificed for their fellow Canadians throughout the years. We also need to continue to build on our sense of Canadian pride as a peaceful and loving nation. So, in 2014, we began an annual cross-Canada tribute initiative named "Veteran Voices of Canada—Flags of Remembrance."

In October of each year, in many communities across the nation, Veteran Voices of Canada strategically places and raises in a line 128 full-sized Canadian flags, each representing 1,000 Canadian soldiers who died or were declared missing in action, dating from the Boer War to the current day. Our first Flags of Remembrance tribute site was in my hometown of Sylvan Lake, Alberta. We've now expanded into British Columbia, Ontario, Prince Edward Island, Nova Scotia and New Brunswick, but we hope to have the tribute represented in every Canadian province and territory.

The idea is that when Canadians drive past or visit a Flags of Remembrance site, they will gain a stronger sense of patriotism and better understand the number of Canadian lives lost in times of war and conflict, and during peacekeeping actions.

Sponsors who wish to pay tribute to a veteran or military hero can have what we call a "hero plaque" attached to one of the flagpoles for all to see, read and remember. Featuring an acrylic Canadian maple leaf, the plaque includes the hero's name and rank, with whom the hero served, and his/her years of service. The heroes named can be still serving, retired or passed on. We say that the names of our heroes on these plaques act as guardians for the 1,000 souls that one flag represents. Because Royal Canadian Mounted Police are veterans, too, we include them as part of our annual initiative.

Each flag can be sponsored by anyone who wants to pay tribute to our veterans—a friend, family member, kindly individual or business. Everyone who believes it is important to honour and remember our veterans is welcome to participate.

At each of our tribute sites across Canada, all flags are raised simultaneously at moving ceremonies with hundreds of community members, local veterans, their families and representatives from a variety of service agencies and youth groups in attendance. The flags remain in place until just after November 11, at which time the tribute site is closed for another year. The flags and commemorative hero plaques are subsequently handed over to the sponsors or their designates as a keepsake at a closing ceremony held later in each community. We always strive to have a large youth presence at the closing ceremony, where "Last Post" is played, to impress upon them the importance of remembrance. With that in mind, we also bring our project and our message into schools at every opportunity.

Through this initiative, we aim to ensure that Canadians throughout the country of all ages and walks of life continue to understand and appreciate the sacrifices that our veterans have made on behalf of the country we all call home. Through the coming years, we intend to grow our Flags of Remembrance tribute into as many communities across Canada as possible. We promise to never forget.

*—by **Allan Cameron**, Sylvan Lake, Alberta*

A War Vet's Best Friend

Thanks to Vantage and Canadian Guide Dogs for the Blind, life is better for this wounded veteran

William Goodwin grew up in Thompson, Manitoba, and moved to Ontario when he was 20. A year later he joined the military, becoming Cpl. Goodwin of the 1st Battalion, The Royal Canadian Regiment, stationed at Canadian Forces Base Petawawa. The Royal Canadian Regiment was formed as the Infantry School Corps in 1883. Since that date, the regiment has been involved in nearly every conflict and operation involving the deployment of Canadian Forces units or personnel.

William was wounded while serving in Afghanistan. Despite the challenges involved with his long recovery, he has made enormous progress and his spirits are high. He is now paired with a dog named Vantage, from the Assistance Dogs Division of Canadian Guide Dogs for the Blind.

William says, "A couple of months after my injury, my occupational therapist suggested that I might be eligible for an assistance dog. I was immediately interested, but I had just started physiotherapy and learning to walk on prosthetics. I felt it was not the right time. It was about a year later that I sent in the paperwork."

Shortly thereafter, William met with a trainer from Canadian Guide Dogs for the Blind's Assistance Dogs Division, and he was introduced to a couple of dogs. He still felt uncertain about how much he would be walking, so he decided to wait until this was a little clearer. The training started about a year later, when William could work on handling a dog from both the wheelchair and in a standing position. His walking was still very unstable, but he started with the chair and adjusted to the legs as he could.

"The training was extremely educational, learning how a dog's mind works and all the different commands he is capable of," says William. He received Vantage on the second day of training and the dog was permitted to stay at William's home from that point as he continued the training course. William was advised that it could take from three to six months before Vantage would bond with him. He says, even knowing what to expect, he questioned whether he had made a mistake.

"It was probably in the fourth month that I really started to notice Vantage was bonding to me and that was a pretty incredible feeling. In my day-to-day activities, Vantage is capable of doing all sorts of tasks, but the biggest help he can give me is also the simplest—picking things up for me and just being around, drawing my attention enough to help with any anxiety I might be having. It is almost guaranteed that I will drop something when I am walking as I try to juggle my two canes, wallet and phone." William adds, "It has gotten to the point that I don't even have to say anything. If Vantage sees me drop something, he immediately retrieves it for me. It makes me smile every time."

William tries to encourage people as much as he can when they ask about an assistance dog. "I usually tell people how difficult the first few months can feel. I never had a pet before, so it kind of caught me off guard just how much work is involved. It is tough to describe just how incredible having Vantage in my life is. He gives me a reason to wake up every morning and keeps me smiling throughout the day. He also forces me to get outside and be more active."

While there are dogs that are used to assist individuals suffering from long-term post-traumatic stress disorder (PTSD), it is important to note that Vantage is used to assist with mobility issues, as are all dogs in the Assistance Dogs Division of Canadian Guide Dogs for the Blind. While there may be some unintentional overlap, such as Vantage providing William with a caring companion and the responsibility of having a dog to care for, the main intention is for Vantage to assist William with mobility and tasks that he cannot perform himself. Canadian Guide Dogs for the Blind does not train dogs for PTSD; however, the Assistance Dogs Division continues to assist individuals with mobility-related disabilities within a 200-kilometre radius of Ottawa, within Canada. And there's no doubt that both William and Vantage are very happy about that fact.

*—by **Steven Doucette**, Manotick, Ontario*

Vets in Transition

The men and women who defended our home should never be without one

I am a veteran of the Canadian Armed Forces and served my country for 15 years until an accident at work ended my career. I loved being in the military and signed up for two tours in Bosnia.

I was assigned to the HMCS *Halifax* on a NATO mission and we were sailing off the coast of Spain on 9/11 when the planes hit the Twin Towers. Everything changed for our military then. Our ship broke from the NATO fleet and sailed up the Gulf of Oman towards Afghanistan. We boarded all ships coming into and leaving the gulf, which conjured up nightmares from my Bosnia days.

I was scheduled for my Junior Leadership course in October 2002, so I caught a flight back to Canada to take it. I was going to be promoted to master corporal and the training course was mandatory. I was happy to get home, but the cork had popped and everything I had buried deep inside was coming to the surface. I struggled to understand what was wrong with me.

I made an appointment to see the doctor and he told me I had post-traumatic stress disorder (PTSD). He prescribed medication to help relieve the all-consuming lack of sleep, nightmares and mood swings. I was gradually becoming deeply depressed.

In February 2003, I was managing the supply ration room on base when I accidently fell from a 15-foot ladder, tore my arm from its socket and crushed two discs in my back. I hit my head so hard on the cement floor that I now have a condition called TBI—traumatic brain injury. I was put on medical leave and underwent several operations over a two-year period, after which I was retired with a 3b medical classification.

I was very lucky to have a loving family who helped me deal with my PTSD, which, in spite of professional help, was growing worse. I had my wife, Debbie, a little boy and two stepchildren; I can only imagine how difficult it must have been for them to cope with my depression, pain and mood swings. I felt like my life was over.

I was seeing a physiologist who told me to get out of the house and volunteer in the community, something I used to do regularly before my Bosnia tours. I found a church that served Sunday dinners to the homeless in Halifax. I thought I could just go in and start helping—not the case. I drove by the church seven Sundays in a row before I could pull myself together enough to go in and offer to help. After I started working, it felt great to help others and be useful again.

While serving the dinner, I noticed a familiar face. It was a guy I had served with in the military and I assumed he was there helping out like me. I went to say hello and we started chatting. When I asked him how long he had been volunteering, he told me he came here for something to eat.

After a bit more talk, he finally admitted he was homeless and at the end of his rope with family, friends and life. I was floored when he pointed out three other homeless veterans at the dinner. I told him I would try to get them some help and gave him the money I had in my pocket.

When I got home, I told Debbie. She couldn't believe it and started looking up homeless veterans in Canada and found other similar cases online. We set up a meeting with case workers at Veterans Affairs Canada to discuss our situation at the church. Their response was, "We don't have homeless veterans in Canada." I brought in the four veterans I had found at the dinner and the case managers were amazed. They said they had put out flyers in shelters and no one had come forward. I explained that veterans are proud and it isn't easy for them to ask for help.

I thought if it was that easy to find four homeless veterans, there were probably others. I called some military friends and we patrolled downtown Halifax, checking shelters and talking to any homeless people we could find. Everyone seemed to be aware of veterans living on the streets.

We ended up at another church dinner, where we found seven homeless veterans. Actually, they found us, drawn to the particular mannerisms most military people have.

The media became aware of the situation and went public with the story. Through Facebook and other media, we began receiving calls from several other provinces to help homeless veterans. I found it hard to believe people were calling us in Nova Scotia to help a veteran in British Columbia. I put the word out to my military friends there that veterans needed help and, within three hours, we had volunteers at the door, and we were really under way.

We felt the best way going forward would be to work with a business plan to keep us on track, so Debbie and I decided to form Veterans Emergency Transition Services, or VETS Canada.

We contacted Veterans Affairs, the Canadian Legion and social services in an effort to find our homeless veterans some temporary assistance and to get them off the street. We found, however, the bureaucracy in government and large agencies slow to react and the paperwork seemed endless. We decided to do what we could with small donations and work to get the large agencies more involved at a later date.

It was a difficult beginning, but eventually we put together a strong team. In 2010, we applied to the federal government for charity status, which was granted, transforming us from a small, local grassroots group into a national veterans organization. We have since formed chapters in every province in Canada. Veterans Affairs Canada, the Canadian Legion, Wounded Warriors, the Military Family Resource Centres and the RCMP Command have now partnered with us. Our overriding goal is to take veterans off the streets and give them the chance to become productive and contributing members of our society once again.

*—by **Jim Lowther**, Dartmouth, Nova Scotia*

MEMORIES

From lakeside in summer to hockey in winter, and from characters that inspired us to the games we love, here are places and memories that have touched us the most

Memory-Go-Round

One teacher's devotion continues to inspire her student almost 50 years later

Even as a 55-year-old man, one of my most poignant memories is that of being an eight-year-old boy in Grade 3 at St. Vincent School in Chatham, Ontario, taught by a wonderful teacher, Ms. Mary Wolanski. Somehow, she knew how to help me learn where other teachers could not. I didn't know I had a learning disorder back in those days, but Ms. Wolanski managed to understand how I learned.

From whatever criteria an eight-year-old boy can draw as far as appreciating beauty, I admit that perhaps I also had a bit of a crush on her, and one day, I decided to act on that crush. I used to take a bus to school from a rural area in a collection of houses, barely a village, called Louisville, meeting a group of other rural students at an impromptu bus stop in front of our home. One morning, while waiting for the bus, I thought I'd pick some small wildflowers from the bank of a broad ditch by the road to give to Ms. Wolanski. I have no idea what kind of flowers they were, but it hardly mattered. All I could think of was that I was going to make her happy with a gift of flowers.

While holding them in my hand as I waited for the bus, a taller, older boy teased me incessantly about the flowers; when I spoke out in my defence, he grabbed me from behind, holding my arms, laughing at my inability to get away. As hard as I could, I kicked his right shin with the heel of my shoe and he tossed me into the gravel, shredding my flowers as he held his aching shin. The fight was over.

I saw the school bus approaching, so I dashed into the ditch again, undeterred, and picked a handful of flowers again and ran to board the bus. I carried those flowers in my left hand as proud as anyone would an earned trophy. I even remember how the flowers' stems felt in my hand.

Once at school, my heart pounded in anticipation of what Ms. Wolanski would think of my gift. As I rounded the doorway of the classroom, I was stopped dead in my tracks at the sight of a female classmate giving Ms. Wolanski roses. She seemed so happy to receive them, and the girl was so happy with her reaction. I stood in disbelief and could feel my heart sink as I looked at the tiny flowers in my hand and thought she would never like my flowers after having received roses. I went out into the hallway and tossed the flowers into the trash can. For whatever reason, that memory, and the disappointment, has stuck with me for almost half a century and I can rewind and play it over as freshly as the day it happened.

Fast-forward nearly 50 years. I am living on Vancouver Island and I get an email from my sister in Chatham, where she is working as a personal trainer at a national-chain fitness centre. Apparently the gym had a member who inquired about her last name, to which the member remarked, "I taught a young boy in Grade 3 a long time ago with the same surname. Ugo was his first name." My sister said, "That's my brother."

Yes, that gym member was Mary Wolanski, who told my sister that she remembered me and my name to that day! My sister emailed me Ms. Wolanski's email address and I wrote her, recounting the story of my crush on her, the flowers...all of it. She had no idea that I had brought her hand-picked wildflowers, nor that I had thrown them out when I saw the girl give her roses. It was an emotional moment for both of us. She empathized, even after all this time, with that heartbroken little boy. She is such a wonderful human being.

She wrote me back and told me I should have given her the flowers on that day years ago, that she would have loved them as much as the roses, but what does an eight-year-old boy know of such things? That was her first year as a teacher; I was in her first class.

She also told me a personal story of her own, about her favourite flowers, violets. A little while later, I contacted my sister to call Ms. Wolanski to her gym for a parcel pickup. Curious, she arrived to find a floral arrangement of violets waiting for her. I had decided that it was time for this little boy to give her, a most wonderful teacher, the flowers she wanted and deserved.

Just last week, I moved my mother to Ontario to live beside my sister, but I could only stay a handful of days before having to come back to the island to work. After a small farewell gathering of family at my sister's place, who should come to my sister's door but Ms. Wolanski! I was stunned speechless, and although decades had passed, I knew her eyes—they were as familiar as if I'd seen them yesterday.

What a wonderful reunion of student and teacher, now as adults with a common, powerful memory. I gave her the hug that waited 50 years to happen.

It became clear to me that achieving success in my career as an instructor was all because Ms. Wolanski had taught me that in order to be a good teacher, one has to first learn how each student learns, adapt a teaching method to suit each student's needs and care for the student's success. I wholeheartedly agree and have seen the successes of my own students because of it.

Lives are inextricably and inexplicably linked, and memories are tied to commonalities that we must be willing to seek out, because they are there and they have meaning and purpose. We are all connected. I could not imagine a more profound experience than that one poignant day in my life as a young boy coming home to roost, by sharing that memorable day again, in person, with Ms. Wolanski. Her influence on me survived in me for decades and surfaced just when I needed it. For me, it has been a true memory-go-round, one for which I remain truly grateful.

*—by **Ugo DeBiasi**, Nanaimo, British Columbia*

Facing Off Against a Blizzard

A hockey team saves its best moves for the postgame by guiding cars to safety through a blinding storm

It was a typical winter day in 1947 in south Saskatchewan—and I mean south Saskatchewan—only 60 miles or so from the American border. It was cold, with lots of snow already on the ground. Weather forecasts being what they were in those days, we didn't let them dictate our activities. We just carried on with whatever we had planned.

Several nearby towns had a hockey team, and my hometown of Gravelbourg had two—a community team and a college team. On this particular night, the college team was playing. My dad was a hockey fan in his own right, and he knew that my kid brother was wild about the sport. He also knew that I, the eldest teenage daughter, was a hockey fan—but really more a fan of my boyfriend, who played on the college team. So my father piled us into the car—me, my friend, my kid brother and a pal of his—and off we went on the 30-mile trip to watch the game.

The match was exciting, with the usual boisterous hockey fans, and my boyfriend played beautifully. Soon, though, it was time to pile back into the car and head home. Unfortunately, we walked out of the arena straight into a blizzard.

My dad gathered the two priests who helped run the college team and were providing lifts for players and fans and, if I recall correctly, one other man who had also volunteered to drive people. My dad suggested that we all follow one another very closely to avoid getting lost in the whiteout. Within a few miles of starting out, it became obvious that we were in for a pretty rough night, for the road was all but invisible. It was then decided that the bigger, older and stronger hockey players would get out and guide the little convoy of cars. So the boys bundled up and worked in teams of three. One boy stood in the centre of the road with one boy on each side, relaying one another and guiding the cars. The vehicles moved at a snail's pace, but at least we all stayed on the road.

After about 12 miles of this, we arrived at a small town, which, happily, had a hotel...although I use the term loosely. At the very least, it was shelter from the storm, for which we were thankful. Dad and the two priests went to seek out the local parish priest in the middle of the night, asking for a bit of Mass wine to be heated and given to the boys to ward off colds or flu. Needless to say, none of us got much sleep: We were having too much fun! We had managed to dig up some music, and we started dancing. I can't quite remember how the hotel owner reacted to all this, but knowing my dad, I'm sure the owner was generously compensated for his hospitality.

The next morning, after little or no sleep but having had an experience that in those days was pretty special, we set off for home. The snow had stopped; the Saskatchewan skies were clear and blue, and the sunshine glorious, so the remaining 18 miles home were easier to navigate, despite a bit of shovelling along the way to clear particularly high snowdrifts.

We wandered into class that day after the lunch break a bit sheepishly, facing stern looks from the nuns, our teachers. Under the circumstances, though, there were no scoldings or punishment, for it really was beyond our control, and I'm sure Dad had a little talk with the nuns to explain and placate them.

The memory of those events popped into my mind suddenly one fall day, even though they took place almost 70 years ago. Things were different back then; we took the weather in our stride and just went on with our lives. Nowadays, in the cities and surely in the country, a snowstorm closes schools and offices, the weather dominates headlines and life is disrupted until the snowplows have cleared the way. It's a shame that today's teenagers are unlikely to experience something so unique as being guided home through a snowstorm by hockey players. Those were simpler times, and this is a memory that I will always treasure.

*—by **Jeanne Emelyanov**, Ottawa, Ontario*

The Coldest Day in Canadian History

In February 1947, the temperature in the Yukon plunged to a bone-chilling and record-breaking –81.4°F

My father, Wilfred Blezard, joined Transport Canada in 1946, a year after he arrived home from Europe after serving six years in the Canadian Army. He willingly accepted postings as a weather technician to various northern stations in the Yukon and Northwest Territories, very grateful for the solitude and quietness of these lonely outposts, in sharp contrast to his devastating experiences overseas.

The first weather station my father was posted to was called Snag Airport, located approximately 30 kilometres east of the Alaska-Yukon border, near Beaver Creek, Yukon. He was one of four young weathermen stationed there during 1946-47. Snag Airport was part of the Northwest Staging Route of emergency landing strips and observation stations established during World War II to facilitate travel from Alaska and the Yukon to Central Canada and the United States.

The weather station operated from 1943 to 1966. It was while my father was there that the temperature plummeted to –81.4°F on February 3, 1947, a record-breaking low for all of North America. He, along with the officer in charge, Gord Toole, had the dubious honour of recording this unbelievable temperature. According to astronomy experts, on that day, Snag was colder than the average surface temperature of Mars. Telegrams of congratulations were received from many countries around the world, with several messages referring to Snag as North America's new "cold pole."

Mark Twain once remarked, "Cold! If the thermometer had been an inch longer, we'd all have frozen to death." My father and Gord Toole immediately noticed that the tiny sliding scale inside the glass thermometer column had fallen into the bulb at the end, well below the lowest reading on the thermometer (–80°F). After marking the thermometer sheath using a fine, sharp file (ink does not flow at that temperature), it was sent to a Toronto laboratory, where it was recalibrated at –81.4°F.

Three months later, the weather service accepted this as the correct temperature, the lowest official temperature ever recorded in North America. According to my father, the men were excited by the news, saying, "We had to put a little lock on the door to the instrument screen because everyone was rushing out and looking at the thermometers. Even the slightest bit of body heat would cause the alcohol to jump." Now, all official alcohol thermometers in Canada have markings to –94°F, a thermometer redesign due to the coldest day in Canadian history.

Just how cold is –81.4°F? In order to give you a clear idea of the answer to this question, I am including several anecdotal, once-in-a-lifetime observations, as recorded by my father and Gord Toole in several interviews given over the years since this historic event. Will Snag remain North America's "cold pole"? Only time will tell.

- At –80°F, the people's voices and barking dogs in the village of Snag could be plainly heard at the airport four miles away.
- An aircraft that flew over Snag that day at 10,000 feet was first heard when still more than 20 miles away, and later, when overhead, still at 10,000 feet, the engine roar was deafening. It woke everyone who was sleeping at the time because they thought the airplane was landing at the airport.
- A piece of ice, when broken, sounded exactly like breaking glass.
- Ice on the White River, about a mile east of the airport, cracked and boomed loudly, like gunfire, amplified by a cap of warmer air lying over intensely cold air on the ground, bouncing sound waves across great distances.
- The extreme cold air generated intense radio static, much like the crackling sounds heard during a thunderstorm.
- Exhaled breath instantly froze with a hissing noise, and stayed suspended in the air at head level in long vapour streaks several hundred metres long, like miniature condensation trails from a jet aircraft. These patches of human "fog" remained in the still air for three to four minutes before falling to the ground as powdery ice crystals. One observer found such a trail still marking his path when he returned along the same route 15 minutes later. Becoming lost was of no concern!

- For days, a small fog or steam patch would appear over the sled dogs, at a height of 15 to 20 feet. It would disappear only in the warm part of the day when the temperature warmed up to –60°F.
- A chunk of ice was so cold that, when brought into a warm room, it took five full minutes before there was any trace of moisture.
- A cupful of cold water was thrown high into the air, just to see what would happen. Before it hit the ground, it made a hissing noise, froze and fell as tiny round pellets of ice the size of wheat kernels. Spit also froze before hitting the ground.
- At such temperatures, metal snapped like ice and wood became petrified, even paper became brittle and rubber was just like cement. The sled dogs' leather harnesses would break if bent.
- After seconds outdoors, nose hairs froze rigidly and eyes would tear. Facial hair and glasses become thickly crusted with frozen breath. You had to be careful not to inhale too deeply for fear of freezing or scalding your lungs from the frigid air. Another discomfort were numerous cases of beginning frostbite, particularly the familiar "ping" as the tip of one's nose froze. "It was easy to freeze your nose at –70°F without even knowing it was cold."
- The animals didn't appear to suffer too much during this two-week spell when the temperatures never climbed above –64°F. Two horses, owned by a local trapper, used to visit the cookhouse every morning. It was amazing the things they would eat: apple pie, wieners, buns and cakes, and as an extra treat the cook even fed them ice cream one morning at –76°F. During their wandering around outside, almost eight inches of ice would build up on their hooves, making it look like they were up on stilts.
- The stamina of the sled dogs was remarkable. They never went into their kennels, preferring to lay on top of their kennels, curled up with their heads tucked in towards their bellies. A band of frost fog formed over their heads, keeping them reasonably warm.
- Starting machinery was a chore. Getting an engine started was no guarantee it would continue to run. At that temperature, the oil and transmission fluid would coagulate.
- And finally, truck tires could splay open when they hit ruts in the road.

*—by **Carman Scherlie**, Wembley, Alberta*

The Fabric of Her Life

Practicing the noble art of embroidery

During the Depression, when I was a preschooler, Mom taught me to embroider. We didn't have warm, cozy clothes to wear to go out and play in the snowdrifts and my sister Tena had rheumatic fever, so I needed to be kept quiet and busy. Fortunately, the *Free Press* printed a weekly "Farm Life" quilt pattern. We traced it on bleached flour sack squares. Mom showed me how to thread a needle, knot the yarn and outline stitch the animal of the week. There were 21 blocks to complete, which I proudly did. Mom sewed these together on her old sewing machine and it became a bedspread that we enjoyed showing to visitors.

As I grew older, my sisters and I embroidered tea towels, pillowcases, curtains and tablecloths with fancy floral designs. For centuries, it was popular for ladies to do this kind of handiwork. It was often done by the heroine in historic novels.

In 2000, while travelling in Europe, we saw religious themes neatly stitched on prayer kneeler covers in several cathedrals. After crossing through the Chunnel, I was pleased that our tour of Britain included some embroidery exhibitions. To my delight, I got into a needlework festival in York. The altar cloths and priestly vestments were very impressive. Rich satin and velvet banners, highlighted with intricate patterns, added elegance to the show.

Even Queen Elizabeth II's Holyrood Palace in Edinburgh has beautifully stitched bench covers—they were originally a gift to her parents (Queen Elizabeth and King George VI) upon their coronation.

As a young child, I discovered how much prettier things look when you decorate them with coloured thread. Now, in my 80s, I still like to cross-stitch a motto or French knot, and satin stitch a crewel embroidered bouquet.

*—by **Hilda J. Born**, Abbotsford, British Columbia*

My Early Education

Despite the chilly seats and "boot soup," life in a one-room schoolhouse was not so bad after all

Education as I knew it some 70 years ago was much different from what it is today. No warm, comfortable buses stopped at the gate, ready to whisk us away to a modern learning centre. No centrally heated and cooled multi-roomed complex awaited our imminent arrival or catered to our every educational need. No vast array of teachers armed with teaching aids attempted to keep our inquisitive little minds occupied. We made do with what we had, and we created our own learning experiences—for better or for worse.

While we didn't trudge five miles uphill through waist-deep snow barefoot, we really did walk a fair way to the local stone schoolhouse. Built on a hill, it was just outside the hamlet of Osaca, Ontario. It was a drafty, dank, one-room building, serving students of all ages and grades. Just inside the main back door sat a huge, black, wood-eating monster that was our version of central heating. A long line of stovepipes below the ceiling that ended in the front bracket chimney attempted to keep the frost at bay for those forced to sit near the front of the room. Surrounding the stove was a three-sided galvanized heat shield designed to keep awkward young bodies from getting fried, but it really just served as our own built-in clothes dryer. During winter months, a row of matted mittens, soggy socks and fetid footwear adorned its surface. Responsibility for feeding the fiery beast fell to the senior boys, but try as we might, the front seating area almost always felt like a suburb of Siberia.

While the school building did have the recently installed luxury of good overhead electric lights, there was no indoor plumbing. Drinking water was obtained from a blue-enamelled, communal drinking cup dipped into a large pail that sat on the windowsill. Germs were something only city folk worried about. The washroom facilities were located outdoors in two little shacks at the far corner of the playground. The seats were known for their lack of comfort and a cold updraft was always waiting to bite occupants where it hurt the most. If the call of nature became too insistent during class, you learned to hurriedly trek back and forth through the drifting snow. Great relief was experienced when you finally arrived back to the warmth of the classroom.

In those days, clothing was more about function than form. We wore anything that would keep us warm; fashion wasn't yet one of our priorities. Layering, even then, was a useful and practiced concept. First came a fuzzy pair of woollen long johns—buttoned trap door in back—over which we added a shirt, a sweater and a pair of bibbed overalls. Our feet were encased by at least two layers of hand-knit wool socks pulled up over our pant legs and stuffed into oversized, hand-me-down rubber boots.

I'm not sure what the girls used for their first layer, but I know they always wore long, full skirts. For warmth, trousers were sometimes worn underneath, and then came a blouse and lots of wool sweaters. Their footwear was similar to ours—socks and rubber boots. Almost everybody kept another pair of slippers or old shoes to wear inside.

Since there were eight grades to be taught and only one teacher, that usually allowed us a bit of free time between lessons. This was spent by helping the younger grades practice their math and hearing them read from books that were all about the adventures of Dick, Jane, baby Sally and Spot the dog.

If time permitted, we were encouraged to practice our penmanship. I suspect it was a futile attempt to keep our eager little minds employed while the teacher was occupied elsewhere. Since ballpoint pens were not yet invented, the tools of the trade consisted of an ink bottle, nib and straight pen. After doodling and drawing became dull, a new use for the straight pen was discovered: It made an excellent projectile. If lobbed with just the correct trajectory, the pen would fly and silently stick straight up in the wooden floor. If the angles were calculated incorrectly, however, the missile would clatter noisily onto the planks. The game then ended abruptly, sometimes for several days, if the teacher was not in a good mood.

During winter months, the government, in its wisdom, supplied us with cod liver oil capsules, supposedly to increase our vitamin D levels. With a practiced flick of a finger, when the teacher wasn't looking, those vile concoctions could be reduced to harmless, smelly, smoldering smudges on the hot stove.

In keeping with the spirit of the times, the community also organized a system of hot school lunches to help augment our afternoon learning experiences. Since there were ten families represented in this school section, it was agreed that each family would supply something hot one day in a two-week rotation. The rules were simple: Each of us would bring a bowl and spoon from home and the senior girls would dole out the heated ingredients from a huge pot simmering on the stove. We were supposed to consume it, along with the capsuled cod and our sandwich from home. After lunch, we'd wash our utensils, place them in the cupboard and finally escape outside for the remainder of the noon hour.

For me, this posed a problem; I don't really like soup at the best of times, but my freedom outside was precious. While probably nutritious, the quality of those offerings varied greatly. Mother's contribution to the hot lunch program was more of a hearty stew than a soup. At my request, it contained extra meat, carrots and onions, but no tomatoes.

Although somewhat biased, I considered Mother's creative cuisine, if one had to eat soup, as quite palatable. Other contributions were passable, some semi-edible and a few barely so, but there was one family's concoction that defied description. It was a greasy gruel in which floated a couple of bloated, dead tomatoes, a few scraggly bits of limp onion parts and some chunks of what I think used to be stale bread. This, I determined, I was not going to eat!

The problem for me, though, was that it had to be consumed before I was allowed outside. What to do? How was I going to follow the rules, show an empty bowl and escape to freedom if I didn't choke it down? There had to be a solution! Then inspiration struck. After much blowing and stirring to cool the gruel, I secretly slipped the slimy contents down the open top of my rubber boots when nobody was looking. Dutifully, I showed my empty bowl, rinsed it, grabbed my coat and hat, and, foot sloshing in gruesome gruel, hurried outside.

My first stop was at the hand pump on the well. There I pulled off my boots and socks, pumped them full of water and tried to rinse away the evidence. The operation was a success! I'd escaped having to eat any dead tomatoes, gained my freedom and my footwear would be dry by the time I needed it for the homeward trek. This little episode was repeated faithfully every other Wednesday all winter with no apparent repercussions. Mother did mention, however, that she often wondered why my feet frequently seemed to smell a little swampy.

Now, as I look back from the perspective of more than seven decades, I must admit that I actually enjoyed the trials and tribulations of my early education. In a one-room rural school, I was started on the proper path to higher "learnin'" and given the basic tools for success. The rest was left up to me. Now, after working 35 years in education, and earning three university degrees along the way, I hope I haven't let anybody down.

*—by **Jim Soul**, Erin, Ontario*

Hockey Night in Hedley

Fond memories of a small but vibrant town and its love of Canada's favourite pastime

I grew up in the tiny but mighty (back then) town of Hedley, British Columbia. The town's two gold mines and two mills drew workers from around the world before, during and after the Great Depression.

Any boy who could skate could join the Hedley scrub hockey team in the late 1930s. With no official coaches, the boys' abilities improved by playing shinny—not through drill practices. Some of the dads with previous hockey experience, and who showed up in town for mining work, volunteered tips at irregular intervals. Occasionally, even the company superintendent shared his hockey expertise. Other times, the butcher's helper leaped onto the ice. The boys would shout, "Hey, Syd, show us how to do stuff." He'd stickhandle, zoom around and shoot past the startled goalie. My brother Donnie would shout, "Hey! When Syd skates backwards, I can't catch him!" Syd would reply, "Okay, boys, let's play the game. They're fired up now."

Adult volunteers would take turns refereeing, but they didn't have to work too hard, as the ice had no blue line, red line, crease line—or any other lines. Any spot was a faceoff spot. Mostly, the referee whistled to signal time, or when the puck arced over the wooden fence. He'd ignore minor infractions. But body checking, checking into the boards, slashing, high sticking and fighting were disallowed because only the goalie, my other brother, Alex, could brag of having padding at company cost. He and a couple of others wore padded gloves. Otherwise, the boys' uniforms consisted of toques, sweaters and knitted mitts, as well as trousers with newspaper stuffed up the pant legs. When Donnie, a right winger, took a turn at being captain, he goaded his teammates into playing harder and skating faster through any zone—his only offensive strategy.

The rink, of unknown dimensions, was built on a pond partially comprising runoff from the mill, and featured a couple of floodlights. The one penalty box gate opened onto a snowbank, which served as seating. But it was seldom used and there were few injuries because games were weekend "friendlies" with scrub teams from nearby neighbouring towns.

Family and friends, who attended evening home games without fail, stood ankle-deep in snow at the railings and whooped as loud as any *Hockey Night in Canada* crowd we'd hear on our static-filled mantel radio. A volunteer stood behind each goal and held up a hand when the puck slid, wobbled or flew into the net. Another volunteer scraped the ice with a makeshift Zamboni made of boards nailed to a two-by-four.

Our team's trips to surrounding towns—Blakeburn, Princeton, Copper Mountain and Keremeos—each no more than an hour's drive away, were composed of carpooling dads, the few who could afford a sedan big enough for players to cram into; coupes with rumble seats lose their appeal in sub-zero temperatures.

I recall my friend Finlay's 1937 Hudson Terraplane with swooping fenders and a bulbous rear end, as well as my dad's dented Ford with the cracked windshield. Frozen ruts beneath fresh snow showed their true nature when the cars skidded and fishtailed along narrow mountain roads. Flat tires were not unheard of.

The Hedley rink at the town's heart thrived due to the skaters' shack. Its worn benches lining the walls appeared plush to tired players and spectators alike. The potbelly heater full of crackling and spitting frost-coated wood warmed noses and toes. Some of the miners who rode the skip into town on weekends enjoyed the banter with rink rats of all ages. There were no flashing scoreboards, twirling towels or thundering music to celebrate our team's win, just glowing hearts amid the falling snowflakes winking in the lights.

*—by **Gloria Barkley**, Coquitlam, British Columbia*

Ice Dreams

Skating along the Rideau Canal caps off a perfect Canadian winter day

As I drove along the glorious, winding road leading away from Toronto and towards Ottawa, I could feel the tension from a month of challenges at work melting away in the warm air blasting from the car heater. Lost in the beauty of the Canadian countryside, I contentedly drove by meandering rivers, frozen lakes and snow-capped trees towards my destination.

The pink light of the setting sun was melting away over the far horizon of trees as I pulled into the driveway of my friend's country-cottage home. I frowned momentarily as I thought of the last-minute bombardment of paperwork that had delayed my arrival by an hour and prevented me from seeing an unobstructed sunset from her kitchen window, which overlooks an open country field. I tried to conjure up an image of the majestic sight I had missed as I grabbed my backpack from the trunk.

My good friend Stefany welcomed me and, after I freshened up, we grabbed a late dinner at a Chinese restaurant in town. The atmosphere of the small Renfrew establishment instantly brought me back to my years teaching English overseas in Beijing, China. I breathed in the familiar aromas of garlic broccoli and other stir-fries as Stefany and I caught up on our news.

Early the next morning, we were on our way into Ottawa, where we were joined by Stefany's sister Kat to enjoy the winter festivities. Scattered throughout the city were ice sculpture competitions in progress and parties hosted at restaurants. The city was buzzing with excitement and we followed the electricity towards the frozen canal.

The Rideau Canal freezes over in winter and locals skate it for fun and as an alternate route to work or school. I was told that, on occasion, you would see a business person gliding along the frozen river to work, briefcase in hand.

We strapped on our skates and joined the crowds already skating, sliding and stumbling along the ice and past booths where you could buy cocoa, soup and Beaver Tails; the scent of the pancake dessert wafted in the air, trying to entice us to skate over and buy some.

As we gracefully skated towards the heart of activity, I caught glimpses of the happy faces of people as they whirred past me in the oncoming lane of skating traffic. My parents, keeping with Canadian tradition, had made sure that I had my first pair of skates as soon as I was stumbling-walking. As children, we would skate no less than three times a week at the local community centre or on a friend's backyard rink. I was signed up for figure skating lessons long before I was attending school full time.

My education started on the cold ponds of Canada, where I experienced "toe freeze" and runny noses, and learned how to properly bundle up to protect against the winter elements. Then, as a young teenager, my mother decided we should all enroll in speed-skating lessons. Every Friday night for three years, my older brothers and I would load into our station wagon and together, as a family of five, we would learn another great Canadian tradition. As a result of all of my years on skates, I could easily navigate the roughest ice; thus, where the river nearer to Ottawa's downtown region got choppier from the greater number of skaters, my body instinctively picked through the ice with ease.

The sun was nearly setting as we walked off the ice, skates slung over our shoulders and our feet happy to be back in boots. The air was cool, but we were both warmed through and through, thanks to our invigorating skate. I smiled back at the skaters and holiday-makers still on the canal as we grabbed a cup of cocoa and walked up the staircase back to the car. French music, blasting from a booth below, reminded us that the celebrations would go on well into the night as we continued with our outing.

Tired, warmed and relaxed, we were content to wander into a few shops before heading homewards to cuddle down into our warm beds for a long sleep and to dream of what else we might do the rest of our Canadian winter weekend.

—by ***Leesha Nikkanen****, Newmarket, Ontario*

This Old Sugar Shack

Making syrup, sharing stories and building memories for generations

Our sugar shack is located in Bloomingdale, Ontario, and has been in the family for five generations. Created in the early 1900s by my great-grandfather Titus, it was passed down to my grandfather George, and then to my father, Gord, and now to me and my siblings and our respective families. Every year, we gather to make our "liquid gold," with my sister Lynda and her family travelling all the way from Alberta to join us.

Maple trees surround our house, so in the spring, we tap the trees and the process begins. In the early days, making syrup entailed cooking the sap in a pan over an open fire in the bush and finishing on a stove in the summer kitchen of the house. Now, it's all done on a wood-fired evaporator in the sugar shack.

We use the traditional method of tapping when spring temperatures are predicted, usually beginning in early March and lasting two to six weeks, ending in April. We watch many weather forecasts, beginning in January, for the correct conditions—warm during the day with a freeze overnight.

The trees are tapped with drills and a spile is inserted into the hole. Adults and children follow with buckets and lids to be hung, sometimes two or three on each tree. During this time, a day is set aside to prepare the sugar shack for the boiling-down process. A large smokestack is erected through the roof and the gathering tanks and evaporator are set up.

It requires at least 40 gallons of sap to produce one gallon of maple syrup, and we collect each bucket by hand. Large gathering tanks are placed on a wagon and pulled behind a tractor, stopping often for the happy, excited young—and older—people, who fill gathering pails and carry them to the wagon. They are emptied into the tanks, then each person refills their pail.

The tractor operator drives the tanks to the sugar shack, emptying them into holding tanks, and then slowly into the evaporator. A wood fire is built under the evaporator pans. The sap boils under close supervision so it does not boil over or burn. A syrup thermometer is used to determine the correct thickness. Next, it's filtered into large cream cans and containers for our family to share.

At the end of the season, each bucket, spout and lid is removed from the trees, thoroughly washed, dried and put away until next spring. The gathering pails, tanks and evaporator are also thoroughly cleaned and the smokestack is taken down. All in all, it's a lot of work for a short season, but it's something we look forward to each year. It's our sign that winter is over and spring has arrived.

As children, we'd listen to the stories of when my father, uncle and grandpa were younger and cooking sap. It's important for our children to hear and know those funny, heartfelt tales—even more so now, as my father passed away suddenly in his sugar bush several years ago.

So many memories have been recorded and shared every season as we come together to tap, collect and boil our sap. The old sugar shack has more stories and more memories to make. If only those old boards could talk, what stories they might tell!

*—by **Sue Weiss**, Bloomingdale, Ontario*

Summer Dreaming

Facing an uncertain future is easier when you hold on to a little bit of the past

I'll always have my childhood in Malachi. My best friend, Sydney, had a cabin on Malachi Lake in Kenora, Ontario. When we were kids, I visited her there many summers, for a week at a time. Lying on the dock, we'd read magazines and gab about what it would be like to be 17 with a car, a boyfriend and fabulous hair. Dragged along on blueberry-picking hikes and staying up till the wee hours of the morning giggling and watching movies, we were not yet aware of how fast time actually passes when you turn 14 and enter the kingdom of high school.

The summers always faded like the freckles on my nose into crisp falls that brought a new beginning, and a new backpack and binder. New friends, crowds and scenes came with the chill of autumn as well. Sydney and I may have drifted from our summertime haze and gotten into arguments or disagreed once or twice. There were times throughout the years in which we stopped talking altogether, but conflicts were always resolved and our friendship lived on.

High school goes by even faster than your older cousins tell you it does, even though most of your classes feel decades long. You blink one day in your freshman year and wake up a senior with a driver's licence. But the summers seem to slow everything down—long enough for us to catch our breath, for wounds to heal and wings to spread.

So, in my 17th summer, I found a free week—between flipping burgers and making cones at the drive-in—to pack a suitcase with books and tanning lotion and board the eastbound train to Malachi.

Just like when we were 11, Sydney and I still gabbed on the dock and read magazines, except now the conversation was about the pointless drama and recent hookups and breakups back in our hometown. We talked about anything but the elephant in the room—our futures. Life was staring back at us in the reflection of the water, except it was nothing but a question mark—so we'd simply push the thought aside and cannonball into the centre of it to shatter the idea of growing up.

Our days were a blur of blackfly bites and coconut oil. Our hair became textured from frequent dips in the cool water to escape the sun's rays. Most days were spent lying in the sun, reading aloud from some romantic mystery novel and drifting in and out of catnaps. Other days, we'd paddle kayaks to a nearby rock island and have fun jumping from the rocks into the water and waving at the shirtless teenage construction crew who passed by on boats. Occasionally, we'd sit in the cabin with a fan directed at our sunburnt bodies, using coloured string to make bracelets for our unfortunate friends back home in Manitoba.

Evenings, after a meal that satisfied every taste bud, we'd go fishing with Sydney's dad, which included watching the sun set and the full moon rise while the minnows on the ends of our lines lured small perch and we cursed the mosquitoes.

Back inside, we'd pick out a corny movie, cuddle up on the couch to munch popcorn and make fun of the bad acting and cheesy lines. We savoured every smell, sight and sound: the loons calling back and forth, the fog on the lake in the morning and the taste of blueberry pie made from berries picked that day.

Neighbours who dropped by in the morning for a cup of coffee and to chat about the weather would jar us back to reality with questions about graduation and university. Croaks rose from our throats in response—we were shy and embarrassed and frankly not ready to answer questions about our futures.

On my last night there, we raced out to the rocky island with soap in hand to wash off the day and cool my burnt shoulders. Standing on the rocks, lathering up, we noticed the dark clouds gathering and the flash of lightning. Adrenaline pumping, we frantically paddled our kayaks back to the cottage and made it just before the downpour and hail.

So maybe, for me, that summer was like the calm before the storm. The storm being growing up and making decisions—arriving quickly in all its terrifying beauty. There's no avoiding it; you just have to do the best you can. Wait out the blowing winds and roll with the punches. And after the storm—even a beautiful storm—the sun comes out again.

Although I may be sad to say goodbye to my childhood days at the lake, or feel scared about the future, I've got to take that step so I'm not left behind. But I'll keep some of my childlike self within me to remind me of where I came from and my dreams for my future self.

*—by **Cassandra Cardy**, Minnedosa, Manitoba*

Larger Than Life

A moving tribute to a special uncle

My uncle Cec—short for Cecil—was a great inspiration to me. I think of him often and the many ways he influenced me. When I last saw him, he had grown a little feeble, unlike the man I had known as a child. I remembered him as a strong man with broad shoulders, big biceps and, wow, could he saw wood with a bucksaw! As we sat that day, Uncle Cec reminisced about all the times he visited when I was young and the triumphs and tragedies of his life.

He was my dad's brother, the second son of five boys growing up in the 1930s in St. Leonard's, now St. Lunaire-Griquet, on Newfoundland's Great Northern Peninsula. Life in Newfoundland during the Depression wasn't easy for anyone, and Uncle Cec had his share of troubles, too. But it was like he always said: "Life is what you make it."

He told me of some really hard times. Like the great nor'wester in '37 that stripped his family clean. My grandfather told me about this tragedy in bits and pieces, but Uncle Cec recalled it more vividly. He told me of winds gusting up to 140 kilometres per hour and two-metre-high waves crashing against the cove. The storm ripped my grandfather's wharf and fishing stage to shreds and tore his old motorboat from its moorings and crashed her to bits against the rocks, along with the little dories and all the fishing gear on the shore. "Lost everything that fall," he said. "Everything, and we didn't have much to begin with."

But Uncle Cec told me he gained courage from my grandmother's Bible and read about the tragedies of Job. He told me how he helped my pops rebuild and how the fish were plentiful that year. "What goes around, comes around," was another of his favourite quotes. I swear he had faith as solid as the old rock his daddy's house was built on.

I remember one summer, he came to live with us at our house in Roddickton, more than 100 kilometres from St. Leonard's. There was only one winding, narrow gravel road connecting the communities in those days, so Uncle Cec elected to take a two-day trip down the coast in an old schooner. He arrived tired and hungry but full of good cheer.

Dad told us Uncle Cec had come to help build our new house. But the way he took the time for my brother and me that summer, I just think he came to be our friend. Tired as he was after working all day, he took the time to joke, tell stories and take us fishing on Saturdays.

I learned a lot from Uncle Cec. He taught me not so much in what he said but in what he didn't say. The old adage "actions speak louder than words" was certainly true for my most-beloved uncle. It seemed that nothing got him down. I honestly never saw him get discouraged. He never saw a situation as a problem, only a challenge to be overcome. Uncle Cec was not a wealthy man. He saw riches not as money but in making people happy and earning a good reputation.

I never saw him get the blues. Blue to Uncle Cec was the Atlantic on a calm, sunny day. Uncle Cec never married. I don't know why. I'm sure he would have made a fine husband and father. Love, responsibility and integrity were just a way of life to him. He certainly was a father figure to me, and the best role model anyone could ask for. He taught me to trust in God and never rely on what I think I know. Lying, he used to say, makes for a hard life because you are always working to cover it up, but honesty gives you a clear conscience and makes life easier. There aren't too many around like him today. We need more Uncle Cecs in this world. "Life is short, live it to the fullest," he said.

Five years had passed since I last saw him, so my wife and I took a trip to the Great Northern Peninsula and a visit with Uncle Cec was a priority. I learned that he had grown more feeble and was now living in a nursing home in St. Anthony. Was he the same man I once knew?

An attendant led us to his room. I knocked gently and waited. He opened the door and we looked at each other for a brief moment. "It's Hec!" he said with a smile as we embraced. His voice, though a little weaker, was still familiar. We talked for hours and he told me about new friends and how he could still beat anyone in checkers. He still went for his daily walk, took gym classes and made trips to the mall. Even though he looked a little old and bent and a little slower than I remembered, he still had that twinkle in his eye and positive persona.

As I said goodbye, I saw a tear in his eye and I fought to not break down, too. "Don't wait five more years to come again," he said with a grin. "I won't," I promised. I know that when his time comes he'll be buried in the family plot, but part of him will also be buried in my heart.

*—by **Hector M. Earle**, Stoneville, Newfoundland and Labrador*

A Man Named "Apples"

A memorable summer spent with a real-life hero

Way back in 1941 or maybe '42, I experienced the most exciting summer of my life. This was back in the days before television, air conditioners, refrigerators and cellphones. Back when Borden's milk was delivered by a horse-drawn milk wagon, as were the 25-pound blocks of ice for your icebox. Party lines were normal; we all had our own number of rings. Food tasted better. Everything was grown naturally.

My sister Betty and I lived with my grandparents in Amherstburg, Ontario, while my mother and dad worked at John Inglis in Toronto, making guns for World War II.

I had a rat terrier named Teddy and tiny metal toy soldiers to play with. The radio was our only source of entertainment. My favourite programs centred around the cowboy heroes of the day: *The Lone Ranger, Hopalong Cassidy* and Gene Autry—they were the good guys. You used your imagination and the Wild West magically came to life.

Back then, my grandparents had what you might call a hobby farm. A black man by the name of Oswald Simpson, a.k.a. Apples, was the man who worked the land for them. He was a large man—he weighed more than 300 pounds—and he had a team of horses he called by name. Mr. Simpson would show up at sunrise and leave at sunset. He wore bib overalls and a straw hat. The work was hot and difficult. Mr. Simpson and his team would work the ground as he sat perched on a spring-loaded seat on his three-furrow plow. Back and forth, back and forth, as the sun punished all three of them.

For breakfast, my grandma made oatmeal porridge. This stuff would not only stick to your ribs but it could also be used in wallpapering. I didn't much care for oatmeal porridge, so when Grandma went to her sewing room while Betty and I had breakfast, I would take my bowl and place it on the floor for Teddy to gorge himself. Thank goodness for Teddy; I ate the toast, he ate the porridge.

After breakfast, Grandma would suggest I go outside and play. With straw hat in hand, I would make my way out to the field and watch

Mr. Simpson. Wherever he happened to be, he would yell "whoa" to the team and motion for me to come over. Once I arrived, "Apples" would put my hat on my head and pick me up, placing me on the back of one of his giant steeds. He told me to "hold onto the horse's mane and hang on tight!"

Boy, it was a long way to the ground. The smell of a horse and freshly ploughed earth are odours you never forget. It was wonderful. When Apples said "giddy-up," the two matching drafts knew it was time to work. They plodded along, ploughing their furrows, but imagination enabled me to be whomever I chose. I could pretend to be any one of my cowboy heroes. I whiled away my time in a cloud of dreams on a horse that could fly.

"Whoa, whoa," Apples would shout; my dream interrupted, it was time for lunch. Apples lifted me like a feather and placed me back on earth. It's hard to walk after you've been riding a horse at breakneck speed. I got my balance as I walked over to the shade of a tree.

Before any lunch was eaten, Apples took care of his dutiful drafts. They came first because, as he said, "they worked the hardest." The two of us sat under the shade of the tree and ate our lunch. Oh, my, if anyone ever wondered why Apples weighed 300 pounds, I think I found the answer! Notwithstanding the fact that he had brought both his lunch and dinner, Apples unleashed a cornucopia of food. Most of it was homegrown or homemade, except for the half roll of bologna. Anything served on homemade bread is delicious.

Once lunch was finished, he would tell me to lie down and take a nap. He'd place my straw hat over my face and the next thing I knew, I'd wake up to see Apples and his horses hard at work. Now, Hollywood can have all of their cowboy radio heroes, but for me, that summer, Mr. Simpson was my real-live hero. Thank you, Apples.

*—by **Wyman Atkinson**, Cottam, Ontario*

Cowboys, Flapjacks and Fun!

An inside look at the "Greatest Outdoor Show on Earth!"

Growing up in a small town in southwestern Ontario, the Calgary Stampede barely made a blip on my radar. I knew that it happened every summer and I'd watch reports that aired on the national news. They showed dusty cowboys roping wild bucking broncos and bulls, and chuckwagons being driven at breakneck speeds around a dirt racetrack. Every now and then, I would hear about one friend or another taking a road trip out to Calgary to visit the "Stampede" for their summer vacation. I never once thought that one day I'd look forward to attending it as well, but in August of 2008 my husband Glen and I moved to Calgary for work and that move brought me one step closer to attending my first Stampede.

The Calgary Stampede, billed as the "Greatest Outdoor Show on Earth," happens every year for ten days in July and has been going on for more than a century. Beginning in June, city residents awaken from the long Alberta winter and break out their Western gear and decorations to celebrate the big event. Hay bales and farm fences, saddles and milk cans are displayed in bank lobbies, on restaurant patios and in shopping malls. Business establishments have their windows painted with cowboy and saloon scenes. Party tents help convert downtown parking lots into huge outdoor saloons. Companies put on barbecue lunches, and at work we happily wear jeans, cowboy boots and cowboy hats for the entire duration of the Stampede.

Free pancake breakfasts are put on in neighbourhoods throughout the city. You could have a free Stampede pancake breakfast every day if you wanted to, and many do! Those ten days of excitement begin with a parade through the downtown core of the city. Each year, different celebrities lead the parade; such as Kaillie Humphries, a Canadian bobsled champion, and Calgary's Mayor Naheed Nenshi on his horse Garfield. After the parade winds down, it's party time for the next ten days. The excitement is contagious.

My first summer living in Calgary, I watched the events on TV from our living room and secretly wished I was there. Finally, after living in Calgary for three years, I decided it was time to check it out for myself. Glen and I left our car at home and took the train downtown; when the doors opened, we squeezed out with hundreds of other people, all heading towards the grounds. The line moved quickly and the heat wasn't too bad. The weather during the Stampede is notoriously unpredictable. The sky could be clear and blue one minute, only to change at a moment's notice to drenching downpours, or even nasty hailstorms that pelt down marble-sized icy stingers. That day was hot and dry and, thankfully, stayed that way.

I immediately fell in love with the carnival-like atmosphere; the sweet smell of cotton candy and zesty aroma of barbecue tempt you at every turn—that is, until you tour the stables, with their funky farm smell. That first year, despite not attending the rodeo events in the afternoon or the grandstand show in the evening, I was hooked and knew I'd be back the following summer.

After that first visit, I made sure that I was able to get down to the Stampede every year, either to watch the rodeo events, the Rangeland Derby and grandstand show, or just to wander around the grounds, people-watching. I love seeing and feeling the energy and excitement that takes over the city for those ten days.

One year, I entered a photography contest organized through the Stampede's Instagram account. Ten photographers were chosen to post their snapshots online. I was lucky enough to be chosen and was assigned to cover the final day of the Stampede. What a thrill that was! I spent time in the Indian Village, wandered the entire grounds, enjoyed a few rides and indulged in some exotic food. Well, maybe the pulled pork poutine and deep-fried Snickers bar weren't all that exotic. All the same, they were delicious! I finished off the day with a good friend and I taking in the Reba McEntire show at the Saddledome. I'm not much of a country music fan, but I can't lie, it was quite a thrilling concert!

Another year, I attended a pancake breakfast held in my Calgary neighbourhood of Country Hills. I was given a behind-the-scenes pass from a friend of mine who is with the Stampede Caravan, a community group that has organized free Stampede breakfasts for more than 85 years. I learned that it takes a dedicated army of volunteers to organize the marching bands, country music outfits and line dancers that are featured at these breakfasts. Not to mention all the cooking it takes to produce a mountain of bacon, sausages, eggs and baked beans, as well as the stacks and stacks of pancakes drenched in syrup! Mayor Nenshi was there, flipping pancakes and grinning for all of the people trying to take his photo. The Stampede queen and her princesses wandered around greeting folks, and of course everyone wanted to pose for a photo with Harry the Horse—the official mascot of the Calgary Stampede.

It was a fun-filled morning in our neighbourhood and I finally felt like I truly belonged in the city—I was now a Calgarian. As such, I cordially invite everyone to visit the Calgary Stampede. Come and discover for yourself what the Greatest Outdoor Show on Earth has to offer. Try the pancakes and maybe the lobster corn dogs. And don't forget the world-famous mini-doughnuts dusted in sugar and cinnamon powder. Cheer on the rodeo competitors, feel your heart race on the midway rides and enjoy some of the best country music in the world. I think every Canadian should attend the Stampede at least once in their lifetime!

—by ***Leanne Smith****, Calgary, Alberta*

The Saturday Matinee

Recalling a favourite childhood ritual

These days, we can instantly communicate and entertain ourselves through the Internet, cellphones and video games, but this "high-tech" generation may not know how an older generation of Canadians entertained themselves on Saturday afternoons.

In the 1930s, '40s and '50s, many cities had a matinee movie theatre. They went by many names—the Capitol, Empire, Bijou, Roxy or Regent—and the experience was always memorable.

My Saturday matinees during the late '40s and early '50s were at the Empire Theatre, part of the Charlottetown Market Building before it burned down in April 1958. The Empire Theatre opened in October 1941 and, like many Maritime theatres owned by Saint John entrepreneur F.G. Spencer, the Empire offered a Saturday matinee consisting of a cartoon, short comedy and feature film—all for 10 cents.

Millions of kids across the country enjoyed these types of matinees in their hometowns. What made it so memorable for many in my generation was—like going to confession in church—that the Saturday matinee had certain rituals. I had to line up, and the line snaked around the Durango Kid poster at the corner of the Market Building. I also had to be "worthy," so I'd patiently clutch my dime as the line moved up to reach the huge steps leading to the heavy, church-like doors through which I passed into the "sanctuary." On the right was the box office where the short lady with the nun-like wispy hair sold me my ticket. Having paid my fare, I'd race up the wide staircase with its ornate banister to the landing where the usher tore my ticket in two—no sneaking in here!

My seat had a plywood back and was curved, so my legs dangled over the dusty floor. Some said creatures—rats from the Market—watched the movies with us, but I found that hard to believe; I never saw one. Besides, what would a rat have to do with Tom Mix, Hopalong Cassidy or my favourite, the Durango Kid? They were already chasing "rats" in the movies, like one who appeared in almost every Western, Roy Barcroft!

Rituals don't change, so the Westerns were always the same. The film always opened with a stagecoach bouncing along the same terrain; the bad guys came from behind a familiar rock and the stagecoach guard always got nailed first. Then along came the Durango Kid, fanning his gun and knocking off the robbers while Smiley Burnette, riding his horse Ring Eye and clutching his hat, lagged behind the Kid.

Those stagecoach scenes, along with very familiar-looking ranch houses, and even the dishes in the kitchen of the fair damsel, recurred in most Westerns. That's how Charles Starrett as the Durango Kid could make 65 Westerns between 1945 and 1952. The producers of these movies churned out "B" Westerns quickly and economically. Of course, I didn't know all this as I watched Durango leap from his horse onto the villains, or when the Cisco Kid bullwhipped the gun out of the bad guy's hand.

It didn't matter that the structure of the Western never changed. I didn't want it to change. I didn't want the Empire Theatre to change. Outside was all the change we needed: the Korean War, the Cold War and, thanks to the buildup of enough nuclear arms to blow the world up two or three times over, nuclear attack drills where we all hid like ostriches under our desks when the siren sounded.

The Saturday matinee was a place where joy and escape danced together—it was all so innocent.

*—by **Bernard J. Callaghan**, Charlottetown, Prince Edward Island*

Going Home to "Lost Villages"

One of the costs of building the St. Lawrence Seaway was a devastating loss of communities—and history

For most of us, going back to our childhood hometowns, often to share memories with our children and future generations, is something we take for granted. The former citizens of the "Lost Villages" of the St. Lawrence River and their families, however, can never truly go home again.

Born in Cornwall, Ontario, I, like many young people, never really took much interest in where I came from or what the history of the area meant in the context of our Canadian identity. To me it was just the place I lived. Only now, as history and genealogy have become popular, have I realized that my history is not only tied to the beautiful St. Lawrence River but also lies beneath it.

The Lost Villages, as they came to be known, were nine well-established communities in the former townships of Cornwall and Osnabruck that were dismantled and then flooded in July 1958—the "price of progress" as the St. Lawrence Seaway and an Ontario Hydro power project were being implemented. These were, however, places of our earliest history.

At the founding of Upper Canada, the United Empire Loyalists made their exodus from conflict during the American Revolution to lands along the St. Lawrence to forge a new home for their descendants. Predating the arrival of the Loyalists, the area had been the traditional lands of the Mohawk people for centuries. Yet, despite their significance to our collective history as Canadians, these places now lie under dark waters.

A recent trip to the Lost Villages Museum, located in Long Sault, Ontario, revealed just how lingering the loss is. The museum—a collection of original buildings from the various villages—had just opened for the day when a woman, appearing to be in her late 80s, aided by a walker and her grown son, made her way to the little red train station from the village of Moulinette. Of all the buildings there, this was the one I was most tied to as well: My grandmother Mary, more than 80 years earlier, would wait on the small station platform to catch "The Moccasin" steam train for the ride to high school in Cornwall.

Wondering if the woman was a tourist, with one gesture, I knew she was not. Removing one hand from her walker, she gently placed it on the outside of the building. I knew she was reconnecting with an "old friend" from a beloved time and place. As I watched, I noticed more people of the same generation appearing and going to what must have been their respective "places." They, like my grandmother, no longer had a home to go back to.

Many people I meet assume the Lost Villages story was written long ago and only has regional importance. To set the record straight, I explain that where the St. Lawrence River flows today, west of Cornwall, is not its natural path; at one time, six villages, three hamlets and parts of towns existed there and were home to about 6,500 people. Soon the inevitable question comes, "When did this happen, the 1800s?" When I reply, "1958," it always elicits a look of shock. I then ask them to imagine their hometowns being dismantled, burned or moved in pieces, and I can see a flicker of understanding wash over them. I then remind them how our history was changed forever when the Lost Villages were submerged in 1958:

- Ancient lands of the Mohawk People—obliterated.
- Locales where United Empire Loyalists forged a new future—lost.
- Fertile farmland, abundant orchards, old growth forests—drowned.
- Historic site of 1813 Battle of Crysler's Farm—submerged.
- The thundering and once-famous Long Sault Rapids—silenced.
- Loved ones at rest in their graves, including my grandmother's "mama," whom she lost to tuberculosis at age 14—never to be visited again.

This is a region rich in buried history, with many stories to tell. The more people visit, the better the chances that the Lost Villages will be remembered always.

*—by **Jennifer DeBruin**, Smiths Falls, Ontario*

The Last Steam Donkey

Preserving the memories of a bygone era

For years, the relic lay rusting and rotting in the West Coast rainforest. Then, in 2008, old-time logging legend Jack James decided that at the age of 77, he'd better get cracking if he wanted to preserve the memories of a bygone working world. After all, some things can't wait.

The relic was a 1929 Washington Iron Works steam donkey, last operated by the R.B. McLean Lumber Company (1926-1965) in the Alberni Valley on Vancouver Island. It was the last steam donkey working when they closed down; all the other donkeys were scrapped or retired after the Second World War and replaced by diesel and gas machines.

The steam donkey—steam-powered winches mounted on wooden skids for mobility—was the workhorse of the British Columbia woods prior to the Second World War. Once the timber was felled, donkey engines provided the power to "yard" the logs out of the woods to be loaded for transport to the mills.

The engineer, or "donkey puncher," was an essential person in camp. Every donkey had a team of workers to keep the steam up that included woodcutters, wood splitters and stackers; a fireman; and a "spark chaser," whose job it was to extinguish fires caused by the machine. And then there was the "whistle punk"—either a beginner or an older worker who was no longer agile—who relayed signals by steam whistle from the crew in the woods to the donkey.

Jack James began work in the forests of Vancouver Island seven decades ago as a spark chaser. He went on to become a well-known woods foreman and lived through all of the technological change that followed the steam era. Now, well into retirement, he found himself about to start all over again on a steam donkey.

The first order of business was to build a new sled—the platform on which you fastened the steam engine and winches that yarded the logs out of the forest, a forgotten skill. A sled was made from two giant logs bolted together and tapered at the ends to allow them to slide over debris and the rough terrain in the forest to get to the next work site. Powered by the steam engine bolted onto the sled, the steam donkey would winch itself through the forest via a cable attached to a distant tree. A local company, Island Timberlands, donated two big fir logs and Jack and crew set to work.

A steam engineer and his brother restored the steam engine, which was then jacked up and slid onto the new sled—just a few tons! Jack's dream included setting up an old-time steam-logging operation so that visitors to the McLean Mill National Historic Site would get a more complete picture of the forest industry of that era. Not only would they see logs being sawn into lumber in the vintage steam mill but they'd also see how the old-time loggers yarded the logs out of the forest in the first place.

The next step was to rig a spar tree—a tall, strong tree located in the middle of the patch of trees to be logged—to be able to demonstrate "high-lead" logging. The spar acted as a giant fishing rod that extended the reach of the donkey far into the forest.

In the old days of logging, the logs were dragged out of the forest along the ground, bumping into rocks and stumps and through mud. This was called "ground-lead" logging. Originally, they used oxen and horses before the brute power of the steam donkey was adopted. Then, some innovative American logger came up with the idea of trying to get at least one end of the log up in the air—thus the spar tree was born, modelled on the mast of a sailing ship.

"High rigging"—the art of climbing a tall tree to limb it, top it, then rig it with guy lines and blocks to yard in the big logs—is another vanished skill. The "high rigger," an elite logger in those days who was not afraid of heights, would put on his climbing spurs and wrap his climbing rope around the tree, cutting off the branches on his way up.

At up to 160 feet, the high rigger would top the tree, which sometimes swung back and forth violently when the top snapped off. As riggers were sometimes pretty cocky, they might then sit on top of the tree for a smoke, or show off by standing on their heads before coming back down. The rigger next rigged the tree with steel cables, including the lines from the steam donkey winches.

In our case, Jack coached Aaron Thom, a local arborist, and also scrounged up the rigging (cables) and other ironwork, some of it scrap recycled from 60 years ago. We, as Jack's crew, were rediscovering an entire lost way of working as well as recreating the old technology.

June 26, 2009, was a special day at the McLean Mill National Historic Site. For the first time in 45 years, a steam whistle echoed through the forest as the whistle punk gave the signal to the donkey engineer to "skin it back"—send the rigging into the forest—for the first "turn" of logs. The punk on duty on that particular day was none other than Jack James himself.

—by ***David Hooper****, Port Alberni, British Columbia*

A Treasure Reclaimed

Cherishing these small but precious books that chronicle the sentiments of youth

Being a book lover, the first things I look for at flea markets are books—new, old, shiny or shopworn. What matters to me is the content. At a recent sale, I spied a small box under a table with some dusty old books in it that had obviously been ignored by other buyers. Inquiring about it, the vendor said, "Take it as is and it's yours."

Returning home and dying of curiosity, I immediately delved into the ragged box. On top were some old, outdated reference books, a calculus book, an old, worn Bible and several novels written by unknown authors. Some tattered newspapers were folded in two, and beneath them—to my amazement—I discovered a well-worn black leather book with the word "Autographs" written in faded gold letters across the cover.

From what I've read, autograph books originated back in the mid-16th century among European university students who wished to preserve memories of their classmates and teachers upon graduation. These took the form of sketches, poetry and verse, and although they were chiefly confined to Dutch and Germanic cultures, by the late 18th century they were popular in America and flourished until school yearbooks replaced them.

Carefully turning the fragile pages of this book, I realized it was someone's treasure of memories. Who would trash something like this? I wondered. The dates range from 1915 to 1926 and appear to have been written by friends who attended Provincial Normal School (for teacher training) in Vancouver from 1925-26—over 90 years ago!

One by one, I gently turned the faded gold-rimmed pages and began to read the beautiful sentiments, which were accompanied by some extraordinary coloured sketches.

The first page shows a delicate black-and-white sketch of a lovely dogwood flower, followed on the next page by a poem written in December 1915 and signed "Yours as ever, Dad."

The following pages, 43 in all, with most written on both sides, reflect the affection with which this lady was held by her classmates. On one page, there is a King George V two-cent stamp, which reads, "By gum—it sticks!" signed "Howard Brown." There is also a painted picture of orange poppies decorating another page, a sailboat and lighthouse on still another, a whole page devoted to an owl in full dress sitting in a tree, and many more, all with loving sentiments.

These are truly little works of art and should be preserved. The last entry in the book is from the recipient herself and reads: "This ends the book of affection, the album of beauty and truth, this ends the sweet collection of gems that were gathered in youth." It's signed "May Cornwall, June 11th, 1926."

After reading this exquisite little book, I remembered that I, too, have an autograph book somewhere in the recesses of a trunk that I had largely forgotten existed. Upon retrieving it, I saw that it was dated 1942 to 1945, my elementary school years at Sir Richard McBride, over 70 years ago!

Although it doesn't contain any works of art, it has many of the same sentiments, poems and sayings as May's does. My favourite teacher wrote: "Choose not thy friends from outward show, feathers float but pearls lie low." The same verse occurs in May's book as well, 20 years earlier.

Reading over the names of these friends brought back old memories of days gone by when we were all young and eager to face the future with our dreams and aspirations. I can't help but wonder where they've all gone and whether their dreams came true.

Our autograph books are truly a record of our past as surely as a diary or journal and should be treasured as such. These are words and sentiments that were written in our youth and should be forever remembered. It is sad that May's book was destined to end up in a dusty old box, but I shall treasure it for her.

*—by **Jo-Anne Sheanh**, Sechelt, British Columbia*

Remembering RCAF Station Namao

A fond look back at a special piece of Canadian history

Who would have thought that the construction of an airfield back in 1943 would be the start of so many memories? That little air force base in the Alberta countryside became home for many. It seems like yesterday that crews were standing around hangars and buildings ready for duty—rag-wrench crews with screw-drivers at hand to launch another flight into the sunset. All part of the air force family who made life at the Namao base interesting.

During happier times, we remember the moms and dads, sons and daughters of the community. We recall the concerts at Guthrie school, nights at the swimming pool, the kids' hockey and the figure skating club. Then there was the base theatre for movie night and our pint-sized grocery store with matching library. These helped meld the lives around us each day as our families grew.

Eventually the young people left, spreading through our city, province and country, where you will now find them in all areas of life. It has been our legacy, you might say, and one of which we are justly proud.

During our tour at Namao, many visitors were welcomed. Who could forget the numerous refugees who flew into Canada and whose first look at this country was the tarmac at Namao airport? There was never a dull moment and the community was like the Alberta weather: If you stood around long enough, something newsworthy was bound to happen.

How many remember Operation Morning Light, which took place in the late 1970s? Morning Light, for those who don't remember, was the name of the mission to recover a Russian satellite that came down over the North, spreading its radioactive payload over much of the area. Many of us had to put down our rag wrenches and head off to the Northwest Territories to help in the cleanup.

Our airport hosted many famous visitors over the years, including a royal visit during the Commonwealth Games and an outdoor Mass during Pope John Paul II's visit to Canada in 1984.

Our air force family deployed to many corners of the world and, following tradition, we served in many UN and NATO roles, including resupply trips to Alert in the Canadian Arctic during winter, as well as assisting with many humanitarian flights. In addition, there were many search and rescue operations.

Many in the community and province remember with us the thrill of the air force days and the big air shows, where we got to strut our stuff. When the gates opened, you wouldn't know it by our demeanour, but we were all proud of the role we played and happy to have the chance to show off a bit.

In other cases, the work was quite serious. After all was said and done, though, the best memories are of family and our community with its cast of characters who, on a daily basis, completed all the tasks that needed to be done.

These, then, are my memories—a view that reflects a snapshot of the life and times at one of Canada's major air force stations. There are still many of us in the community who remember RCAF Namao. We watched with a large degree of sadness as the final curtain came down with the knowledge that all the air force personnel and their families made this such a great place. We know that the legacy of this fine airbase will live on long after the sounds of aircraft such as the mighty Hercules, the trusty Twin Otter and the great Chinook helicopter have faded away.

Now called CFB Edmonton, we watch with pride as present-day members carry on these great traditions. On Canada's National Day of Remembrance in November, please pause a moment to remember the dedicated air force personnel from RCAF Station Namao, whose ranks are fast depleting.

*—by **RJ Goodfellow**, St. Albert, Alberta*

Sowing the Future

The Tree Planting Car brought nature education to four generations

Some of my earliest and fondest childhood memories go back to the times when I would accompany my dad, Alan Beaven, to search for the Tree Planting Car (TPC) located somewhere among the hundreds of railcars at the Canadian Pacific Railway (CPR) yards in Winnipeg. It always felt like an adventure. Dad was the longest-serving lecturer on the TPC, beginning his career in 1926 and ending in 1946. By the time I came on the scene, he had completed his stint on the car but was still responsible for its operation.

The saga of the TPC began in 1919 when the Canadian Forestry Association, in cooperation with the CPR and Canadian National Railway (CNR), launched one of the most innovative and longest-surviving education programs to be undertaken on the Canadian Prairies. From 1919 to 1973, the TPC travelled 263,000 miles and played host to four generations, numbering more than 1.5 million people across Alberta, Saskatchewan and Manitoba. During those years, about half a billion trees were planted on approximately 100,000 farms.

The TPC was a railcar equipped by the CPR as a "travelling schoolhouse," with accommodation for the lecturer and an assistant or, in the case of my dad, for his family. My mom and brother toured with Dad for several seasons until my brother started school. Being considerably younger, I missed this experience and have often felt cheated because of that! I was very privileged, however, to have the opportunity to meet many of the fine men who served as lecturers during the later years, as they were frequently entertained at our home.

Knowledgeable staff engaged rural people in their own communities and encouraged them to plant trees, thus making the TPC program unique. Over the years, all available teaching tools were used, including slides, silent films, radio broadcasts and "talkies" to enhance the program. Presentations included a grade-appropriate series for schoolchildren who visited the car during the day, and a program for adults in the evening. In addition, for 40 years, from 1933 to 1973, the TPC doubled as the Conservation Car and travelled through the parkland regions to promote the wise use of renewable resources, emphasizing the importance of forests and trees.

Each spring, the car would leave on a pre-arranged itinerary, stopping at small towns and villages. There was great excitement and anticipation among the population when they knew the car was coming to their town, particularly in the early years when there was little or no other entertainment. If the first evening program was "sold out," families would wait in the heat and dust or in the rain for up to two hours until a second show was presented later that evening. At times, they would stand on wagons or the back of trucks and peer in the windows to catch a glimpse of what was going on inside the car.

Lecturers were required to keep a daily diary and their reports provide entertaining scenarios.

> ***Friday, July 29, 1938****, Irvine, Alberta:*
>
> *"It was one of the hottest days of the summer, with heat in the car intense. Yet so many turned out, two meetings were necessary, a remarkable showing for this small place. Watching the program was like taking a Turkish bath, and running it was even worse. None remained for the question period!"*
>
> ***Wednesday, July 12, 1939****, Oxbow, Saskatchewan:*
>
> *"Just to keep it from being too perfect, about a million mosquitoes invaded the car when the lights went on for the lecture, and I couldn't tell whether the people were applauding me or slapping the insects!"*

So many passionate people contributed to making the TPC a successful endeavour, including the lecturers who served with dedication and conviction; the railway personnel from both CPR and CNR; the staff at the federal tree nursery at Indian Head, Saskatchewan, which supplied the trees and shrubs that the farmers planted; private nursery operators, who expanded the variety of plant materials available; and, most importantly, the farmers themselves who bought into the dream of "planting the Prairies" and helped make it a reality.

The TPC was retired in 1973 and donated by the CPR to the Manitoba Forestry Association. The car was moved to the Sandilands Forest Discovery Centre near Hadashville, Manitoba, where it now resides.

*—by **Dianne J. Beaven**, Winnipeg, Manitoba*

ADVENTURE

Ordinary Canadians doing extraordinary things—from camping on the tundra to paddling mighty streams, here are tall tales for intrepid adventurers

High Hopes

Remaining calm while skydiving is essential—especially when your chute fails to open

Skydiving in the '60s was a relatively new sport. It was so new, in fact, that it barely qualified as a sport at all. The equipment we used was military surplus that was not designed for skydiving. A few modifications were made to adapt the equipment to this new civilian pastime, which included cutting panels out of the back of the canopies to give us some forward speed and the ability to steer.

The parachutes were 28 feet in diameter and were intended to save a pilot who had to bail out of his aircraft. A skydiver could reach speeds in free fall in excess of 120 miles per hour and, depending on your body position, the opening shock could be violent. A deployment sleeve was designed to impede the speed of the opening, thus eliminating this rather unpleasant experience.

The only emergencies we trained for were those involving a malfunction of the main parachute. We couldn't detach the main chute, as is the procedure today, so we would have to deploy the reserve while we were still attached to a malfunctioning main. This deployment procedure was basically quite simple, but it was not always successful. You'd pull the ripcord handle on the reserve chute, reach under the canopy, grab the reserve and throw it away from you, hoping that air would find its way into the reserve canopy.

By 1969, I'd been skydiving for two years and had 164 jumps under my belt. I had learned about parachutes in the RCAF, when I was trained as a safety systems technician. I took my training in parachuting and skydiving at the Abbotsford Sport Parachute Centre in Abbotsford, British Columbia.

One winter day, three buddies and I had been waiting for hours at the centre for the weather to improve. The clouds had been hovering at around 1,500 feet, but we needed 2,200 feet before we could go up. The wind was blowing at 20 miles per hour, which was too strong for us to safely jump. Sometimes, days could go by while we'd sit at the drop zone waiting for the weather to change—and we weren't a patient group. The weather on the west coast of British Columbia in winter could be grey and dismal for weeks at a time.

So, there we were: The wind was up, the clouds were low and the pilot, who had been threatening to leave for a while, now had one foot out the door heading for his plane and home. So, we decided by a vote of four to none that the wind had in fact dropped and the ceiling was at 2,200 feet. Off to the plane we headed, not feeling much better about the weather, as nothing had changed, but at least we were doing something.

We'd planned a "hop and pop," which is basically exiting the aircraft one after the other on one pass. I was second out the door with a normal and stable exit. I waited five seconds and pulled the ripcord. So far, so good—except something didn't feel quite right. There was no opening shock at all. My deployment sleeve had rolled up around the bottom of the main canopy. I found myself on my back, staring up at a snarled main parachute that didn't appear to have any hope of opening. It was very quiet and everything seemed to be happening in slow motion. Time stood still, but there was no feeling of panic or urgency. I just floated in some kind of limbo.

Finally, I grabbed the reserve ripcord handle, pulled it and reached under the canopy to deploy it. The parachute was damp from days of rain, so all I could see was this lump of white flopping around in front of me. Still in slow motion, I could see people on the ground pointing up at me as I fell to earth at 80 to 90 miles per hour.

I reached out to grab a hold of the risers and gave them a shake. Air began to find its way into the bottom of the canopy and, finally, at what was estimated to be about 400 feet above ground, the reserve chute deployed.

The wind was still up, and after a ten-second canopy ride, I was approaching a cornfield where pointy cornstalks were sticking up out of the ground like spikes. I was falling downward and sideways at about the same speed and those cornstalks certainly had my attention at that point.

When I was about 50 feet above the ground, the wind suddenly stopped. For the first time that day, the wind ceased blowing and remained calm long enough for me to land and gather up my parachutes. The wind then began to blow again and didn't abate the rest of the day.

I have thought of that experience many times over the years. I never really understood what happened in those long moments before the reserve parachute opened, but I've always had the feeling that someone or something greater than myself was looking out for me that day—and probably still is.

*—by **Darryl W. Lyons**, Sayward, British Columbia*

My Struggle With the Nahanni

Canoeing down the beautiful but treacherous Nahanni River was both exhilarating and daunting

It was many years ago when I first read about the Nahanni River in Pierre Berton's book *The Mysterious North*. In it, Berton describes canyons along the river rivalling those of the Grand Canyon, mystical and mysterious valleys, and a waterfall twice as high as Niagara—Virginia Falls. As a UNESCO World Heritage Site in our Canadian North, it was a region I just had to see; at age 74, I couldn't leave it any longer.

The only way to do it is via canoe using a licenced outfitter. You are also required to register with Parks Canada. In the back of my mind was a desire to get some wonderful photographs; I even wanted to use my specially devised 3-D camera to share the beauty I experienced. Attending an adventure show in midwinter, I shared with the outfitter my desire to take pictures. He suggested that two boats be attached together catamaran-style to stabilize a rig for that purpose.

While I was experienced with canoeing, I had never done any white-water, so the outfitter advised me to take a course that spring on the Madawaska River, which I did. The teachers devoted a considerable part of the discussion afterwards to the Nahanni River, and the conclusion they came to was to expect fairly large, standing waves, nothing more. They also assured me that with a guide in the stern, all would be fine.

I flew to Yellowknife and met my nine fellow adventurers. They weren't very young either, but all were younger than me. From there we all flew to Fort Simpson, Northwest Territories, our journey's official starting point for our two-week adventure. There we met our two guides—I was to be paired in a canoe with one of them—along with adventurers from the previous trip. The latter remarked, "The water levels are so low you'll have no trouble at all."

The pilot of the Twin Otter float plane that was to take us to our launch point assured us we'd have fair weather for the coming week. After the first day of our trip, however, it started to rain. And it continued raining day after day as if it would never end. An east wind at Virginia Falls signalled further bad weather. The staff of Parks Canada declared we'd have wet weather for nearly a week. The only good thing was that the forest fires had been extinguished. Some of us calculated we'd already had four inches of rain and the river had risen six feet. The river was now a raging torrent—the very worst scenario possible.

We knew that Fourth Canyon (which is actually the first one you come to—they go from Fourth down to First) immediately after Virginia Falls would be the most challenging. In an attempt to minimize the risk, we joined our boat and another together catamaran-style. We strapped two narrow logs to the boats as tightly as we could, leaving the boats about five feet apart, and set out.

It wasn't very long before we got into trouble. We were faced with the wildest, most turbulent water I had ever seen, with waves as high as seven feet breaking in front of us. One of the four attachments had come loose and we couldn't fix it. That meant the two canoes could no longer remain parallel.

Meanwhile, a huge wave was about to break over the bow. My guide and partner Adrian Smith shouted "Backpaddle!" which I did, but when I leaned back to do this, I couldn't keep the spray skirt sealed in front of me and a huge quantity of water got in the boat. With our boat nearly full of cargo, it didn't take many waves of this size to fill it. By now both attachments on the other boat were quite loose. Adrian, more agile than a monkey, ran across on the logs to the other boat to loosen them, and believe it or not he succeeded. Now the other boat was free, but ours, with two poles hanging out to the left, was completely swamped.

The river, still raging, was not as bad as before. Adrian then said, "John, get onto the other boat and lie with your chest in the middle and remain perfectly still."

I had an adrenaline rush and responded immediately and smoothly to his command. Any other time my ankles would be sore and stiff after getting up after kneeling, but not this time. Remaining still as the dead, I lay face down at a slight diagonal behind the bow paddler. My two new canoemates paddled like mad to ferry the three of us across the current to shallow, safe water in front of some trees. Only then did I move my head, and what a joy it was to see land.

Next, Adrian had to deal with our swamped boat with the two logs hanging out. Fortunately, these acted like a paddle, turning the canoe towards shore. All the same, it was all he could do to bring it in. The other guide came to his assistance, and the two of them bailed out the boat and brought it back to where I was on the opposite shore. We then resumed our journey.

But that wasn't the end our troubles. The following day, one couple lost control of their canoe between Third and Fourth canyons and capsized. With help from the other guide, the woman made it to shore, albeit cold, wet and shaken up emotionally. Her male partner remained floating in midstream, carrying the two paddles. It was up to Adrian and me to rescue him. He caught our line and we ferried him to shore—but it wasn't easy. Ferrying across that current is really tough even without towing anyone. With a 250-pound man in tow, my arms were nearly pulled out of their sockets, but we made it. The two victims warmed up and put on dry clothes—all our clothing and personal items had been stored in food barrels to stay dry—and the journey resumed.

The next day was a repeat performance, only worse. Our boats got out of line leaving the Pulpit Rock campsite, in an area called "The Gate." The same couple capsized again, and ended up together holding hands in midstream between steep-walled canyons. Their capsized canoe was headed straight towards the canyon wall, and it was only thanks to the quick action of the other guide that it was saved. It was once again left to Adrian and me to rescue the pair in the water. We did get them, but they were forced to remain there for about three minutes, as there was no safe area to land, and Adrian and I weren't strong enough to ferry them any faster. More than five minutes in that icy water can cause death.

We came on the trip expecting to need our wetsuits for the Third and Fourth canyons, but with this kind of water we needed them for all four. These, together with warm, insulating clothing, were the best we could do if we fell in. Nonetheless, it became plain to us that a victim in the water had little chance of being rescued, unless a guide in a canoe went after him immediately. Trying to ferry yourself across the current while swimming in that frigid water was next to impossible.

I had been well-fed on the trip but still ended up losing 12 pounds. The psychological stress had taken its toll. In fact, the reality of this experience was such that had one more thing gone wrong, we would have been in serious trouble.

While I couldn't take all the pictures I wanted to, I did achieve my primary goal of experiencing the Nahanni. I got to see the magnificence of Virginia Falls, the legendary valleys and the stark beauty of the many canyons. But never was I so glad to return home from a vacation.

Here are a few interesting facts, that I would like to share with you, about the Nahanni National Park Reserve:

- It is one of the largest parks in the world.
- Virginia Falls is nearly twice the height of Niagara Falls.
- In 1908, the disappearance of two prospecting brothers in the Nahanni Valley, and the subsequent finding of their headless bodies, resulted in place names such as Headless Creek and Deadmen Valley.
- Prime Minister Pierre Elliot Trudeau championed the formation of Nahanni National Park Reserve after paddling the river in 1970.

*—by **John G. Attridge**, Hamilton, Ontario*

Climb Every Mountain

Conquering these rugged peaks gave this newcomer to Canada confidence, strength and purpose

In early 2010, wheezing from the exertion of carrying my two 30-pound suitcases—which contained all of my worldly possessions at that time—up a couple of flights of stairs, I walked into my new home in Squamish, British Columbia. Arriving here from Ireland, my bulky frame weighed more than 300 pounds from many years of being sedentary. Now, as I stared out at the snow-capped mountains rising up around me, the sight of them filled a hole inside me I'd been unaware of before. Although I had not come to this place with an interest in mountains, I was suddenly bitten with the desire to touch those shining summits.

Living in Ireland, I did not grow up in a culture of athleticism. I was never very coordinated, so any team sports I tried I usually failed at. The circle of friends I kept would kick a ball around on a Sunday and then follow it up with a trip to the pub to gain back any calories expended. No physical exercise would occur again until the next Sunday, and if it was raining too hard, which it frequently does in Ireland, we'd skip soccer and head straight to the pub.

Eventually, through a poor diet and a complete lack of exercise, I looked down at the scale and realized I'd passed the maximum weight of 280 pounds on it. I stopped weighing myself after that, ashamed at the thought of having to buy a scale with larger numbers.

After the Irish recession in 2008, though, I got an itch to move somewhere different, as progression in my career stalled. My wife Spring is originally from Alberta and, while living in Ireland, we'd always talked about starting a new life in her home country. On a whim, we decided to move to the small town of Squamish and left Ireland behind.

I can't explain what changed when I got here. Maybe I'd been idle for too long, but like a siren on the rocks, the wind blowing spray off those high ridges and summits beckoned me. Mountains no longer looked like scenery but rather an arena in which to test myself.

I'd never backpacked before, so I needed to learn about tents and sleeping bags. I'd never climbed before either, so I read about climbing knots and harnesses. Words that I previously had never said aloud, such as "crampon" or "crux," became a daily part of my lexicon. My thirst to understand how other people were getting to these summits was insatiable.

As I pushed myself higher and further, not even slowing down in winter, I finally realized what my talent was. I could suffer longer than others around me. I could endure the cold; I could endure the sleepless nights inside a tent being beaten by the wind; I could smile while being swarmed by clouds of mosquitoes as I pushed through the dense rainforest of British Columbia—and I could get up and do it all again the next day. I didn't need a couple of weeks' rest to forget the tortures that led to reaching that summit. I could always see the next summit rising up behind the one I was currently reaching.

It is said that the mountains have gifts for those who wrestle with them and I believe this is true. The mountains have taken my self-doubt and over 130 pounds off of my body; in return, they've given me confidence, strength and purpose. While there, I found a passion for photography and writing, and for that I will be eternally grateful. As author John Muir once said: "Climb the mountains and get their good tidings."

*—by **Leigh McClurg**, Garibaldi Highlands, British Columbia*

The Yukon Is Gold

It's the best of times—even in the coldest climes

"The Yukon? In March? Isn't it still winter up there at that time of year?" I smiled at my friend and nodded my head. When our "Wild Women of the Yukon" group first suggested holding our annual reunion back in Dawson City, I balked a bit at the idea of heading north when most people head for sunnier climes. But it turned out to be the best of all times.

March is the month when the sun returns in the Yukon. After the long, grey days of winter, everyone smiles as the warmth of the sun increases. In Dawson, water drips from log cabin roofs, the streets get a bit muddy and the locals start speculating on when the ice in the Yukon River will begin to crack. People are eager to be out and about, but the summer tourist season is still just a thought in the back of the mind. Some shops are opening their doors, getting ready for the season ahead, and often prices are good, as they are clearing out last year's stock.

We had come back to Dawson to celebrate the tenth anniversary of our annual Wild Women reunion and to help a few friends celebrate a milestone birthday. Usually there are six of us who get together once a year to renew our friendship and talk about those "old Dawson days." We first met in the small northern community in the early 1970s and have remained tied together by those memories, the kind that solidify friendships into lifelong relationships.

But this time, there were more than six of us. We joined friends who still live in Dawson, and invited a few from Whitehorse as well. The numbers grew to the point where we had to find an alternate place to host the birthday party. When the time came, we packed a local establishment, presented a handmade quilt to one of the birthday girls and feasted on a variety of dishes supplied by our Dawson friends, including a huge and very delicious birthday cake.

The party didn't stop there, however, as we were invited out for dinner every night or met friends at local eateries and continued to present gifts to those hitting that significant milestone. The week flew by, filled with hugs and kisses and the often-heard expression, "Do you remember when...?"

We even managed to squeeze in a trip up the Dempster Highway as far as the Tombstone Valley. Layered in warm clothing, we lit a campfire at the campground, feasted again on everything from moose jerky to fresh oranges, and then drove to the summit to take in the view. There is nothing as stunning as a clear Yukon sky with the gleaming, snow-covered mountains reaching out to it. The Tombstone Valley in March is a beautiful sight to behold. A special bonus was spotting two lynx as we journeyed back down the highway.

All too soon, it was time to say goodbye to Dawson and its people and make the six-hour drive back to Whitehorse and our flights home. We chatted easily as we drove, already filing away more memories that would last until our next get together. Dawson in March? Oh, yes. I recommend it!

Here are a few interesting facts about Dawson City:

- Dawson City gets about 5.5 hours of daylight in January, and about 21.5 in June.
- The Yukon encompasses 483,450 square kilometres—more than the Netherlands, Belgium, Denmark and Germany combined.
- Dawson City's population grew to nearly 40,000 during the Klondike Gold Rush in the 1890s but fell to about 5,000 by the time it was incorporated in 1902. About 1,300 people now call it home.
- Dawson City is named for Canadian geologist George Mercer Dawson. "Yukon" comes from the Gwich'in word Yuk-un-ah, meaning "Great River."
- The Yukon boasts three national parks—Ivvavik, Kluane and Vuntut—as well as numerous National Historic Sites.

*—by **Marcia Lee Laycock**, Blackfalds, Alberta*

Life in Igloolik

Impressed by the people of the North

In 2007, we took another of our numerous trips north of 60. This time, we went to a small hamlet on the edge of Foxe Basin called Igloolik. This area has a history that dates back 4,000 years. We were interested in seeing the wildlife, such as birds, walruses, whales and hopefully a polar bear. We were well-rewarded thanks to two Inuit guides, Manasi and Lainiki. A komatik (sled), pulled by a snowmobile rather than a dog team, took us to the ice edge, where the guides were waiting with modern boats to take us wildlife viewing.

While we loved seeing the amazing wildlife, we also met and learned much about the local people and culture. In winter, the residents of Igloolik live in southern-style homes with conveniences such as TV, microwaves, dishwashers and computers. In summer, however, some abandon all this and head to the edge of the ice at Igloolik Point to live in the traditional Inuit way with no power, phones or plumbing. We were camped beside these people and had a first-hand experience of their way of life.

The family we grew to know consisted of five generations: Rachael (106 years old), Atoa (72), Tam (38), Daniel (25) and Neil (three). Four family members lived in one tent, which consisted of a sleeping platform and cooking area. A kudlik (oil lamp), usually carved from soapstone, filled with seal oil and a wick of arctic cotton, gives warmth and light and is used to boil water for cooking. The wick is attended to constantly to avoid it burning too high. If this happened inside an igloo, it would melt the inside, causing it to ice over and transmit the outside cold in.

We watched Atoa sewing a new tent with a hand-crank sewing machine and repairing her other grandson Nathan's shoes. She also prepared the hide of a second seal using an ulu to scrape the fat off. It was then scrubbed many times to get rid of the grease and then stretched to dry. The finished product would be used to make mitts for Nathan. Rachael was busy cutting and cleaning the meat, saving the oil for the kudlik. She also made a duster from the feathers of the goose that had been cooked for dinner.

Bill and I played many games of double solitaire on Sunday, sitting in the tent with our legs straight out. Atoa didn't go to church that Sunday, even though she is a lay minister in the Anglican church. Her mother, Rachael, sat humming and singing hymns in Inuktitut. We all got along fine, even though we spoke different languages.

When we were taken to the airport at the end of our stay, we went early because Brad, Tam's partner, had to meet the plane to get groceries and deliver them to Northern Store. This, we learned, is fairly typical of the North, where people often have two or three jobs.

We will always remember the warmth, friendliness and hospitality we experienced from these people. It was so kind of Tam and Brad, our official hosts, to share their family with us.

*—by **Joan Prunkl**, Edmonton, Alberta*

Beauty and the Barrens

Canoeing unnamed Arctic rivers and trekking the treeline tundra

Superlatives are inadequate. The Barren Lands (also called Barren Grounds) of the Canadian Arctic that I visited in the late summer of 2014 are inadequately described with words and photographs. Nonetheless, I wish to piece some phrases together and convey a glimpse into the magnificence of this pristine place.

David, my companion in all things important for 40 years, had an unfulfilled yearning to canoe the Arctic waters explored by the likes of Samuel Hearne in 1771. I had no such interest. Agreeing to accompany him was one of the better decisions I have made.

The area we flew into with our guide, outfitter and bannock baker extraordinaire Alex Hall, is a spectacular, roadless wilderness that is yet untouched by mineral and petroleum exploration.

We canoed nameless rivers; unbelievable but true that a number of rivers and lakes we travelled have no name. We tented on numerous sandy beaches scattered with caribou antlers. If you like the beaches of Prince Edward Island, you will love the beaches of the central Arctic. Our group has been sworn to secrecy about the precise location of this expedition. Ever since Alex, with his company Canoe Arctic Inc., began flying enthusiasts into this area from Fort Smith in the 1970s, he has never met another traveller. And he wants to keep it that way.

Including Alex, our group consisted of ten adults in five canoes. Lucy from Boston was an outlier age-wise at 31, while the average age for the remainder of us was 65. The journey commenced in Fort Smith, Northwest Territories, where all the gear and my fellow Canoe Arctic adventurers were loaded on three planes bound for our first night of beachfront camping. Alex is the boss and he determines, based on weather factors, if the day is to be spent canoeing or trekking the vast eskers to view wildlife. Over 11 days, our group paddled 100 kilometres. Alex hosts a number of groups every summer. Guests early in the season will be awed with sightings of muskoxen and migrating caribou. Not so awesome at this time are also hordes of pesky insects.

The beasts and bugs were mostly absent during our excursion dates from late August to early September; however, the fall season presents other unique gifts. Autumn happens quickly in the north and the beauty of each day was breathtaking. The land was turning crimson with dwarf birch and bearberry, among other vegetation. This was in dramatic contrast to the silver lichen ground cover. If you love the fall colours of New Brunswick, the Arctic will leave you weak in the knees.

Comparable was the exquisiteness of the night. Countless stars illuminated an endless sky and the aurora borealis is downright dreamy. One night, a red moon was reflected twice in the lake. While unsure of the physics involved, I am sure the image existed, as David saw it, too.

There were other surprises. The water is so pure that you can dip your container into the lake and simply drink. It is so quiet that when the planes arrived to pick up our group, I had to cover my ears. I'm positive they were less loud the week before. There are no bright screens, smart phones, electrical towers or aircraft overhead. Simply a vast expanse of land, small trees hugging the shoreline and lakes upon lakes as far as the eye could see. It is an unreservedly lovely place. After several centuries, explorer Samuel Hearne might conclude that not much has changed.

If you believe that this type of tenting and canoeing is beyond your physical capacity, I can identify with you. Years ago, I did some tenting but always in a civilized campground with bathrooms and rain shelters adjacent to designated parking. Then last year, David and I enrolled in a day of canoeing lessons. Still, knowing Alex had emergency contacts, I believed I would be the first shipped back to Fort Smith!

If you are considering a visit to this majestic Arctic corridor, don't put it off. Visiting the Canadian Barren Lands is an experience that is seen with the eye, felt in the heart, and permanently settles in the soul.

Here are a few interesting facts about the Barren Lands:

- The Barren Lands (or the Barrens) in the Canadian Arctic is a vast, subarctic prairie.
- It lies mainly in Nunavut, but it also includes the eastern part of the Northwest Territories, extending west from Hudson Bay to Great Slave and Great Bear lakes, north to the Arctic Ocean and south along the Hudson Bay coastal plain.

- Its surface is covered with grass, moss and lichen, interspersed with granitic outcrops. It's also dotted with countless lakes and streams, many of them unnamed.
- Wildlife includes caribou, muskoxen, foxes and bears, while most of the permanent human inhabitants are Inuit people living in the coastal areas.

*—by **Barbara Leroy**, Delta, British Columbia*

Searching for Wild Bill

The hunt for the legendary mountain man's secret cabin took years

"I headed downslope below where the cubs were feeding and came up at them, hoping to scare them into one or another of my mining shafts for protection. It worked perfectly, as they ran for the nearest dark hole, and I went in with my ropes on the ready to see if I could catch one. I could hear the little fellows squealing in the dark and I had to pause a moment to let my eyes adjust. Just then I heard a tremendous roar and knew the sow was coming on the run looking for her wayward offspring. It didn't take her a moment to pick up the scent and she headed straight for the mouth of the shaft, bent on destruction..."

—Entry from Bill Peyto's mountain journal, "Ain't It Hell", May 15, 1910

Anyone who's ever been to Banff National Park has encountered Bill Peyto, even if they weren't aware of it. His likeness adorns the "Welcome to Banff" signs that greet visitors as they enter town. The raucous saloon on the corner of Banff Avenue and Caribou Street borrowed his famous moniker for its name: Wild Bill's. Bill Peyto's Café, a restaurant in Lake Louise that's quickly becoming a favourite among locals, also bears his title. He even has a lake, a glacier, a mountain and an Alpine Club of Canada hut named in his honour. The man has reached legendary status in the wilds of Alberta.

Ebenezer William "Bill" Peyto was born in England in 1869 and immigrated to Canada in 1887 at the young age of 18. He eventually made his way to the Rocky Mountains of Alberta, where he proved to be a proficient outfitter and mountaineer. Between enlistments in the Boer War and World War I, Peyto joined the Warden Service, making him one of the first wardens in Banff, which was known as Rocky Mountains Park at that time. He married Emily Wood in 1902 and the birth of their son Robert soon followed. Emily suddenly passed away in 1906, and Robert was sent to live with his mother's family for a time. Peyto remained with the Warden Service until his retirement in 1934. After retiring, he led a very private life until his death in 1943.

The stories about his exploits, embellished or not, are sure to lure even the most indifferent bystander into the mystique that is Bill Peyto. There's the one where he walked into a Banff bar with a live lynx strapped to his back, sending the patrons running for the exits and giving Peyto the place to himself. Or the winter he raised two orphaned cougar kittens in one of his secluded cabins so they wouldn't perish. Or how he would regularly leave clients alone for the night during outfitting expeditions so he could have some solitude. It was his need for privacy and seclusion that drove him deeper into the wilderness, where he could coexist with the natural world instead of the man-made one that was rapidly developing around him. Peyto erected several cabins in the Healy Creek area of Banff National Park, where he could be alone and maintain his other interests, such as trapping, prospecting and mining.

Several years ago, I learned at least one of Peyto's cabins was still standing, hidden away from the public, as Peyto himself had intended. I'm not referencing his fully restored cabin that sits on the grounds of the Whyte Museum but rather a cabin that remains exactly as it was when Peyto left it for the final time. I immediately started researching, hoping to uncover the location, but like surviving a harsh winter in the Canadian backcountry, finding the cabin proved exceedingly difficult.

Google searches only revealed veiled references to the cabin's existence; nothing was concrete in terms of an actual location. Discouraged but not defeated, I turned to word-of-mouth tactics and began talking with folks who knew about the cabin and some who had even been there. Despite my best efforts, I was only able to uncover the fact that the cabin truly does exist and that it was in the vicinity of Simpson Pass. It appeared that the cabin's location was a closely guarded secret; without specific details, searching that vast, forested area would be the equivalent of looking for the proverbial needle in a haystack. I didn't give up entirely on standing in Peyto's forgotten cabin, but my hopes were diminishing rapidly.

A few years passed and my plans went into hibernation until I caught a break one summer. As the outdoor editor for a Calgary publication, I was invited to Sunshine Meadows for a media-day program they were hosting. Our guide for the day, Alex, was supplied by White Mountain Adventures and knew of Peyto's cabin but hadn't actually been there himself. He, too, was interested in finding the elusive cabin, so we joined forces, gathering intel from a variety of places. One of the biggest pieces of the puzzle came in the form of a cryptic, eight-line poem written by Jim Deegan, a guest of Peyto's at the cabin, which he refers to as "Bookrest." The poem describes the cabin using obscure references to the area, loosely hinting at its secret location.

> *"On Simpson Pass,*
> *atop the Divide,*
> *among the yellow tamarack*
> *stands a cabin in a meadow,*
> *a lone prospector's shack.*
> *Weathering in the elements,*
> *abandoned in the vale,*
> *a sod-roofed fortress, built*
> *beside an old packtrail."*

Armed with the poem and a rough map indicating the cabin's approximate location within a large circle, Alex and I put boots on the ground and set off in search of Peyto's mysterious cabin. On a typical day, the stunning hike towards Simpson Pass would have been reward enough, but the prospect of finally finding Bookrest was all-consuming.

We began our search as the sun sat low in the sky, making several passes through dense forest, always remaining within auditory contact of each other. I expected to see the cabin around every corner, but we kept coming up empty-handed. Although we observed evidence of previous human existence in the area, such as hand-sawn tree stumps, the cabin continued to elude us. With hunger panging our stomachs like a drum, we decided to refuel and refocus while appreciating an unmatched view of the Monarch.

Once our bellies were full, we took another look at the map and the poem, hoping to uncover additional clues that we'd originally missed. We formulated a new plan and again set off into the forest. Quicker than either of us had imagined, we stumbled upon an overgrown trail that obviously hadn't been used in quite some time. With rekindled enthusiasm, we hurried down the trail, hoping we were finally on the right one. The old trail was so overrun with brush that eventually it became impassable. We split up, one going left, one right, to search for a way around the barrier. As if by some coincidence, while checking in with each other, we both stopped mid-sentence and stared off into the distance, trying to process what we were seeing. Tucked away in a stand of larch and pine, scarcely visible from our respective locations, sat the ramshackle remains of Bill Peyto's Bookrest cabin. We had found it! Just by laying eyes on this obscure refuge, we had joined a select fraternity with very few members.

Eager to thoroughly explore the cabin's derelict remains, but hyper-aware of the rapidly fading daylight, we made the most out of the short time we allotted ourselves at the cabin. As our time expired and we began hiking back to the trailhead, I couldn't help but smile.

My ambitious search for the colourful character that was Bill Peyto had ended. This pioneer of the wilderness, who made the mountains his home and worked hard to maintain an isolated lifestyle, just had the curtains pulled back on a small part of his mysterious existence. My venture was not out of disrespect but out of curiosity and an inquisitiveness to learn more about the man and how he prospered in a very different time. Don't worry, Bill, your secret is safe with me.

—by ***Tyler Dixon****, Calgary, Alberta*

Epic Winter Race

Battling extreme conditions, endurance racers celebrate human resilience

In February of each year since 2012, men and women gather in the dead of winter to bike or run 130 kilometres through unforgiving temperatures, brutal winds and the wild and barren landscapes of southern Manitoba.

The Actif Epica race was started by local sportsman Ian Hall after he realized that a winter ultra-marathon could be created right here in Manitoba with a unique urban finish. Before Actif Epica, local ultra-marathoners had to travel to Minnesota, North Dakota and other places to compete. Ian's idea utilized the historic Crow Wing Trail, a trading route previously used by Manitoba's Indigenous peoples and early settlers. This event now draws participants from as far away as Delaware, Colorado and California.

The race starts 130 kilometres south of Winnipeg in St. Malo, Manitoba, and routes through St-Pierre-Jolys, the Crystal Springs Hutterite colony, Niverville and St. Adolphe, ending at the historic Forks in Winnipeg. Each town has washrooms, food, water and hot/cold drinks for the racers, plus a warm place to meet and get checked by safety staff. It's also during these stops that racers greatly appreciate the help and encouragement from the volunteers.

I'm a local city bus driver and community journalist and I wanted to cover the event like an embedded journalist. I have been involved in running, cycling and duathlons for a few years, but only in a recreational capacity. To train properly for the event, I ran 16 kilometres every other day in up to –45°C temperatures and completed one long 45-kilometre run in the cold just a week prior to the race. I also took part in the pre-race "recon ride" in which we ran or biked 32 kilometres and tested our equipment. I estimate that my gear weighed about 18 to 22 kilograms. I took more than most people, including snowshoes, which I didn't end up needing. I also had my camera and a few extra items, because the army taught me not to scrimp when it comes to survival equipment!

"Runners have half an hour until the start," announced one of the race directors, Dwayne Sandall. He oversaw the runners, checking that everyone was alert and physically able to tackle the day. There were 15 of us runners and almost 50 cyclists who were starting an hour later. Some participants were the high-performance types, and others were regular people like myself—just active citizens. There were some people trying out different ways to race, like cross-country skiing and relay teams. A local Hutterite female competitor showed up to the start wearing a gorgeous traditional dress. And I thought I was tough!

My running partner, Ryan, and I witnessed the passing of the first cyclists. They were not happy. We ran through some very deep snow, so the cyclists would have been pushing their fatbikes, which can weigh up to 27 kilograms with their gear, through the same snow.

I saw that Ryan was starting to limp about 24 kilometres into the race, so I told him I was going to go ahead. It was daylight and the weather was good. Around 40 kilometres into the race, blizzard conditions appeared. My hands were getting terribly cold, so I took off a glove to get out a chemical warmer pack—the muscle in between my fingers was firming up, like thawing steak. I was scared by what was happening at first, but thankful when the chemical pack began generating heat.

Twenty minutes later, I saw another runner heading in the other direction, back to Crystal Springs, holding his frozen hand in his glove. He had to drop out.

At the halfway point, I entered the Niverville Arena, where everyone cheered every time a racer entered. While resting there, I dropped out and then re-entered the race, thanks to the encouragement from a volunteer. Ryan appeared, and we agreed to continue together and finish the race. Off we went.

A few hours later, though, Ryan's foot was getting worse. How he managed to make it to that point, I have no idea. My body temperature was dropping steadily and we had to keep moving to stay warm.

When we arrived at the second-to-last checkpoint, the University of Manitoba, Tom from the safety staff checked Ryan's feet. Ryan had no choice but to drop out, but as he did so, he encouraged me to continue on. I was very sad, but at least he was in no danger.

Towards the end of the race, shuffling through the night, I was worried I wouldn't make the 25-hour limit. Fast runners do the event in

17 hours; normal people in around 22. The tracks of the cyclists and fast runners had already been blown away, so the moonlight reflected off a smooth sea of snow. With the light on my head, I looked and felt like an astronaut exploring another planet.

I bumped into two female runners who were out on the Riverwalk for a short run. After they took a look at me, one of them said, "Are you in Epica? Still?" It turned out that one of the women had a son in the event and was thinking of entering next year. I told her to bring hand warmers.

I was the very last person to finish the race, arriving at the table to receive my snowflake medal at 24 hours and 45 minutes. It was just before sunrise when I left St. Malo and it was sunrise when I arrived in Winnipeg. What a spiritual experience. At one point in the race, I don't know why, but I started crying. I wasn't feeling any pain and there was nobody around me. I was by myself. I was living. I was free.

*—by **Gregory McNeill**, Winnipeg, Manitoba*

The Motorcycle Diaries

Passion for the open road and cross-country adventures

As I write this, it is –20°C and my motorcycle—a Yamaha Roadstar Canadian Special Edition—is under wraps in the garage, ready to go as soon as spring arrives. So I am dreaming of sun, pavement and two-wheeled trips. I have been riding for 40 years and will ride until I can no longer hold my bike up.

Motorcycle riding is a passion that has taken me many places in Canada. I have ridden, on different trips, from British Columbia to Newfoundland and through much of the United States. For the most part, I ride alone: just me, my motorcycle and the open highway. Not that I would mind riding with others, but as a solo rider I only have one bladder and one gas tank to consider.

Why do I ride? With riding comes pleasure, fear, exhilaration and relaxation. When I ride, I have a sense of freedom, a sense of being on the open road with no "cage" around me. It's hard to explain if you have never ridden a motorcycle. It's like trying to understand why the dog likes to hang his head out of the car window.

Riding is a banquet for all of the senses. I have feasted my eyes on magnificent scenery from the Rocky Mountains and the hoodoos in Alberta to the fields of wheat and canola in the Prairie provinces and the lowlands along the St. Lawrence River, and from the flower pots at the Bay of Fundy to the cliffs at Bonavista.

I can smell everything from the cow manure when the barns are cleaned in the eastern counties of Quebec to the wild roses in Alberta. Then there's the honeysuckle in bloom and the pine trees in the Acadian forest of Nova Scotia, the fresh bread from the local boulangerie and the crispness of the approaching fall in northern Ontario. I also love the smell of salty ocean air as you ride around the Bay of Fundy, the mushroom farms in Manitoba and the large feedlots in Saskatchewan. Of course, there's nothing like the smell of rain in the air before it actually starts.

I sense every nuance of the weather. Temperatures change dramatically when riding up one mountain range and down the other. While riding through the Rockies from Jasper to Cranbrook, I made multiple stops to put on extra clothing and then remove that clothing.

Once, over Canada Day weekend, it was so cold and windy along Lake Superior to Sault Ste. Marie, I wore four layers of clothes! I notice slight temperature drops while riding along a tree-lined road, such as the one near Black River, Ontario, or towards Sandbanks Provincial Park. It is much appreciated during the midsummer heat waves.

Wearing so many layers of protective clothing has its advantages and disadvantages. It keeps you warm and somewhat protected from the elements. Outfitted in long johns, jeans, chaps, a sweatshirt and a jacket—and covered entirely by a rainsuit—feels bulky but helps keep me warm and dry. I have ridden in rainstorms where everything was wet by the end of the day.

I meet the greatest people while travelling on a motorcycle. I met a fellow rider on the ferry from Prince Edward Island to New Brunswick and we rode together for three days. As we parted ways, I realized I only knew his first name and the state he came from. While riding through Alberta, I stopped for a gas break and as I paid inside the service station, I noticed half a dozen retirement-age cowboys sitting with their cups of coffee. I was asked where I was from, where I was going and warned that I should be carrying a gun. In Godbout waiting for a ferry, I was questioned as to why I ride alone, as it is considered much too dangerous for a woman.

In the over 150,000 kilometres I've covered, I only once wondered what the heck I was doing. In Newfoundland, it was day eight of riding in the rain. I'd enjoyed a beautiful ride through the Avalon Peninsula under overcast skies. Midday saw the start of rain. As I made my way back to St. John's, I stopped at more than a dozen motels only to discover there was no vacancy. It was well past dark and I had been on the road for 12 hours with more than 800 kilometres under my belt. As I parked under an overpass to get out of the rain, I lamented ever having ridden to this godforsaken land and thought I would never get dry again. I picked myself up and kept riding. Within an hour, I rode into a truck stop near Whitbourne and walked into a combination motel, grocery store and gas station. As I stood in the foyer with water streaming from my clothing, the receptionist said, "Oh, me love, you need a room!" I was treated royally, with my room beside the laundry so I could dry everything. I will definitely be going back to this great province.

As a rider, I am never 100 percent relaxed, nor am I a nervous rider. I have to look ahead, behind and at my dash and be prepared for anything on the road. I am on the watch for other vehicles and animals that can step in front of me. British Columbia came complete with herds of wild mountain sheep to navigate around. Near the Saint John River in New Brunswick, I encountered a bear! Moose abound in New Brunswick and Newfoundland. I am always on alert for wildlife.

You hear nothing but white noise while riding—the wind, your bike and the world around you combine in musical harmony. Your brain tries to make sense of outside sounds such as airplanes, other vehicles, dogs barking and the crash of ocean waves and distinguish one from the other. Until, that is, you relax and it all turns into a kind of music you have never heard before.

One of my absolute favourite rides is on new pavement. There's nothing like the thrill of riding on freshly blackened road with the fragrance of asphalt wafting up. Corners and hills are another favourite—discovering what is around the bend or on the other side. The route around Quebec's Gaspésie has roads with steep inclines as compared to the Prairie provinces, where, thanks to the straight roads, you can see for miles.

I have been lost. I have been turned around and gone the wrong way. I have agonized about oil drips. I have fretted that the next gas stop may be too far away. I have asked myself why I drank that extra mug of tea. I have voiced my displeasure at not having the weight to trigger stop lights. I have lamented over the weather.

There comes a point when you no longer focus on the details of riding and you become one with your bike. I glide around corners and up and over mountains while shifting my weight slightly, countersteering and changing gears. I am in total harmony with the world.

I love the freedom and excitement, the clearing of the mind and leaving all the stress of life behind. Motorcycle riding is a romance that comes with the twist of the throttle. I challenge myself. I learn something new every day. It never fails to bring a smile to my face. Riding motorcycles is my passion.

*—by **Anne Hagerman**, Picton, Ontario*

Grand Manan, New Brunswick

A mother-daughter duo go cliff-edge camping

My daughter, Julie, and I have been taking a mother-daughter summer vacation for more than 20 years. Sometimes it is only a long weekend, but we always find a way to make it happen. Tenting has become something we love doing together. It satisfies us both on so many levels. We cocoon when the weather is bad, meditate, read, listen to music, walk on the beach, enjoy nature and try to get some painting in. We always choose a place near a beach, which is not hard to do when you live on the East Coast.

I have to admit, we are not purists when it comes to tenting—we cheat. We have cereal and fruit for breakfast at the campsite and we make sandwiches for lunch. Then we are off to look for a coffee shop and do some sightseeing in the afternoon. For supper, we look for a family-owned restaurant where fresh fish is the house specialty.

Last year, we waited too long to get a reservation at New River Beach Provincial Park, which is one of our favourite spots. We did an Internet search to see what else would be available for Labour Day weekend and found a wilderness campground called Hole-in-the-Wall, on Grand Manan Island.

It offers cliff-edge and clifftop campsites overlooking the Bay of Fundy. Some of the cliffs are 100 to 200 feet high. Their website boasted of the possibility of actually being able to see and hear whales feeding at the weirs at the foot of the cliffs. This was a magnet straight to my heart. I had seen and heard whales once at St. Mary's bird sanctuary outside of St. John's, Newfoundland. It felt like a spiritual experience to me, so even the slight chance of repeating it was appealing.

We immediately looked into the long-range weather forecast, because Grand Manan has a notorious reputation for being foggy. The prediction was clear skies ahead and warm temperatures. We made a reservation and checked out the New Brunswick ferry schedule from St. George to Grand Manan Island. It is a 90-minute crossing on a beautiful new ferry with wonderful facilities, lounges and a restaurant, but best of all, it provides outside seating. Sometimes whales can be seen from the ferry.

We sat out on the deck inhaling the smell of the salt water, feeling the sun on our faces and the wind in our hair. Looking at the beautiful water of the Bay of Fundy, we felt so good, so invigorated and so pleased with our adventurous selves.

We couldn't wait to get there, and it was not a disappointment. We were delighted with our cliff-edge campsite. It was large, with both sunny and shady areas, and it was private. We had a gorgeous view of the water from our site, including a view of one of the three lighthouses on the island. At night we could see the ferry—all lit up—crossing against the dark sky and water. The scenery was stunning!

There was no danger of us falling off the cliff, as there is a comfortable distance and a barrier of trees between the campsite and the cliff edge. However, I would not be comfortable bringing children there.

The campground is called Hole-in-the-Wall because there is a large hole in a huge rock caused by thousands of years of tides. It is one of the suggested lookouts and it is well worth the 15 minutes it takes to get there, even if the tree roots and rocks make it tricky walking in places.

Over the following three days, we visited the other lighthouses and four beaches. We were delighted to find charming, family-owned restaurants and local coffee shops—there are no coffee chains on the island. There are bike rentals, sea kayaking tours and an art gallery to enjoy. Grand Manan is also famous for birdwatching and it's an artist's paradise. There is a great bakery and several fish shops, of which you can be sure we took advantage. We couldn't return home without lobster for our husbands. Speaking of our men, we were excited to introduce them to wilderness camping at Hole-in-the-Wall the following spring!

*—by **Evelyn Godin**, Saint John, New Brunswick*

The Mystique of Sable Island

Famous for its shipwrecks and wild horses, this strip of sand off the coast of Nova Scotia is on many Canadians' bucket lists

My roommate and I rose from our comfy berths aboard the *Sea Adventurer* when we heard the anchor chain being released. We sprang from our beds, threw on some warm clothes and raced to the top deck. The sun was just beginning to peer over the horizon, turning the vast sky various shades of purple. Just over 180 kilometres off the coast of Nova Scotia, the 42-kilometre-long, crescent-shaped sliver of sand known as Sable Island glistened in the morning sun.

Sitting barely above the ocean's surface with its widest point only 1.5 kilometres, we could now tell why it inherited the name "the Graveyard of the Atlantic" due to the numerous shipwrecks off its coast over the years. Soon we would feel the island's sand between our toes and hopefully witness with our own eyes the famous Sable Island horses that share the shores with one of the largest colonies of grey seals in the world, and the rare Ipswich sparrow that makes the sandbar its only breeding ground.

Years ago, when I had attempted to reach the island to photograph the horses for my first Scholastic Canada book, a nonfiction book about horse breeds, I discovered that to fly there was both expensive and difficult. There was no guarantee when you could take off from the island due to the omnipresent fog that rolls in and possibly stays for days or weeks. In 2013, the island's care was transferred from the Canadian Coast Guard to Parks Canada, making Sable Island Canada's 43rd national park.

After much deliberation, the tour company Adventure Canada came to an agreement with Parks Canada to allow a group of approximately 100 tourists to land on its beaches, transported from the ship by Zodiacs, a method that would impact the island's environment the least.

After breakfast, we loaded our gear into waterproof sacks and were safely transported to the island's shore in groups of six to ten. Greeted by Parks Canada staff, we were led down a narrow horse path, being careful to stay in one another's footprints in the sand. After walking for half an hour with no horses in sight, we climbed a dune only to spot a foal frolicking down the beach with its mother close behind. My heart skipped a beat to know that I could finally tick that box off my bucket list. Walking a little farther, we witnessed many more small herds of horses.

Believed to be descendants of animals that were seized by the British from the Acadians during their expulsion from Nova Scotia, these horses now exist in numbers ranging from 300 to 500. These wild horses feed off the marram beach grass and know by instinct where to dig for underground freshwater reservoirs when the surface ponds are contaminated with saltwater from the Atlantic Ocean after storms.

From 1801 to 1958, before modern navigational systems, a human presence existed on the island as a lifesaving station for shipwrecks. Originally used for riding and farming, the herd was destined to be rounded up and auctioned off for use as pit ponies in the coal mines, or alternatively slaughtered for dog food.

In 1961, a movement to convince then Canadian Prime Minister John Diefenbaker to save the horses was successful after numerous children sent collections of drawings and letters begging for the herds' protection. More than 50 years later, one of those children was able to witness the result of her efforts and stepped ashore with us.

The horses have never received modern veterinary care and the herd is completely unmanaged. Parks Canada has mandated that a 20-metre distance be observed between human and equine, allowing the horses to maintain their wild instincts.

There is a controversy with Parks Canada in regard to the horses, as the general rule is to remove any alien species. Since these horses have been there for so long, however, who is to determine if they are alien or native? Permanent dwellings used for research and housing for Parks Canada staff dot the island and many of the original buildings remain, disappearing in the windswept sand only to reappear years later. In 1901, the federal government planted more than 80,000 trees on the island in an attempt to stabilize the soil, but they all died, with the exception of one pine that still stands near the weather station.

I felt honoured to meet Zoe Lucas, a researcher who has lived on and off the island since she first stepped foot on it in 1971. Since the early '80s, Zoe has made Sable her home for ten to 12 months of the year. I asked Zoe if she had the chance to tell the world something about the horses, what it would be. Her reply was, "To be aware of what is going on around you. The horses of Sable Island will be fine for now, but there are so many other wild horses out there that need our help."

Many of the passengers aboard the *Sea Adventurer* had dreamed of this opportunity since they were young children and had now fulfilled that dream.

—by ***Shawn Hamilton****, Campbellcroft, Ontario*

Swimming Great Bear

Three dedicated swimmers take on British Columbia's Great Bear Sea, seeking adventure and generating awareness

To say we've been called just a little crazy a couple of times would be an understatement. Indeed, it probably isn't your average summer vacation to go swim the Great Bear Sea, but that's exactly what three close friends did one summer.

We departed from Port Hardy, British Columbia, by ferry to travel to British Columbia's central coast to attempt a two-day, staged swim from Ocean Falls to Bella Bella. Starting from the foot of the falls on day one, we swam the length of Cousins Inlet into Fisher Channel, veering off into Gunboat Passage, where we exited the water for the day. The next morning, we picked up where we left off in hopes of catching the tidal current through the narrows of Gunboat, past the town of Shearwater, across Lama Passage, landing on the shores of Bella Bella, completing two back-to-back 25-kilometre swims.

This was the first time these waters have been swum, and probably for good reason. The water registered surface temperatures in the range of 12°C to 17°C. Careful planning was implemented before the swim to accommodate surface and tidal currents.

So why would anyone want to do such a thing, you might ask? Well, that's a really good question. We were asked this question many times as we put the wheels in motion to make this little adventure happen. Of course, if you ask each of us that question, we'd likely each give you a different answer. Simply put, though, we're just a bunch of swimmers who love to swim in unique and wonderful places. We love the challenges and freedoms we confront when we're in the open water, especially when surrounded by such natural beauty. So I guess the easy answer is, why not do it?

Of course, there is a lot more to it than that. For Dale Robinson, swimming has always played a huge role in his life, both as an athlete and a coach. As he gets older, he finds himself seeking out new and more exciting ways to challenge himself within the sport, and the Great Bear Swim seemed liked a pretty good way to do just that. The swim was also his way of helping in the fight to bring attention to the wonder that is the Great Bear ecosystem and the local-to-global need for its conservation.

There is incredible diversity of life in the Great Bear, much of which is hidden below the waterline. He believes that as a human race, we'd better start collectively understanding just how critical maintaining that biological diversity is to our own continued existence on this planet.

For Susan Simmons, swimming has healing power. About 20 years ago, Susan was diagnosed with multiple sclerosis and was advised to avoid strenuous exercise, only to watch helplessly as her body began to fail. She decided a different approach was warranted and now uses swimming as an effective management tool for her symptoms. And by all measures it appears her approach has worked, as she can lay claim to being one of the world's most accomplished open-water, ultra-marathon swimmers. Her longest nonstop swim to date took more than 30 hours while swimming a total of 70 kilometres. One day, she's hoping to set another benchmark by attempting to swim more than 100 kilometres without stopping, other than to feed and hydrate. So, the Great Bear Swim was just an easy warm-up for her.

In my case, especially in light of my past experiences as a Canadian record-holding freediver, this was a rare opportunity to swim and dive in the pristine and abundant waters along the British Columbia coast. I've been freediving in California among the sea lions, with manta rays in the Cayman Islands and along a salmon run in Campbell River, and I was absolutely thrilled to see humpback whales in the Great Bear Sea. For me, this swim was also very much about having an opportunity to meet, engage and share stories with the people in the communities along the route.

The waterways we were swimming in are part of the Heiltsuk First Nation's traditional territory, with the town of Bella Bella being a focal point of their people and culture. Ocean Falls holds a special place in the Canadian swimming community for being called hometown to a disproportionately large number of our Olympians in the 1960s. Now, with barely 20 or so remaining residents, Ocean Falls has fallen largely idle as an abandoned ghost town.

Our adventure took about a year to plan and train for, and we ended up with an amazing 12-member crew who supplied our navigation, safety and emergency support. We also chose to support three charitable and nonprofit causes: the MS Society of Canada; Pacific Wild, which is dedicated to developing conservation solutions for the Great Bear; and QQS Projects Society, which runs Koeye Camp, an innovative educational camp for Heiltsuk youth that helps promote and foster scientific and traditional cultural knowledge.

All in all, it was a labour of love and, more importantly, an opportunity for personal growth and reflection, with each one of us realizing that we all have our own unique demons to confront in taking on a challenge of this nature. Of course, the flip side is that we have also learned about our individual strengths, and how that helps in comforting and supporting one another. It was such an amazing ride, and our hope is that this will turn into a project that takes on a life of its own as we seek out new and extraordinary places to go swimming.

*—by **Jill Yoneda**, Victoria, British Columbia*

Wild About Horses

Photographing magnificent "wildies"

I enjoy photographing everything in nature, but wild horses are my passion. When I first heard about Alberta's wild horses 20 years ago, I wanted to photograph them. A friend of mine, who loves and advocates for "wildies," heard about my wish and I was fortunate to accompany him to see the wild horses in the Williams Creek area of Alberta.

It was an incredible experience. We saw more than 100 majestic horses—I was in heaven. We spent a day there on our first visit, and have been back to the same area often.

On one occasion, while taking photos of a band of around 30 horses, I didn't realize that not 20 feet away, a foal was sleeping behind a tree. All at once, he awoke, jumped up and just stood there allowing me to get several great shots of him. As I was snapping away, the herd stud realized how close the little guy was to me and came running over, snaking his neck with his ears back, as if warning the colt, "Danger, get away!" The colt didn't seem to understand what he was being told and stayed put until his mom came over to get him. I didn't feel threatened at all by the stallion being close to me and kept taking photos. It was an encounter that I will always cherish.

Another time, I managed to capture a great shot of a foal running and jumping for the sheer joy of it. He was having such fun all by himself while the rest of his herd grazed peacefully—it brought a smile to my face. Once, I snapped a funny pic of a red roan stallion with a cowbird perched on his back. Later, the same roan was with another bachelor stud and they were both very tolerant of our presence, allowing us plenty of time to take photos.

Having spent time with the wildies, I hope to visit as often as possible! They're magnificent and truly nurture my soul. I'm so thankful for the privilege. These horses are born wild and free, and deserve to always remain so.

*—by **Julie Birch**, Didsbury, Alberta*

COMMUNITY

Canadians celebrate their country, culture and inclusiveness in poignant stories of struggle and achievement

Canada, Do You Have Room for Us?

Fleeing persecution, this Mennonite preacher and his family found freedom on these welcoming shores

Dietrich waited until dark, and then jumped on his horse and galloped away. He had an important mission, and it would not do for other villagers to see him. Everyone lived in fear. Who would be next on the government arrest list? Where would the marauders strike next?

It was 1929, in a part of the U.S.S.R. that is now Ukraine. Government forces kept tabs on everyone, while wild bandits roamed the country. Dietrich didn't know which peril he feared more. His name was on the government blacklist (all preachers were), and the ruthless bandits didn't care that they were preachers. They rode into villages at random, looting and killing.

Dietrich and Agatha (my parents) had relatives in Canada, and thought of immigrating there with their little ones—my baby brother Walter and me, Mary, 1½ years old at the time. We were living with my mother's parents, owners of the village mill. They were kulaks (landowners) and could be a target soon. Leaving without them would be heart-wrenching, but they wanted to sell their business and home before they would think of leaving. Now in the dead of night, Dietrich sought advice from a friend in a distant village who had gone to Moscow and was encouraging people to emigrate. To his horror, police barged in and arrested his friend. Dietrich reached home breathless. "We're leaving!" he said.

Now we were not immigrants—we were refugees, fleeing our country. We boarded a train for Moscow from a neighbouring town. Thousands gathered in makeshift camps, applying to leave their homeland.

Every night, police barged in. Breasts heaved in fear as the police called out names. Always men. Broken-hearted wives gathered their crying children and returned to their villages. They could not, would not, leave the country without their husbands. Thousands were shipped in cattle cars to Siberia.

One night, the dreaded knock came to our door. Dietrich trembled as police entered and called out every name in the room. The next announcement stunned them: "You may leave!" Audible cries and cheers! Tears rolled down even the policemen's cheeks. Dietrich, Agatha, baby Walter and I were among the survivors.

My parents feared for our lives even as we rode the train to the border. Desired destination? Canada! We arrived at the Red Gate—freedom awaited beyond. Later, Dietrich heard that our train was the last one through the Red Gate before the Iron Curtain descended. How he thanked God for deliverance!

Months later, our family stood on the pier, waiting to board the *Marylebone.* I pointed to the water spouting from the ship's side and said, "Look, Papa! The boat is peeing!"

After a transfer in England to the SS *Montcalm,* we finally arrived in Saint John, New Brunswick, Canada.

At customs, however, we were taken to a hospital on Partridge Island. I had scarlet fever. Our family was separated, as I was quarantined and my father stayed with me. Mother and baby Walter were allowed to see us through a window. We spoke no English, and now we couldn't even speak to one another.

Canada was in the midst of the Great Depression, so we lived in poverty for our first few years, but we were free. Free of fear, free to worship God.

The Niagara Peninsula seemed a good place to live in this free country. My parents grew fruit and vegetables, and raised pigs. There was always plenty of work to keep us (now) six children busy. Evenings, neighbourhood kids gathered to play games of "Andy, Andy, Over!"

On hot days, while picking ten acres of tomatoes, Father would inspire us kids with, "If you work hard, we'll head to the Niagara River for a swim in the evening." He always kept his word, although this one time, on the way to the river, a part of the harness broke, stabbing our horse in the stomach. With kids screaming, the horse took off like the wind—but we all survived.

Our family farmed for a living, but Father was also a preacher in the local Mennonite church. Freedom to worship is one of Canada's greatest gifts to refugees. In those days, children all sat in front rows during services. When they started getting restless, or misbehaving, Deitrich would stop his sermon and say, "Listen, children! Here's a story for you," and all would be calm once more.

Eventually, my grandparents and many others also found refuge in Canada after World War II. Canada had room for all. It was indeed the land of freedom and opportunity. No more starving. No more fear of attacks or imprisonment. My parents proudly raised their children and enjoyed their 24 grandchildren here. Today, this country still makes room for refugees—thank you, Canada.

*—by **Mary Derksen**, Abbotsford, British Columbia*

Salami and Popsicles

Savouring the tastes of home, both old and new

I was ten years old when my family and I arrived in Quebec from Oldenburg, Germany. It was August, 1953, and our nine-day crossing aboard the *Beaverbrae* had been somewhat stormy. Although my older brother Baldur fared well, as did our parents, Alfred and Johanna Boenke, my younger sister Marlen and I both got very seasick.

After a few days, the ship's doctor came to check on us. He asked Marlen if there was any food that might make her feel better and she requested a traditional favourite—sauerkraut and beer—which the doctor somehow managed to find. After she consumed some of both, Marlen felt better and wasn't seasick anymore. Unfortunately, it only made me worse.

Once off the ship, we had to go through customs and immigration. A dear friend of my parents had asked them to bring along a whole smoked salami from our hometown. At that time, it was not possible to readily purchase such cold cuts in Canada.

So, my mother had the big salami among her personal belongings, but as we looked around, we saw buckets and buckets full of all kinds of sausages and cheeses that had been confiscated from the new immigrants.

When the customs officer spotted the salami, he informed Mom that she would not be allowed to bring it into Canada. My mother said, "If I'm not allowed to take this all the way to our final destination in Edmonton, I will at least enjoy a bite," and then took a big bite right out of the centre of the sausage. The shocked customs agent said, "Well, once it has been started (or bitten into), we cannot take it away from you." The agent let Mom keep the salami.

We then boarded a train for a four-day trip to Edmonton. After our first night on the train, my father woke up to discover he had gone deaf in one ear. Upon closer inspection, we discovered his ear was completely clogged with soot, which had come in through the window during the night. We cleaned out his ear and he never had another hearing problem in all of his 91 years.

After a few days on the train, we had a layover in Winnipeg. It was very hot that summer, so my friend Rosemarie, whom I'd met on the ship, her dad and I went shopping for ice cream. None of us spoke any English. We stopped at a store and asked for *eis,* which is the German word for ice cream. The employee looked at us, puzzled, and proceeded to give us a huge block of ice, which would have easily fit into an icebox, if we had one. I don't remember what we did with the ice, but we went to a café, where we were able to purchase purple popsicles—they were pictured on a poster on the wall. To this day, they are still my favourite popsicles.

We finally arrived safely in Edmonton, and have never regretted coming to Canada.

—by ***Gerlind Koesling****, Edmonton, Alberta*

A Fairy Tale of Ice and Magic

Transitioning from 36° above to 36° below

Sitting across the desk from an HR representative for a Canadian oil company, my husband, Charles, and I wondered if what we were hearing was true. The woman patiently explained how the temperature in Fort McMurray, Alberta, can reach –40°C in winter, that the town is surrounded by forest and cars have to be plugged in! Looking out the window at the sun reflecting off the metal burglar bars and security gates across the bustling Johannesburg street, it seemed unimaginable, but this was where we were heading.

Tired of living behind locked security gates and sleeping with a gun under our pillow, the final straw was when a nephew of ours had to fight for his life after being shot through his car door and dragged onto the pavement before the thieves sped away in his car.

On January 15, 2005, it was 36°C outside as we boarded the aircraft for our trip to Canada. When we arrived some 42 hours later, the pilot cheerfully announced the temperature as a balmy –36°C! Stepping outside into a white wilderness, exhausted and reeling from jet lag, we wondered what we had done.

As we soon discovered, you needed to bundle up in multiple layers just to stay warm, use a remote starter to get the car going in the morning without freezing to death and always remember to plug the car in at night. Why did we choose to live here again?

Well, there really is a lovely boreal forest encircling Fort McMurray, but that's only part of the beauty of this place. One morning, we awoke to the view of a child's bicycle lying undisturbed on the side of the road...and it was still there the next day! In our former home, it would have been taken in a flash.

When our first Christmas arrived, we were amazed to see ornaments and lights outside and trees gleaming brightly behind uncovered windows. Back in South Africa, we would have put the tree in the corner farthest from the window or door, so as not to advertise the presents beneath it.

It seemed we had fallen into a fairy-tale land, but it didn't take long to realize our previous "normal" had not been normal at all. We decided to explore all the wonders of our new country at every opportunity.

Have you ever visited the Great White North, where the inukshuk stands in the blowing snow, polar bear cubs slide down snowbanks and the northern lights dance overhead? You should! As you slowly crawl over the winter ice road on your trip north, you'll do so at five kilometres an hour, so as not to cause an under-surface wave to well up, break the ice and send you into the frozen depths.

You'll also come across sand dunes in a desert-like area of fine sand left behind by the receding glaciers. Then you can head to the mountains to find treasures behind those snow-capped peaks: grand glaciers, tumbling waterfalls and emerald lakes, whose fine silt sediment hides the remains of creatures from bygone eras.

Over the mountains and down to the west, you'll pass smooth, black-slate cliffs, alive with clear, trickling water that seemingly oozes from the very pores of the hard stone. Winding mountain passes give way to sparkling beaches, covered in bird life, where the waters resound with the calls of giant whales.

I no longer question why I am here. As I wait for the rumbling crack of the frozen river's surface to explode, throwing chunks of ice up the banks, heralding the arrival of spring, I cannot wait to start off on another adventure in this land where ice gives way to magic.

*—by **Patricia Wilsenach**, Fort McMurray, Alberta*

Reflections on Canada

Arriving with his family in 1989, an emigrant from India expresses his heartfelt love of Canada

Cold weather and hockey may be internationally recognized symbols of Canada, but beyond its climate and recreational activities, this great nation has a lot to offer newcomers.

I chose to immigrate to Canada because of the wonderful and helpful Canadians I had met along my life's journey. When I first arrived from India in 1989 with my family, everyone was extremely nice and kind, and tolerant of my language difficulties, helping me to speak and read English very quickly.

Canada is successful as a nation because it has always been a country founded and built by people who came here by choice, who immigrated for a chance at a new life, and who have worked hard, generation after generation, to build a tolerant society. Unlike many other places, here in Canada everyone is free to dress as they wish, speak English or the language of their birth or ancestry, worship and live in peace.

Canada is a nation where the culture of peace has the deepest roots. People here can freely express their ideas, participate in politics and depend on a fair judicial system to protect their rights. The country's multicultural policies also help everyone to find their place in society.

Ours is one of the greatest countries in the world, with free health care, accessible schooling for kids with physical handicaps or intellectual disabilities, and many helpful nonprofit organizations such as The Friendship Circle, which helps people develop a social life without having to resort to cyberspace. And, yes, we love the game of hockey and our four distinct seasons. Add into the mix the natural tendency of Canadians towards peace and love—and you can see that we have it all here, in abundance.

I find it fascinating to live in a multicultural environment such as the Greater Toronto Area because, as a journalist, I have the opportunity to meet people with very different backgrounds and learn about their cultures. I believe that Canada as a whole draws strength from its multicultural spirit.

The people of Canada have worked hard to build a country that opens its doors to include all, regardless of race, religion or community, and, as such, is a country that respects and gives equality to all.

While violence is prevalent in many parts of the world, and takes many forms, Canada has built a culture of peace by adopting and developing values, ways of thinking and attitudes that are in keeping with equality, tolerance, sharing, generosity and respect.

Canada is my home now and I have a lot of fondness and love for such a fantastic country. It has given me hundreds of special moments and the opportunity to forge incredible friendships and continually make new acquaintances.

I would say that Canadians get along with everyone, unless someone tries to step on us or our friends, in which case, look out, because we will stand up for one another. Overall, though, Canadians are easy-going, blessed with a vast amount of land and lots of clean water for drinking, swimming and fishing. Our forests are rich with timber and scenic beauty, and our farms are fruitful with good harvests. We do indeed have to face the cold and snow in winter, but that is bearable for most and enjoyable for many.

I'm proud to say I am a Canadian, proud also that my children will be able to say the same. There is no other country in the world with the freedom and choices our Canada has to offer.

—by ***Surjit Singh Flora****, Brampton, Ontario*

Loving Peace River

Heading west meant new experiences and a different way of life

It was Easter weekend 1960. I felt a little apprehensive as my journey from Toronto to Fort St. John, British Columbia, was coming to an end. I was on my own now and on my way to a strange town, having accepted a position as an X-ray technologist at Providence Hospital in Fort St. John. Bridging the gap between working in a large Toronto hospital and new employment in a very small hospital would be challenging.

I was positive the taxi driver had deposited me at the wrong location as I gazed at the building. It was an ancient, three-storey house situated on the main street. I was soon to discover this old building housed the friendliest people I would ever meet.

The Sisters of Providence owned and operated the hospital, giving of themselves in every possible instance, all for the safety and well-being of patients and staff. They had a very limited income, relying time and again on the townspeople's generosity. Financial donations from Fort St. John organizations and its citizens provided for necessary, if not elaborate, medical equipment.

After being warmly welcomed and fed by the Sisters, I was given a tour of the hospital. The main floor housed the office, dining room, emergency room (basically a hallway), X-ray room, lab and about ten patient beds. The second floor accommodated maternity patients and operating rooms.

The X-ray room was where I would be working. The X-ray table resembled a steel hammock. Little did I realize that this room held many surprises for me in the days to come. Normally, examinations, including X-rays of the stomach and colon, are performed by a radiologist. In those days, however, the nearest radiologist was in Edmonton. I, therefore, was elected to do these on my own; my greatest accomplishment was to dislodge patients from that hammock and get them quickly to a bathroom down the hall after the procedure.

Another result of the hospital being quite small was that there was no space for a morgue. This caused me to have a couple of unnerving experiences. On two separate occasions, I arrived at work to find what I presumed to be a bag of soiled laundry on the X-ray table. Upon closer inspection, however, I realized it contained something other than soiled sheets.

In spite of these rare occurrences, the hospital was a lively and spirited workplace. We all needed strong backs to help transport patients up about 20 steps to the floor above. These stairs proved to be an eventful climb for maternity patients on their way to the labour room.

Everything was about to change, however, as a new hospital was being constructed. The Sisters of Providence were buzzing with excitement at the prospect of a new, larger space. Many gracious and capable townspeople joined in moving equipment and records into the new hospital. Fortunately for me, the antiquated X-ray table stayed behind. The Sisters were sad to leave their old building, but were nevertheless joyful at the prospect of a new era in health care.

During this time, two co-workers and I had promised to transport an elderly patient, Gus, home from the hospital to his cabin in Hudson's Hope, British Columbia. His eyes twinkled as he warned us about driving the Hope road—especially with women drivers at the wheel. When we reached the top of Bear Flats, single-lane traffic on a narrow, winding road was the order of the day. Gus kept telling me to watch the road and not the scenery, but it was so spectacular! The fall colours of red, yellow and orange, combined with the sight of the mighty Peace River winding its way below the cliffs, created a stunning, postcard-like picture. I'm sure Gus was trembling as he called out in a shaky voice, "We'll all be killed!" But we made it safely to Gus's cabin. He served us tea in dainty china cups, a strong contrast to his bachelor way of life.

In the 1960s, Hudson's Hope was a quiet little town and many bachelors lived a simple life in small log cabins. Their doors were always open to old and young alike; the younger children were enthralled with numerous events of bygone days. These residents had endured difficult times over the years, having existed without modern conveniences and basic health care. Travel was a major challenge, with the gravel roads deemed impassable on many occasions. But all of this was about to change, as plans were under way to dam the Peace River.

After leaving Gus that day, we decided to continue on to Gold Bar—a sprawling jewel of a homestead at the foot of the Rockies. At one point, the narrow gravel road disappeared and we were forced to cross a fast-moving creek, no easy task for three city girls. Finally, we arrived at Gold Bar, where moose, deer and stone sheep roamed the hills bordering this unique log home.

We were warmly greeted by Elizabeth Beattie, the feisty but gracious matriarch of Gold Bar. She'd raised eight children in this home, which also housed many trappers and prospectors at different times of the year. Vegetables and flowers were abundant; apple and plum trees provided fruit for family and trappers alike. The home itself had its own water system, a first for the area. A huge wood cookstove heated the roomy kitchen and a long wooden table was laden with hearty meals all year long. But a drastic change was coming and you could see it in Elizabeth's eyes.

By around 1961, BC Hydro had begun construction on the W.A.C. Bennett Dam and extraordinary changes were about to transform this pristine valley into an underwater oasis. Some would call it progress, but many would disagree. How could the uniqueness of Gold Bar be measured in dollars? How many miles would majestic mountain sheep and moose have to travel in order to escape the rising waters? A very great number of them would perish in underwater graves.

The Beattie family discussed the pros and cons of saving their huge log home, but it would be an insurmountable task and so, as planned, the buildings were burned before the flooding. Elizabeth could not bring herself to return to her home for months prior to the flooding, knowing in her heart the pain she would endure. The engineer for BC Hydro called on her afterwards and even he had tears in his eyes.

Although the dam took more than five years to complete, the changes came too suddenly for many others who made their living on the river. These people would be forced to completely change their way of life and, sadly, some simply could not adapt.

I married into the Beattie family, and Jim and I spent our honeymoon at Gold Bar before the devastation. We continued our life in Hudson's Hope and are so proud to call the beautiful Peace River our home.

*—by **Mary Lou Beattie**, Hudson's Hope, British Columbia*

Come From Away

Learning to navigate the ways of Nova Scotians

As a "come from away" in the 1970s, I was interested in the Gaelic language still spoken by elders in rural Cape Breton where my husband, Aaron, our two sons and I had settled. One Saturday, D.J. "Beag" MacDonald stopped by to say that the Sunday service in St. Andrews Church would feature the North Shore Gaelic Men's Choir and a sermon preached entirely in Gaelic by Charlie "Holy" MacDonald.

I talked Saul, my five-year-old, into accompanying me with a promise of lots of singing. But I didn't know that the sermon itself would be more than an hour long, and that the only seats available when we arrived would be in the middle of the centre section, hardly the ideal place for an active five-year-old and his nervous mother.

When the lengthy service ended, I pulled Saul outside, where we were stopped by a group of local women gathered to welcome us to the church. One leaned over my son and asked loudly in lilting English, "Did you enjoy the service, dear?"

He answered politely: "Yes," he said and I patted his shoulder approvingly.

"And did you understand what the man was saying, dear?"

"No, but my mother told me."

I gasped. The women raised eyebrows and looked at me in surprise. Everyone knew I didn't speak a word of Gaelic, and I hoped that the obvious next question wouldn't come. But it did.

"And what did she say the man said, dear?"

Saul smiled brightly. "He said, 'Sit down and be quiet!'"

N.D. Carmichael was a backhoe driver who helped many of us who immigrated to Victoria County in the 1970s. He was a quiet man and an artist with the backhoe who could work in difficult areas. He cleared rocks and trees, opened roads, built septic fields and dug wells. He seldom left the cab of his backhoe when he was working. He wouldn't come to the house for tea and he never gave advice—except, in our case, once.

When we started rebuilding our abandoned Cape Breton farm, we noticed that local people seldom gave advice unless we specifically asked for it. A neighbour might ask Aaron what he planned to do about the old barn, for example, and Aaron would describe what he had in mind and the neighbour would nod. Unless Aaron asked, "Do you think that will work?" nothing more would be said. But when he did ask, we would hear, "Well, I suppose you could do it that way, and I sure couldn't tell you folks what to do, but then you might want to..." and we would get excellent information about how it best could be done and sometimes an offer to help.

N.D. was typical. We needed a well, and we had brought in a hydrologist from the city to help us site it. There was a marsh at the foot of the hill on which our house sat, but we were told to definitely put the well higher up, near the house.

When N.D. arrived with the backhoe, we explained to him what the hydrologist had said.

"Well, those folks are supposed to know," he said, and began to dig near the house. After he'd dug as far as the backhoe could reach, he stopped the machine and climbed down to look at the dry hole, now 12 feet deep.

"That's as far as I can go. Now, you might climb down there and dig a bit deeper with a shovel..." He looked at Aaron. The sides of the hole were beginning to fall in.

Aaron grimaced. "What do you think about the foot of the hill?"

N.D. nodded. "Oh, you'd find water down there, I guess."

He filled the original hole, smoothing the land neatly with the bucket of the backhoe, and drove to the foot of the hill, where he dug into a spring almost immediately. Clear water gushed out and N.D. pulled back the soil as Aaron threw a fibreglass liner into the well.

Pleased with the result, N.D. promised to return with a load of gravel to put in the base of the well. However, he wondered if the bridge that crossed the stream on our driveway was strong enough for a load of gravel. We'd had trouble before with the bridge and had temporarily repaired it. Now, however, Aaron got some railroad ties for stringers and placed heavy boards across them, extending out on both sides.

"How strong is your bridge?" N.D. asked, stopping the loaded truck the day he arrived.

"It's good; I rebuilt it and it's strong."

The truck moved slowly ahead. Suddenly there was a cracking, splintering sound as the boards of the bridge pulled out and the truck slowly tipped into the stream and rested on its side. The truck was wider than the supports of the bridge and had pulled the bridge over as it tipped. Aaron frantically pulled open the door that now faced up and N.D. crawled out. He walked over to Aaron and stood looking at him.

"So, that's your good bridge, is it?"

N.D. hauled the truck out with the backhoe while we levered logs underneath. By afternoon, the truck was standing on its wheels in the driveway. The door on the passenger side was damaged, but the engine started. Gravel was everywhere and the bridge was destroyed. It had to be rebuilt again.

"Oh, I suppose I could get a culvert to go under the drive..." Aaron considered aloud.

N.D. looked at him quickly. "A culvert is the only thing I'll ever drive over again!" That settled it. A culvert was ordered, delivered and placed by N.D. before evening. Forty years later, it's still solid.

N.D. died a few years ago. He is greatly missed by his friends and neighbours. The "come-from-aways" of the 1970s and '80s still talk about all he did to help build our homes and community.

—by ***Ruth Morris Schneider****, Baddeck, Nova Scotia*

Journey From Nepal

Learning to live and thrive in multicultural Canada

Originally from Nepal, we immigrated to Canada in January 2010. We first landed in Toronto, where it was tough for me and my family because of the cultural differences and the difficulty we had communicating. There was no one with whom we could share our feelings, but we also had many interesting experiences, such as figuring out the city bus and metro system and touring the Greater Toronto Area.

After three months, we moved to Fredericton, where I joined the graduate program in the Department of Geodesy and Geomatics Engineering at the University of New Brunswick (UNB). This was a tough decision in my life, but it was an exciting learning process.

I got my driver's licence in Fredericton and we bought our first car. My wife, Sarmila, supported us financially by working at a hotel while she was pregnant. Our elder son, Amitesh, was happy with his school, sports and other activities offered at the Multicultural Association of Fredericton, the YMCA and UNB. While living in Fredericton, our second son, Aariz, was born and we became a family of four.

I received a land-surveyor job offer from an Ontario-based company and we moved back to Toronto. Thanks to my job duties, I had the opportunity to travel to many different places in Ontario and Quebec. I learned about the geography, people and cultural differences across the two provinces. I completed my remaining four courses at Ryerson University and York University to become a professional land surveyor of Ontario.

In 2013, we moved to Edmonton, which has a very strong job market in many disciplines. Every person I met was very happy in their job. The wages are also higher in this part of the country, but the weather is a bit colder!

Amitesh is now in high school and participating in Air Cadets, which he joined in Fredericton. Aariz attends the daycare where Sarmila works full-time while she studies English as a Second Language part-time.

To our surprise, we discovered a noticeable number of Nepalese families in Edmonton. They have their own community building here, which not many other cities have.

We continue to interact with Canadian culture, though sometimes it is difficult. As permanent residents, we feel we have more of a responsibility to Canada and want to contribute towards its strong and positive presence in the world. With Canada being our new home, we also want to feel more secure, especially about our children's future. Cultural and language differences are the immediate barriers for us, and we would appreciate more support from government programs to help make us mentally, physically and economically healthier.

I was well settled in Nepal job-wise, but I immigrated to Canada with my family to better our situation. I often feel we are still in a struggling phase. I continue to work towards securing a better job, perhaps a government position like I had in Nepal. Canada is a highly developed, multicultural country and I am proud to be a part of it.

—by ***Janak Gautam****, Edmonton, Alberta*

A Pioneering Black Nurse

Ona Allen had to work hard to become one of the first black nurses in southern Ontario

"I didn't know where he'd come from, but in 1946, he came to speak at our church in North Buxton, Ontario, urging coloured girls who wanted to take up nursing to apply to a new nine-month, government-funded registered nursing assistant course," Ona Allen told me one recent February day at her lakeside home in Burlington, Ontario.

I was conducting an interview with Ona at the time as part of the services provided by my company, Vintage Histories and Stories, which is designed to keep oral history alive for future generations.

Ona was referring to black advocate Reverend W. Constantine Perry, who explained to her congregation that, with the war over, Ontario hospitals were overwhelmed. Temporary aides had helped nurses cope during the conflict, but they hadn't been trained to assist with the health system's greater and increasingly complex caseloads. In their place, the province had decided to train a new line of medical assistants in Toronto and Hamilton.

Prior to hearing Perry, Ona says she never once considered nursing. After finishing high school in the early 1940s, she had studied to become a secretary. Despite achieving good marks in the course, discrimination prevented her from obtaining employment. Having grown up in nearby Raleigh Township, where poor farmers looked past skin colour to practice mutual aid, she found being shut out of the region's emerging professional economy surprising and bitterly disappointing. She was compelled to seek seasonal labour, picking fruit and canning tomatoes.

Still, the fact that Ona had been raised on a humble family farm and had gone to business school was itself significant. Born in North Buxton in 1925, Ona had been pushed towards higher education throughout her youth by her grandmother. "Don't end up like all these little black girls and boys around here, singing and dancing," Ona's grandmother had insisted. "Get something in your head! Look at all the girls going to the universities. You can be one of them too!"

Ona told me how she would never forget the day she—then Ona Morris—and her friend Cora Prince first arrived in Hamilton. "There we were," she smiled, "a couple of country girls moving to the city."

Having graduated from the program in 1947, the two found work at the Hamilton General, where they came up against racial prejudice that was all too common throughout society back then. Sometimes, the prejudice came from her patients. "Get your black hands off me!" some would cry when she came to help them. Other times it was staff, in particular an assistant head nurse, who took to relegating her department's "second-class jobs" to black staff. "Miss Morris," she used to declare, "you can clean the utility room while the other girls do dressings and give meds."

When it wasn't cleaning the utility room, Ona recalls, it was handing out trays and giving enemas. One day, fed up with the situation, Ona threatened to leave. "In the end, they changed that assistant head nurse and brought in another girl," says Ona, but it was too late; both she and Cora had had enough. It wasn't just the prejudice but also the poor pay and working conditions.

Querying staff at Hamilton's Mountain Sanitorium for employment opportunities led to a meeting in which the young RNAs were well received, treated with dignity and hired.

After serving for just under a year at the sanitorium, Ona and Cora were encouraged to seek out the training required to obtain full nursing certification. They applied and were accepted to Chatham General and began the three-year program there in the summer of 1948.

They graduated from the hospital's rigorous and competitive program in June 1951. Wishing to give back to Chatham General upon graduating, they stayed on an extra year. "We were the first black nurses at the Chatham General," Ona told me. True acceptance of black nurses only came, she believes, as a result of its fully integrated training program. Once local white families recognized that "our colour didn't move off onto their daughters, who were also in training, and discovered that their daughters were really good friends with us, and that we had all trained and worked well together, things began to change."

In the fall of 1952, Ona was rehired at the Hamilton General. The following year, she met and married her now deceased husband, Alphonso Allen. The couple started a family two years later. Seven months into caring for their new son, the two agreed to share child care duties, with Alphonso working as a porter by day and Ona working nights at the Hamilton General. Nine years later, Alphonso found work at Ford, finally freeing up Ona to return to day shifts.

She continued on days until her retirement in 1990. During her career, Ona gained experience in nearly every department of the Hamilton General. "I was accepted well in all the areas and by all the doctors there," she recalls. That she was a people person, she says, accounted for a good part for her acceptance. "The profession pleased me," she says with a smile. "I loved nursing."

Looking back, Ona argues it was in the 1950s that the nursing profession first opened up for black people in Hamilton. The extent to which this was true only became clear to her, however, when local hospitals later began hiring foreign nurses in large numbers. "The new girls would arrive and right away they would say, 'Oh, I'm not doing that; we never had to do that,' and they'd complain and complain, and ask for what they wanted," Ona recalls.

In contrast, in her early years, Ona says she mostly did what she was told. It was at this point she recognized how distinct her own experience of the profession had been. When a new West Indian nurse pointedly asked her one day, "Why are you so different from us?" she recalls answering, "I don't know, but I'm a Canadian, and I worked hard to get where I am, even to get to be a nurse."

By then, she believes, few knew or recalled how hard it once had been for a black woman to enter, survive and thrive as a nurse in southern Ontario.

*—by **John McCurdy**, Hamilton, Ontario*

A Long Tradition of Service

The special bond between firefighters and the community they serve is commemorated in a unique fashion

Firefighters within my hometown of Kelowna, British Columbia, have long held a place of honour in the hearts and minds of the people they serve. In September 2011, timed to coincide with the tenth anniversary of the 9/11 terrorist attacks in the United States, the Kelowna Professional Firefighters Association acknowledged the special relationship they have developed with the community over the years by erecting a commemorative statue in front of Kelowna Fire Hall No. 1. Aptly named "Tradition of Service," the statue was donated to the residents of the city, and, in an artistic and compelling way, bridges the gap between the modern era of Kelowna's fire department and its early days.

The origins of the Kelowna Fire Department can be traced back to a bucket brigade formed in the late 1890s. In 1903, the town had its first major fire, in which a local business was burned to the ground. Residents decided afterwards that they needed to organize an actual fire department. Easier said than done, the task was completed by 1909.

The first truck that the department acquired was a Broderick hand-pump truck, built in San Francisco in 1850, one of the first manufactured in the state of California. It took 20 men to operate, and failed to work at times. On May 28, 1928, Kelowna's very first ladder truck was purchased—a 1928 Graham, one of the finest trucks of its time.

In Kelowna, the term "firefighter" has included women as well as men for a very long time. The Women's Volunteers Brigade, also known as the Ladies Hose Reel Team, came into existence during the First World War (1914-1918), due to the lack of men, who were off fighting the war. The ladies were well equipped with boots, coats and masks, and were always prepared to jump into the fray when needed.

Our first fire hall was built at the corner of Water Street and Lawrence Avenue, and is still in use full time today. A beautiful heritage building, it not only still serves a vital purpose but also attracts a lot of attention from visitors.

In 1976, a new fire hall was built on Enterprise Way and it has been the department's headquarters ever since. Now referred to as Kelowna Fire Hall No. 1, this main station is now home to the "Tradition of Service" tribute.

By now, you must be wondering why I know so much about Kelowna's firefighting services. Well, while I don't recall the actual date that our Volunteer Fire Brigade became active, I do know that my father, Fred Coe, signed up on August 29, 1960, and volunteered until April 16, 1979. By the time he retired, he was a captain of the volunteer brigade.

I have many memories of Dad being called out in the middle of the night to fires, but the most vivid in my mind were the 1964 fires at the Kelowna Growers' Exchange: Four KGE packing houses went up in flames on March 14 of that year, which just so happened to be my dad's birthday. He was helping to fight those fires for more than 24 hours and returned home, totally exhausted, still wearing his fire gear with his sodden pyjamas underneath. I was so upset, as he had missed his birthday and all he wanted to do was sleep.

At the time, he was also fighting for his livelihood, as he and three other partners owned the Rowcliffe Cannery, which was only one block away from where these big fires were raging. Our family was very concerned not only about Dad's safety but also about his business future.

My husband Trevor (Terry) Turner was also a volunteer firefighter, starting in 1963, while he worked full time in other positions with the city of Kelowna. In 1977, he became a full-time firefighter and worked hard at the job he loved until his retirement in December of 1991.

The most devastating wildfire near Kelowna in recent times was the Okanagan Mountain Park Fire in August 2003—some 25,000 hectares of forest and 239 houses were consumed, and approximately 27,000 people had to be evacuated. It took 1,000 firefighters and 1,400 members of the Canadian Armed Forces to put that fire out. And to think it all began with a lightning strike.

The Kelowna Fire Department now has 115 full-time personnel and 66 paid-on-call volunteers operating from seven fire stations. Four stations are manned 24/7 by full-time firefighters, and three additional stations are run by the "paid-on-call" volunteers. In addition, there are two full-time staff members dedicated to training and safety.

The fire department is very involved in our community as well, actively promoting fire safety year-round. The Kelowna Professional Fire Fighters Charitable Society donates money raised at their many events during the year to various charitable organizations and worthy causes throughout the city, including the Burn Fund, muscular dystrophy, the Cancer Fund, and the Adaptive Ski Program at the nearby Big White ski resort.

Above all, and in keeping with its lengthy tradition of service, the Kelowna Fire Department plays a big role in providing leadership and a sense of hope during fires and other natural and man-made catastrophes, for which we as a community are tremendously thankful and proud.

*—by **Barbara Turner**, Kelowna, British Columbia*

The Show Must Go On

Foul weather can't stop this traditional fowl supper!

Recently, I was reminded that a group of pink-aproned, fixed-up-hair, fancy-jean-wearing women from rural Alberta are not to be messed with. Resourceful, strong and able to work a draft horse under the table, these women are reminiscent of a small army. Oh, my! Don't get in their way.

Across our wind-sculpted Prairies, some old traditions hold current today. Years ago, fall suppers where folks gathered in churches to chow down on chicken, salads and potatoes were an important way to connect after the gruelling days of harvest were over. These meals were all prepared without running water and electricity and ladies' groups did just that—grouped together and cooked.

As fundraisers for the women's clubs in churches, fall suppers were a place where neighbour after neighbour would show up to visit, eat and enjoy a short program of entertainment. My grandma remembers as a child being all shined up and waiting upstairs with a nervous stomach for her number to be called to eat. The nerves weren't for the meal, but for the program afterwards that the children helped put on.

Now, our fall suppers are generally a buffet-style spread of deliciousness. Turkey is served instead of chicken, and potatoes, vegetables and salads adorn the plates. Followed by coffee and pie, it's too bad there aren't couches to have a snooze on afterwards.

As a girl, I washed dishes in the back with other girls from the community. You always wondered who you would get to chat with while going through tea towel after soaking-wet tea towel, drying dishes.

Not long ago, I got my own daughters all washed up and ready to head into Swalwell—a hamlet of less than 100 folks about ten minutes from the village of Linden, Alberta—to enjoy a traditional turkey supper. The sun blazed down on the snow left over from two weeks of ice fog that had caused power outages. Folks had been going a little crazy from the lack of brightness in the sky, so the sunshine was welcome. There was almost a spring-like feel in the air as we plowed across muddy gravel roads where the snow was turning to liquid in the ditches.

Heading into the hall, we were greeted with the sound of clattering dishes and the sight of a dim room lit by a few candles on the tables. We might live in the boondocks, but these aren't the pioneer days, no sir. The power, however, was still having major glitches after the weather of the past few weeks.

Apparently, on this day of all days, there was a power outage for several hundred miles around and you could practically hear the women of the town gasping, not daring to open ovens in which turkeys were being browned to perfection. You can imagine the scene: Frayed nerves, nails tapping maniacally on the counter and eyes glued to the clock, waiting for a light to flicker in the kitchen.

In the end, folks from far and wide showed up at our local hall, where turkey was fed to four times the amount of people that live here. These women were something! I have never seen the like, and you would think that I would have been prepared, having grown up in this area—moulded, raised and supported by these ladies.

When the power went out, a stern phone call had been placed to our local electricity provider and a reminder was given to make our teensy hamlet a priority. Forget those communities with hospitals in them—there was near 300 pounds of turkey cookin' around here!

In the hall, murmured conversations led to phone calls and a general consensus that the show must go on! People joke about gas-powered blenders, but folks, with my own eyes, I saw extension cords hauled around, generators brought in and gas-powered blenders actually used. Warnings of "Watch your step!" echoed through the hall.

With blenders whirring to mash potatoes and electric knives coming to life to carve the turkey, these women worked at high speed to make up the time that had been lost to the blackout. At one point, a cheer went up when the lights came on, and like something out of a movie, a collective "Aww!" when the power went off again.

Like an army of ants, these women put a spread on, but I tell you, the process was somewhat scary to behold. I have an awed sort of respect for these gals, in a "heck yes, ma'am, I'll do whatever you say; I know that pink apron means business" kind of way.

If you want to experience a great piece of Prairie history, find a small town in the fall and ask about their turkey supper—you won't be disappointed as you help celebrate the completion of harvest and support a local women's organization.

You might find yourself seated next to an old-timer who'll tell you tales of roundups from years past, or you might meet the tiniest, newest member of the community, swaddled up tight. No matter who you cross paths with, you will be the better for it.

It might not be as exciting as our last supper was, but it will have some sort of tasty pie to punctuate whatever adventure it will hold, and, believe me, all are welcome.

*—by **Cheyenne Stapley**, Linden, Alberta*

Forging New Friendships

Gaining new appreciation for their home country and province through cultural exchange

Just as my husband, Joe, and I retired, a neighbour introduced us to the Friendship Force, an international cultural exchange organization that aims to build global goodwill through personal friendships. Its motto is: "Changing the Way You See the World."

We have always enjoyed travelling and looked upon the Friendship Force experience of cultural homestays as an opportunity to become immersed in the local culture and make new friends with other members in a few of the nearly 60 countries around the world where clubs are located. In the past 11 years, we have had the pleasure of travelling to many countries, including Brazil, Japan, Russia, Hungary, Romania, Australia and Germany, as ambassadors of Canada and our local Winnipeg club. We have made wonderful new friends and had fascinating experiences we would not have enjoyed as normal tourists.

Another benefit of Friendship Force is being able to host ambassadors of other clubs from around the world. We have learned that Canada, with 21 clubs, is the most requested country to visit within the Friendship Force organization. We have been fortunate to host visitors from Mexico, Brazil, the United States, Russia, Peru, Czech Republic, Australia and Japan. They have rewarded us with their friendship and through their eyes we have gained a new appreciation of our city, Winnipeg, and this country of Canada.

Our visitors, especially the Japanese, have been impressed by our vast, flat prairies with vistas that seem to go on forever. Many guests have remarked about the bright blue of our skies and the clean air. Other ambassadors from European countries have been in awe of the huge size of the Prairie farms. Mostly, they have been impressed by the space we have in Canada with such a large land mass and so few people.

Manitoba is noted for its forests and lakes, and our new friends, many of whom have come from large cities, have been delighted to spend time "at the lake" swimming in the pristine waters, learning to paddle a canoe or just relaxing in the tranquility of our great outdoors.

A lot of tropical and semi-tropical countries do not have noticeable seasons and many of our ambassadors to Winnipeg have enjoyed the beautiful colours of autumn. The tree-lined streets of Winnipeg and our country roads and lakes put on a glorious show in the fall season. Our many beautiful parks, rivers and open areas are always appreciated by our guests.

While many Canadians go south to seek warm weather in winter, guests who came from Australia in mid-February to experience a Canadian winter were astounded when walking on our frozen rivers and driving on our frozen lakes. Many of them had never seen snow and the brilliance of the sun on newly fallen snow. The speed of a live hockey game surprised them. Having never seen a game of curling, they tried their skills and soon realized that it was a difficult but fun game to play. A Californian guest remarked that ever since she had learned to sing "Jingle Bells" as a child, she had longed to take a horse-drawn sleigh ride—something we as Canadians largely take for granted. Another commented that coming to Canada in wintertime had been a lifelong dream fulfilled.

The Manitoba Museum always wins accolades for its outstanding representation of our province's history, geography and culture. Our free and peaceful multicultural society is the envy of many countries and we have been happy to highlight a few of our local Winnipeg communities for our guests. A presentation by an Inuit speaker drew rave reviews from our guests. First Nations, Ukrainian and French history, food, colourful costumes and entertainment are always enjoyed. Visits to the Icelandic town of Gimli, to Hutterite colonies and to Mennonite communities have provided glimpses into other local cultures.

The high standard of living in Canada has been praised by our guests. Others have been surprised by the peaceful society in which we live. They were impressed that there is no need for large numbers of police to be visible on our streets and roads, and also that they are approachable and friendly. Still others have remarked on the participation of women in all areas of Canadian life. And, best of all, they have told us how comfortable they feel in our beautiful country.

All of our visiting ambassadors have enriched our lives and given us a new perspective on and appreciation for our city, Winnipeg, and this great land of ours. They have changed the way we see our country: Canada.

*—by **Valerie Keenan**, Winnipeg, Manitoba*

Breaking Boundaries

This mom-and-son pair push their limits every day

I am a single mother of an amazing 16-year-old named Dylan—my world, my inspiration and my motivation. Born with spina bifida and confined to a wheelchair, Dylan refuses to limit himself by the boundaries forced upon him. The honour of being his mother has inspired many of my endeavours in life.

My outlook and perspective have been influenced in such positive ways thanks to Dylan. Obstacles for us are merely opportunities to be creative, learn adaptability and grow stronger together. Dylan is the reason I began my fitness journey in 2005.

I remember sitting in my dining room one morning and thinking about the future. I watched Dylan transfer himself from his chair to the sofa and it dawned on me: "He isn't always going to be this small!" I realized then that I needed to be physically stronger for him—I needed to be his "legs." With the help of a good friend who was a personal trainer, I started weight training for physical strength, but it wasn't long until a healthy lifestyle was my way of life. I became stronger for me!

I watched my first novice-level bodybuilding show in 2007. I realized that very day I wanted to step onstage. I committed to participating in my first show that same year as a wee middleweight contender and placed dead last, fourth out of four ladies. I didn't care about the placement—I had achieved my goal, found new inspiration and was born into a family of fellow competitors and lovers of the sport of bodybuilding.

I have continued to pursue this passion. I switched from being a female bodybuilder to a different category called "Figure." It encompasses both muscularity and feminine beauty, all together as one package onstage. I don't get to flex my way through the shows anymore, but I am always striving to be better than I was before and to inspire others along the way.

I am also proud to be able to share this passion of mine with Dylan. We are a busy, goal-setting mom and son aiming for great things.

Dylan plays competitive wheelchair basketball—he has ambitions to play provincially in the future and a long-term goal of national-level status. Dylan is also an Alberta and Canadian record holder in para-powerlifting; he hopes to participate in the Parapan Am Games and his sights are also set on the Paralympics. Dylan is training, with me as his coach, and hopes to represent Canada in both the junior and men's open divisions in the under 59-kilogram category.

Another aspect of my life is nursing, my professional calling that was driven, again, by Dylan shortly after he was born. As a result of Dylan's ongoing medical needs, I had a desire to be a better parent through education. I knew I could also be a source of strength for others, especially those with a special-needs child. I enrolled in a four-year Bachelor of Science degree in nursing and graduated in 2004. I extended my academic pursuits by specializing in the operating room and have practiced in this area ever since. I am grateful and honoured to be involved in peoples' lives in this way.

I will always be an operating room nurse, but I also involve myself with perioperative nursing education as a clinical nurse educator. I teach and promote this specialty and am continually emphasizing the importance of further education. I have hopes of facilitating research on a few nursing topics, such as developing a program that reduces pediatric anxiety in the operating room, which will hopefully be utilized in health care settings and published in various scholarly nursing journals.

In 2014, I spent time in South America for mission work, providing new hips to people in Ecuador. I had the good fortune to work with the very surgeon who is Dylan's orthopedic specialist, one who has provided numerous life-changing and life-improving operations for my son. This has sparked an intense desire to do more, to give more. I plan to return to Ecuador in the future and am looking to participate in other medical-based mission work as well.

I think I'll always love to lift and to improve myself in all facets of my being. My number one source of inspiration will always be Dylan, who far exceeds any limitations society expects of him or that his own body has set upon him. Through Dylan, I am reminded daily of what we can do when we set our mind and our heart to the task!

*—by **Tracey Rice**, Grande Prairie, Alberta*

Beaver Tails and Bear Paws

Tasty illegal treats?

For the better part of the last century, my family has lived, worked and played in the Canadian wilderness. Our careers and hobbies generally centred around activities that included aspects of the Canadian environment. Wildlife photography, hunting, fishing, outfitting and other outdoor pursuits ranging from canoeing and horseback riding to snowshoeing and dogsledding filled our days. Careers such as park warden, forest ranger, trapper, land use officer, conservation biologist, wildlife rehabilitator and survival teacher are all represented within our immediate family.

I know this type of family life is not common in the urban areas of Canada where I now make my home, so while I may have routinely swum in frigid northern lakes, sucked the nectar from kinnikinnick, dined on muktuk and caribou, and even played with "domesticated" wolves, I don't often encounter others who may have had such wonderful experiences.

It was therefore with some surprise that I had a conversation about eating beaver tail with a friend and colleague. She began by telling me about a recent trip she had taken to Montreal, where she had eaten a deep-fried beaver tail. Realizing that northern fare is often shipped to big cities for special events—fresh arctic char served at a New York gala, for instance—I took her news in stride. I replied that I had never eaten deep-fried beaver tail, but given the amount of fat, it would likely be quite tasty.

"Yes," she agreed, "totally delicious, especially once you pour the maple syrup over it."

"Now, that would taste good!" I answered, remembering my own childhood enjoyment of the simmering pots of beaver tail and beans that my mother would make. I imagined this sweetened with a hint of maple syrup—mmm, delightful! Something of these memories and imaginings must have shown on my face, because my friend looked at me and exclaimed:

"Not real beaver tail! It's a pastry called Beaver Tail."

I stared blankly at her for a few moments while I tried to adjust my thoughts to this new and strange idea. When she started to laugh at my confusion, I couldn't help but join in. We laughed so hard our sides hurt. For me, at least, it was a memorable moment.

A few weeks later, my niece and I were browsing in a local bookstore, and upon finding the Canadian questionnaire in author Will Ferguson's book *How to Be a Canadian,* I shared the story of my social faux pas with her. I guess it was still funny—she laughed and so did a fellow shopper standing next to us. Our fellow shopper felt emboldened enough with this camaraderie to confess that she herself had recently eaten a bear paw for the first time. I gasped; my niece's eyes widened.

"You can't do that," I told the lady quietly, not wishing to cause her too much embarrassment.

"That's so illegal," my niece explained. Taken aback by our obvious horror, our new friend seemed to shrink and back away.

"It's a type of cookie!" she squeaked.

A cookie? Again, a few moments elapsed while my niece and I looked at each other and tried to understand the new reality called a bear paw cookie. Once again I started to laugh, as did my niece. We turned to share our delight with our fellow shopper, but the bear-paw-cookie-eater had quietly and speedily disappeared...still, we're all Canadians, eh?

*—by **Karen Taylor**, Edmonton, Alberta*

Bilingualism at Its Best

Learning to speak two languages in one sentence

I am lucky because my two wonderful grandchildren, Meredith and Benjamin, have always lived next door. They are adults now and have busy lives, but I still see them often. When they were young, they spent a lot of time with me. During our visits together, they often said things I found amusing and, for fun, I started writing about those occurrences.

Ben, at four years old, was already bilingual, but he used both languages in the same sentence. I really noticed it one day when he was playing at our house, pounding nails in a board with a hammer. He stopped pounding, so I looked to see what he was doing. He was trying to balance the hammer on one finger and, when he saw me watching, he said, "Look, I hold the *marteau* with one *doigt;* I gooder than you." Well, maybe he is "gooder" at balancing his hammer on one finger, but I speak "gooder" English!

When Meredith was around two-and-a-half years old, it was hard to have a conversation with her. Her parents spoke both English and French to her and at that time, Meredith wasn't fluent in either language. In fact, when you began your conversation, you first had to try and figure out which language she was using, and then try to determine what she was saying.

Her other grandmother even gave up for a while. Because she didn't see Meredith very often, she couldn't understand her at all and finally declared, "It sounds as if that child is speaking Japanese!"

Just a few examples: "I going out *dehors.*" That one isn't too hard to figure out. Then, *"Je veux un* Ralph." That one means "I want a dog." My sister's dog was named Ralph and Meredith loved him.

My daughter-in-law suggested to Meredith she call her grandfather Pop, but she couldn't get it right and it somehow became "Putt." She called her little brother Ben "DoDo," because when he was a baby everybody was always telling her, *"Il fait dodo."* If you wanted to know if she would like to go swimming, you asked her if she wanted to "Go boom *dans l'eau."* That one is too complicated to explain!

Finally, the day I found myself telling her, "Don't put that in your *bouche* because it is *sale,"* I decided that, after all these many years of struggle, thanks to Meredith, I was finally bilingual. Hurrah!

*—by **Dorothy Hannah**, Lacolle, Quebec*

Boot Camp, Indigenous-Style

The ancient Indigenous art of mukluk-making brings cultures together at the "Storyboot School" in Toronto

As thousands of Canadians slept in on their day off, or headed to brunch with family and friends, a group of people came together on a Sunday for the Manitobah Mukluks Storyboot School at the Bata Shoe Museum in Toronto to embark on a project: the wonderful yet complicated task of creating traditional Indigenous mukluks. This may seem like simply an art class full of crafty people to many, but for this Indigenous woman, it means so much more.

Recently, there has been so much incredible work done around the concept of reconciliation. For many people, Canadian and Indigenous, this word seems like a light of hope at the end of a long, dark tunnel. However, if you sit down and ask someone what reconciliation means to them on a personal or practical level, the answer is often, "I have no idea." It is a concept that is attractive and fills Canadians with a warm, hopeful glow, but it is often difficult to translate into meaningful action.

As an Indigenous person, I have asked myself this question many times. I don't claim to be any great political thinker; however, I am well aware that I am a political being. Most Indigenous people are—we have to be. Our country's history, one of political and cultural interaction, has been tumultuous, to say the least. At the core of this broken relationship was lack of respect, understanding and compassion by the mainstream society towards the Indigenous nations. As an Indigenous person, I can only speak to how this relationship affected Indigenous peoples. Our nations have been impacted at every level: socially, culturally and politically. We've been devastated by the impact and legacy of governmental policies that sought to eradicate who we were. We are still reeling from this today.

However, there is hope. Today there is a new generation of people who optimistically seek an equal, socially just and stronger Canada.

The question remains, though: How do we do this on a foundation with such enormous cracks? How can we reconcile? How can one person embrace reconciliation?

In the words of hereditary Chief Dr. Robert Joseph of the Gwawaenuk First Nation, "Reconciliation has to begin as an inside job," meaning you have to start within you. In your heart and spirit, you have to commit to making change at a personal level.

At the Manitobah Mukluks Storyboot School, 18 youths came together to do just that. This group of both Indigenous and non-Indigenous people got to work on this "inside job." Whether they know it or not, they staked a claim on reconciliation through the act of cultural revitalization.

How is mukluk-making considered reconciliation? I grew up seeing groups of people beading and actively carrying on cultural practices. It would often be around a kitchen table, and there would be tea and gossip and lots of laughs. Through this shared action with my family and friends, we would strengthen our cultural and family ties, as well as share our expertise with one another. This is passed down through generations of Indigenous peoples. This is how we survived and flourished.

For this course, the Bata Shoe Museum, with the generous backing of the TreadRight Foundation, provided guidance with their expertise in sustainability (in particular their support of local artisan activities), hosted students from all walks of life and enabled them to sit down together around a table. They shared a journey. They helped to claw back some of what was lost. They helped to renew a relationship in a very positive way. They shared their personal histories and cultural stories.

In the end, more people know the beautiful art of mukluk-making, and can pass this knowledge on. They learned how hard and time-consuming it is, and developed a hands-on understanding of what generations of Indigenous peoples made to keep their families warm in the winter. They will be proud of their hard work and share in this personal accomplishment with their peers.

Most of all, the reconciliation (through mukluk-making) was done together. It will strengthen the ties between our past, our present and our shared future.

*—by **Waneek Horn Miller**, Ottawa, Ontario*

Heart to Spirit to Hand

From the internal creative process to the creation itself, art is an extension of healing and community-building

I was born in Manitoba of Santee Oglala Sioux parents. I spent my early childhood on my mother's reserve but at the age of six was forced to attend an Indian residential school. I continue to be active in presenting this terrible history to students throughout Canada.

In 1964, I moved to Ontario, where I settled into a career as a legal secretary. I was encouraged by those I worked with to consider taking up law myself. They saw my passion and that I cared about the values of justice and fairness, but after several years in that setting, I realized that the legal system was still a broken thing, in particular in the way it addresses my people's needs and values. Had I stayed in that setting, I knew it would end up making me bitter and angry, which are not what I knew we needed to make the changes my people, and all of the communities we live in, need.

During my time with lawyers, I was asked to take on running a Native Friendship Centre in Cochrane, Ontario. While the Friendship Centres had been established to provide safe places for First Nations peoples, I quickly realized that they had become crisis intervention centres, though without the tools needed to address those crises. Working with the Cree of Northern Ontario, I began to see a direction in my life towards community engagement and healing. It was art, however, that would bring that direction into focus.

Since I was a child, I have drawn from my imagination and from the world. Like breathing itself, perhaps, I would cover whatever spare paper I could find with images and visual stories. Heart to spirit to hand, this just came naturally to me. The drawings were how I would see the world around me, a way of speaking to that world, and slowly over subsequent years, a way of speaking about it.

A chance encounter with internationally-celebrated playwright Tomson Highway while working in Cochrane, where he admired some of my paintings that I hung on my office wall, brought me back to

Toronto, where I took on a position with the Ontario Native Council on Justice, addressing the needs of First Nations inmates in and out of Ontario prisons and jails.

The work, after being specifically approved for the position by the Native Sons group at the Guelph Correctional Centre (formerly known as the Ontario Reformatory Guelph), involved doing research and interviewing First Nations inmates and former inmates throughout Ontario, in detention centres and prisons, in district jails, community resource centres, and even at a logging camp back out in the bush. The project was part of what is still an ongoing process of addressing the destructive relationship between First Nations communities and the criminal justice system.

This work began to sharpen my sense of purpose as a First Nations woman, residential school survivor, and slowly, as an artist. I began working with established artists, developing and refining my skills and my vision, always with a clear sense that whatever the work I was doing, it was about building a healing community for my peoples and all the communities they belong to.

In March of 1980, I had my first solo exhibition, at the Thompson Gallery in Toronto. Since then I have exhibited throughout Canada and the United States. My work is visionary in its embrace of resilience, cooperation, and a deep commitment to the spirit and history of my people and of all peoples. But it has not been art alone that has sustained me and guided my work. Art has been a tool for a broader and deeper engagement with the issues most pressing for all of us.

In 1985 with Mohawk composer John Kim Bell, we created the Canadian Native Arts Foundation, later the National Aboriginal Achievement Foundation. It began with a focus on the arts in First Nations communities, but over time the foundation expanded the scope of its support to acknowledge the achievements and the struggles of First Nations communities in a widening range of fields of accomplishment.

The foundation honoured elders for their lifetime of achievement and encouraged and supported First Nations youth as they set out on their own challenging roads to learn their own stories and develop the skills to tell new ones. I continued my work with the foundation for 20 years, before passing leadership on to a new generation. That commitment to speaking across and supporting generations in collaboration with each other has been a key part of my life since stepping down from the foundation.

While continuing as an artist, I have dedicated my time, energy, and resources to working with children not only in First Nations communities but throughout Ontario. I speak to classes of high school students, encouraging them in their visions and their education. I share my stories and my encouragement with young First Nations artists and entrepreneurs, as well as with community groups working on building strong and resilient futures.

I have lent my voice and my art to projects to improve the health and well-being of First Nations women and girls, whether in projects related to maternal and infant health, or most recently, in a collaboration with the Native Women's Association of Canada in their work to raise awareness of the brutal dangers facing First Nations women. I continue to seek new challenges and opportunities to present my work as witness to the power of reconciliation.

*—by **Maxine Noel**, Stratford, Ontario*

Harmonizing Cultures

A meeting of two generations, music genres and cultures

After presenting a paper at the Society for Teaching and Learning in Higher Education conference in Montreal several years ago, I decided to explore the city. Having heard so much about the charm of Old Montreal and the splendour of the St. Lawrence River, I couldn't wait to begin sightseeing and feast my eyes. I needed to feel the rhythm of the city.

I went to the shopping district along Ste-Catherine Street and, as I browsed for shoes for my son, I heard a familiar Bob Marley song. When I looked up, I saw a Rastafarian man (rasta) across the way, strumming his guitar and belting out "Don't worry 'bout a ting, 'cos every likkle ting's gonna be all right..." I smiled and swayed to the beat of the music.

A salesman approached me and, in his Haitian accent, asked where I was from. I answered, "Originally from Jamaica, but I'm Canadian." After he tried out a few Jamaican expressions with me, I said goodbye and went across the street to enjoy the rasta's Bob Marley renditions. By then, a French-Canadian youth had joined him and was rapping during the pauses. It was an amazing mix of reggae and rap. Both men represented different generations and genres. They had just met for the first time and the music was the glue. It was like being at a street party.

After about three more songs, the impromptu concert ended, and the Canadian youth thanked the rasta for allowing him to sing along. As I dropped a tip in his pan, he said, "Irie. T'ank yu, dawta!" Ah! An authentic Jamaican accent. What serendipity! I thought. "You Jamaican?" I asked. He said yes and then invited me to different upcoming Caribbean events in Montreal.

Before we said goodbye, I asked him if he liked living here. He said, "Yeah, man. Canada nice!" I realized we had two things in common. We were both immigrants from Jamaica and we both loved Canada.

I walked away feeling delighted to have met a countryman and wondering what his story was. Did he even speak French? How did he get to Canada? I began thinking about the numerous immigrants I've met since I've lived in Vancouver and visited other cities for conference presentations. Some came to Canada for financial opportunities, while others came to get away from harsh dictators. Everyone has a different story, but the common thread is a better life.

I came here with my husband and two young sons 11 years ago because I wanted to be free and safe. That was how I felt walking around in Montreal: free and safe.

Seeing the rastaman reminded me that Canada truly is like a smorgasbord, rich with diverse cultures. Watching him and the French Canadian underscored one of the benefits of living in Canada: meeting and sharing with people from different cultures. I've met so many people from different backgrounds since I've lived here; learning about their different cultures has been enriching and rewarding.

I walked away feeling fortunate and proud to have been given the opportunity to be a Canadian. After all, as the rasta said, "Yeah, man. Canada nice!"

*—by **Tanya Haye**, North Vancouver, British Columbia*

Conserving Canada's Wild Species

Studying, understanding and fighting for the protection of Canadian plants and wildlife

There is little I value more than the beauty of the nature that blesses Canada—especially the slice of heaven on the edge of the Canadian Shield in Lanark County, Ontario, where I am grateful to live. From the log house on 17 acres that my wife Mary Lou Carroll and I inhabit, I relish daily gifts such as melodious songbirds and peeping frogs in spring; tail-slapping beavers, sun-soaking turtles and yodelling loons in summer; flaming maples, ashes and aspens in autumn; and deer, coyote and fox tracks in winter.

Thrilling me with their magic and infusing me with joy, wild species are essential to my happiness. No wonder, then, that I count myself among the half of adult Canadians who, according to a 2012 survey, have chosen to live where we do in part to be close to nature.

However, as I enjoy our land and other wild parts of Canada, I am saddened by the fraying of our country's natural heritage. A report I recently co-wrote for the national charity NatureServe Canada, and supported by some of Canada's most accomplished biologists, documents 381 species and 188 subspecies that are at risk of being lost forever to extinction. These include flowers, ferns, beetles and butterflies, as well as dragonflies, fish, turtles and snakes. The list also includes songbirds, seabirds, bats, seals, whales and more. Two hundred and thirteen of these animals, plants and lichens are found only in the "True North strong and free," meaning that Canada alone has responsibility for their fate.

Since 1844, at least 16 animals and plants formerly of Canada have gone extinct, from the famous passenger pigeon to the virtually unknown Macoun's shining moss. Biologists cannot yet be certain, but other flora and fauna may be extinct as well due to human activity. For example, the Vancouver Island blue, a butterfly known only on the island, has not been observed since 1979. Honey-flowered

Solomon's seal, a plant known only from a few sites in Ontario and Michigan, has not been seen since 1937.

Many of Canada's species and subspecies at risk have highly restricted ranges. Kluane draba, for example, is a flower whose worldwide population exists entirely within Kluane National Park and Reserve in the Yukon. False northwestern moonwort is a fern-like plant known only from a few locations along the north shore of Lake Superior. The Ungava seal, uniquely living year-round in freshwater, dwells within a handful of lakes in northern Quebec. They, along with 108 other animals, plants and lichens are "critically imperiled" across their global distribution—perilously close to extinction.

Some other species and subspecies at risk have very wide ranges. Among them are the ghost tiger beetle, known from five provinces and 36 American states; piping plover, a shorebird known from nine provinces and 38 states; and the hoary bat and silver-haired bat, both known from nine provinces and all 50 states. Despite such breadth of geography, each of these is now globally vulnerable to extinction.

The good news is that extinction due to human activity can, in many cases, be prevented. An inspiring example is that of the Vancouver Island marmot, Canada's rarest mammal. Once numbering fewer than 30 in the wild, there are now approximately 200, moving towards a goal of 600 marmots living in three geographically distinct populations. Though still at risk, its future is brighter thanks to the intervention of the Marmot Recovery Foundation and partners such as the Government of British Columbia and several forestry companies.

Looking ahead, I hope Canada will long include room for all of our nation's roughly 140,000 wild species—only about half of which have been scientifically described to date. From the Great Plains ladies' tresses—an orchid found in open grasslands—to the snuffbox, a freshwater mussel persisting in Canada in only two southern Ontario rivers; from the oreas anglewing, a butterfly of the western mountains, to the kiyi, a fish restricted to the depths of Lake Superior; from the hotwater physa, a snail found only in one hotspring complex in Liard River Provincial Park in northern British Columbia, to the Sprague's pipit, a bird of our threatened Prairies; and to so many more species in trouble, I hope that Canada's rich natural heritage—honoured by a maple leaf on our national flag, the common loon on our dollar, and in so many other ways—will persist for generations to come.

*—by **Rob Rainer**, Perth, Ontario*

Recess in the Arctic

A wondrous surprise awaited this teacher from "down south"

From 2003 to 2007, I taught at Moose Kerr School in Aklavik, Northwest Territories, which is west of Inuvik, 20 minutes by air or about an hour by ice road.

Typically, it is too cold for children to play outside at recess during the Arctic winter, but during one particular week, the temperature rose to almost –12°C and outdoor recess had been announced. I shivered at the thought of going outside for a whole 15 minutes; however, I was in for a surprise—a most exhilarating experience, actually!

Did I mention that it was still dark outside? In December, the sun rises in the early afternoon and is out for only an hour or so. At 10:30 a.m., it is still very dark; stars are blinking and at times the moon is shining.

On this day, there was no moon, but the stars were twinkling and the air was so still you could hear wolves howling in the mountains and the neighbourhood dogs answering back. Smoke rose straight into the air from the homes nearby and the smell of burning wood filled my senses and brought back memories of long-ago days in Newfoundland.

Soon it was the excited laughter of children that filled the air. Someone threw a soccer ball and the game began. I had trouble identifying the players, but I knew that they were seven- to ten-year-olds from Grade 3 to Grade 5. Everyone was wearing a bulky snowsuit or a Mother Hubbard parka made by one of the town elders. Toques and face masks covered every bit of exposed skin. Little puffs of air hovered above our heads as we breathed out into the cold morning.

I stood still, enthralled by the surreal scene playing out in front of me. The ball flew back and forth over the snow until the children fell in bunches on top of it and screams and laughter erupted. Someone emerged from the heap with the ball and kicked it, sending everyone scrambling to their feet to race after it again. To my right, the younger children slid down a slide and plopped in the snow at the bottom, emitting excited squeals. The other teacher from "down south" stood there and appeared to be as frozen in wonderment as I was.

Fifteen minutes passed quickly and protests arose when we announced recess had finished. Eventually, all the children lined up and piled inside. Their little faces were bright and red, eyes shining and happy. It was health personified! Everyone grabbed a tissue as they entered the classroom; the cold air had left all of us with a runny nose. I was already looking forward to my next recess-duty day, but most likely the temperature would fall to the normal –25° or –30° and we'd have to stay inside. It had been a rare day.

The experience made me wonder why we're afraid to let our kids play outdoors in a bit of cold weather: I believe we could learn a lesson from north of the Arctic Circle.

*—by **Ann Dwyer Galway**, Paradise, Newfoundland and Labrador*

The Dream of Belonging

Travelling a long road to find his Aboriginal past

This is a story of my journey to seek out my native ancestral heritage. The journey started innocently enough with my mother, Iris Beeler, mentioning she would like to know more about her Aboriginal background. Little did I know the long voyage I would have ahead of me.

As a youngster growing up in Nova Scotia, I always wondered why my sisters and I looked different from the other children. In the schoolyard, and sometimes even in later life, we were taunted and jeered at by our peers.

Being "Indian," the term at the time, was not popular during my mother's childhood either. They were treated with disdain when visiting the general store in town and were not respected by most members of the community. So it was with great surprise that after all these years, my mother finally wanted to be recognized as an Indian under the Indian Act. What a herculean task to undertake.

We gathered what little information we could from libraries, old correspondence and the memories of family members. Then, in 1991, we submitted a request for status under the Indian Act for my mother. We received a letter from the Minister of Aboriginal Affairs and Northern Development denying our request because we didn't have enough proof we were related to an "Indian," as defined in the Indian Act. We were quite disappointed and not knowing what else we could do, the journey seemed at an end.

In 1995, I decided I wanted to claim my heritage and I would not give up until I had a status card in my hand! With the advent of the Internet, I was gradually able to discover more about my grandparents, great-grandparents and so on, through online databases and forums, but especially through email putting me in contact with family.

As anyone who has performed genealogical research will tell you, when you find the answer to one question, you end up with a dozen more. Add to this the fact that records for Aboriginal people are often meagre, lost or destroyed. Many family members existed off the grid, living and dying without ever being registered anywhere. Others got married and changed their names, sometimes more than once! Property changed hands several times and sometimes towns or villages even ceased to exist.

While being in touch with more family members provided a link to my past, much of the information gathered was through storytelling, and was not factual or valuable enough for the government. What my family did provide me with, however, were names and places to begin searching for more information—places such as Elmwood, a town in Nova Scotia I had heard about growing up, as well as the name of my ancestors, the Hammonds.

Throughout the years, I was able to find census records dating back to the 1700s and 1800s, land and birth records, marriage certificates and even ship records from the 1750s when my German and English ancestors came to Canada.

In 2011, my wife and I visited Nova Scotia to discover more. We made an adventure out of it, taking the train from Ottawa to Montreal and then overnight to Halifax. After arriving, we rented a car and went to the South Shore Genealogical Society of Nova Scotia, where I met a distant relative who worked there. I found some information in a book about our family, which we photocopied. I asked if they had a file on my family and they did! Upon opening it, I only found information I had sent them a few years ago. Imagine travelling all that way just to get information from yourself!

We visited other museums and one stood out above all others: the Parkdale/Maplewood Museum. Inside this museum was a large glass cabinet containing artifacts of my great-great-great-great-grandfather, Chief John Hammond! There were also baskets made by the Beelers, my mother's family.

We then visited the old cemetery in Elmwood. Not a lot of people know, including myself for a long time, that Elmwood used to be called the Indian Grant Lands or, officially, the New Germany Indian Reserve 19A. The government of the day told the Indians living there if they wanted to stay, they could, but the lands would become the town of Elmwood and anyone who was Native and married to a white person would lose their status as an Indian. This changed when An Act to Amend the Indian Act, or Bill C-31, was passed in 1985 and restored band membership to thousands of women who lost their Indian status when they married non-Indians.

The Elmwood cemetery is small and surrounded by forest. Walking through the weathered old memorials, I found the moss-covered tombstones of John Hammond, Agnes Hammond and others who I had been searching for all these many years. It was an emotional moment—my journey to find my roots had come full circle.

After some quiet reflection, we continued on our journey, had a wonderful vacation and returned home, armed with all our new information. I assembled all the documents and submitted my application for Native status to the Eastern Woodland Métis Nation Nova Scotia and was accepted.

This organization accepted me as a member and issued a certificate recognizing me as an Aboriginal and I am registered as one in a national registry. My children and my sister's children are now applying as well. I finally have what I always wanted—to be recognized as an Aboriginal in Canada. I am now proud to say, "I am Métis!"

—by ***John A. Gervais****, Embrun, Ontario*

Hunting With Mémère

At 86, this grandma still keeps up with tradition

Finally, a nice day to take Mémère hunting. Every fall, my grandma Gilberte Tremblay and I hunt for partridge. Back in the day, she used to join us for deer and moose hunting as well, but at 86, the long treks in the woods are too much for her now.

I pulled into the driveway of the small house where she lives on her own, and knocked on her door. She greeted me wearing her hunter-orange gear, consisting of her favourite cap and warm jacket—she was raring to go. With a fanny pack around her waist to carry her ammunition, off we went in pursuit of *perdrix,* as partridge are called in French.

These days, we don't do much walking; instead, we drive ever so slowly along trails wide enough for my small pickup truck. When the trail becomes too narrow, we head off on foot in hopes of seeing a partridge or two.

Mémère is always careful not to make too much noise and steps lightly as she scans the bush for any movement. When she sees a bird she wastes no time, aims and kills her supper. She spends little time celebrating and is right back on the search for a second target.

As we walk along enjoying each other's company, we can't help feeling rejuvenated by nature's beauty. We call it a day when Mémère reluctantly complains about leg pains.

I'm so grateful to have such a wonderful grandmother, who enjoys the same hobbies I do. Let's face it...a grandma who hunts is the coolest thing I can think of.

We drive back to her place, clean the birds and fry them up in a pan with butter. We toast each other with one of Mémère's favourite beers as we wonder how many partridges we'll bag next year.

—by ***Carmel McDonald****, Garson, Ontario*

TALENT

Drawing inspiration from their home and native land, gifted Canadians share their creative journeys

Learning to See

Art comes from within, not one's ability to hold a brush

Though not always a career choice, art has always been a passion. When I was young and our family went to the little country church Sunday mornings, I was too young to follow the sermons, so I'd sit next to Grandma and draw on the back of the bulletins. I liked drawing the delicate flowers on the organ or the intricacies of the decorative hat in the pew ahead of me. My kindergarten teacher often commented on how nicely I coloured and I amassed a collection of neatly completed colouring books. Although there was never an "Aha!" moment, those events started me on my lifelong journey into the world of art.

The path that brought me to this point in my art career has been winding. My sister, Luana, and I were born missing some toes and fingers. The doctors told my parents that we would never walk or hold a pencil. I guess I'm like a kid—tell me what I can't do and that's the first thing I'll accomplish!

As a young adult attending Northern Illinois University, I thought about majoring in architecture because I loved precision drafting. But I soon became disillusioned with its rigidity, so I switched to illustration. Ironically, I minored in math and science. This was unusual, as most art majors minored in art history or something related to art.

Events in my life took me away from the world of art for a while but not forever. Moving to Hamilton for my husband Joseph's job in the early '90s, I started my journey back to creative expression. It was there that I was introduced to one of my mentors, Trisha Romance, a watercolour artist, at a local autograph-signing event. This proved to be a turning point for me. I was captivated by Trisha's ability to express beauty and emotion in watercolour, so I decided to pursue that avenue myself.

While Trisha made watercolour look easy, it proved to be a challenge. My precise, calculated style made it difficult to achieve the fluid medium of watercolour. Still, I persisted. I had some success and my love of art was rekindled. I began honing my ability to see shapes, value and proportion—elements that make for beautiful portraiture.

Another turning point came in an unexpected way. I watched *All My Children.* There, I admitted it. But this time, it wasn't a cliffhanger episode that got my attention; rather, it was an interesting profile after the end of one. Back then, Judy Scott Weldon did a series portraying local citizens who made a difference with their profession. Her segment was only a minute or two in length. On this particular day, she spotlighted Mark Tumber, a local photo-realistic portrait artist. I had taped that day's soap episode and I kept rewinding it, but it wasn't to catch the drama of the show—it was to watch Mark and his amazing drawings. I was hooked. It turned out he was doing a show at the local mall and I knew I wanted to meet him.

When the exhibit opened, I went to the mall. I was nervous, but I met Mark, who was a true gentleman and offered to look at some of my work. His generosity sealed my love for photo-realism and I was off and running. Once I turned to coloured-pencil drawing, I never looked back.

I found that I loved not just capturing a likeness but also a personality. Candid shots are so expressive and really give a glimpse into what a person is actually like. Children are especially captivating, since they often express who they really are. Unlike adults, they haven't learned to raise a façade in a given situation—what you see is what you get.

Because my work is so detailed, I work from photographs. I prefer to take my own, but people often have favourite photos they email to me. During Christmas and summer is when I'm busiest with many weddings and anniversaries, but my greatest inspirations are the people I love, so my portfolio is full of family members.

Over the years, I sharpened my portrait-drawing skills. Since pretty much everyone has eyes, a nose and a mouth, the key to capturing a likeness is determining how those features relate to one another. Everyone's proportions are different, even identical twins! My math and science education came in handy here because measuring features accurately enables one to draw a person's unique expression.

When I meet people at shows or events, I inevitably hear, "Oh, I can't even draw a stick person." Anyone can measure eye widths and lip fullness. Being born with fingers missing on each hand, I have to hold my pencils with both hands. People are amazed I can draw, but drawing isn't about holding the pencil—it's about learning to see.

*—by **Marcia Godbout**, Innisfil, Ontario*

Russian–Israeli–Canadian Jazz Singer

Nothing fazes this vocalist, not even losing her voice

In May 2011, I found myself at a studio in New York, cutting a record with some of the greatest jazz players—Randy Brecker, Gil Goldstein, Larry Grenadier—and singing arrangements by the legendary Alan Broadbent and Rob Mounsey. It was an amazing experience and resulted in the strongest album I could ever have hoped to make.

In the Moonlight came out in late September 2011 and shot to the top of the Billboard and iTunes jazz charts in several countries and remained there for weeks. In subsequent months, I toured nonstop. But the journey to that point and up until today has certainly been colourful and I'd like to tell you my story from the beginning.

My career began completely accidentally and no one was more surprised than I! As a full-time, first-year commerce student at the University of Toronto, I only sang on the side at a few shows, purely for fun, and certainly didn't believe a career in music was possible.

I had immigrated to Canada from Israel three years earlier, in 1999, at the age of 16 and my parents had just become employed again. We had no connections in the "biz" or money to invest in my career or pay a lawyer to look over the record deal that was offered to me by the head of Linus Entertainment, who'd heard me at a show. I went for it nonetheless, with the full support of my family. With very little performance experience, I didn't have real confidence per se, but I was excited and curious about what this could turn into. And looking back, I'm happy I took the leap.

My first recording experience was surreal. There I was at the studio, having never even heard my voice on tape before, surrounded by excellent Canadian jazz musicians: Guido Basso, Rob Piltch and Pat LaBarbera. I froze at first, then thought I sounded horrible. I cried a little, but I persevered. My mom would drive me to the sessions and, with each day, I grew happier and happier. If I wasn't studying, I was singing.

I launched my self-titled album at Toronto's famed jazz club the Top of the Senator at the end of 2004, when I was 22 years old. I performed at the club for a full week in December. I remember one particular night when I wrote a three-hour accounting exam in the early evening and then raced to make it to my own show. I think I changed in the bathroom at University College.

I toured Canada's jazz festivals in support of the first album in the summer of 2005 and the response was tremendous. I still recall the first time I played the Montreal International Jazz Festival with the crowd going nuts over each song. Or the first time I went to Japan and discovered huge posters for the record in Tokyo's biggest stores. For a girl who wasn't expecting any of this, to see my face on the cover of national and local papers, to be selling out venues on my first run and hearing my music on the radio was absolutely mind-blowing!

In many ways, however, I wasn't ready. My voice was not prepared to handle an intense touring schedule. Because all of the gigs were high stakes, I pushed myself to the limit to deliver the goods night after night. That's when the muscle-tension patterns I had struggled with for several years became entrenched thereafter.

I went on to record my sophomore album, *Make Someone Happy (MSH)*, at the end of 2006. It was a tremendous growth experience. I was a lot more confident and assertive and felt like I had a lot of emotional energy and some experience to bring to the project.

Steve MacKinnon, my wonderful producer, agreed. The personal and emotional record resonated with people, even though when I listen to *MSH* now, I'm struck by how green I sound, but perhaps that was the appeal. The song "Being Green" touched upon my struggle with and acceptance of, my "otherness." "Undun" dealt with my turbulent inner world and the title track was all about my relationship with my then boyfriend, now husband, Casey.

The album really connected with fans and critics, but when it won the Juno for best vocal jazz album in 2008, I was completely overwhelmed. All I could think about was how far I'd come from Ufa, Russia, my home until my family moved to Israel when I was seven years old.

All along, I continued touring. The audiences got bigger and the venues more prestigious. In December 2008, I was back in the studio to record my third album, *Take Love Easy.* Every minute felt like magic. I would get home from the studio at 2 a.m., feeling elated. I had never been more confident and creative, or sounded better. A few days after we finished recording, Casey proposed. Life couldn't have been better.

Then, in early 2009, I lost my voice. Years of touring, improper technique and stress caught up to me and localized in the most important, most defining place in my body: My voice box. I was devastated! I went for weeks without speaking, refused to go out and had to reschedule important shows. It was a very dark chapter of my life.

Months later, I began playing again, but my mood was still pretty dark. *Take Love Easy,* which I was so proud of, failed to live up to expectations because I couldn't tour or promote it. I was still living in fear of vocal distress.

I took some time off in 2010, had foot surgery and went back to school to finish my commerce degree, which had been on hold. By early 2011, I was ready to go back to music. I was hesitant, but I knew I had to jolt myself back into life!

I finished my last exam in April 2011 and was in New York, singing, by May. I had been in vocal training for four months and all the hard work had paid off. Going in, I knew I wanted to make a lush, romantic album, more interesting in texture than my previous records. The song selection reflects that as well, with *In the Moonlight* leaning more heavily towards ballads and mid-tempo material. I was able to record songs I've always wanted to, such as "Till There Was You" and "No More Blues," as well as songs that were newer to me, such as Feist's "So Sorry," and Gainsbourg's "Ces Petits Riens"—I relish any opportunity to sing in French. Everything came together so beautifully, I couldn't believe it. I was back! The traumatic voice loss had a much weaker hold on me. I had a renewed sense of my place in music.

In April 2012, I returned to Russia to play my first public show in one of Moscow's legendary theatres, a mere stone's throw away from the Kremlin. It was an incredible experience to stand on that stage in front of 1,100 people, singing in English, French and my native Russian with my own band. It was also the first time my grandparents, aunts and uncles had an opportunity to see me perform. It was emotional beyond words and the only time I have ever cried onstage. Miraculously, the waterworks only came at the encore.

I felt like I had come full circle: There I was, in the country where I was born, playing music I love, with and for the people I love, including my Canadian husband, Casey, who flew there with me. My past, future and present collided in a thrilling musical moment.

May 2013, however, brought me the greatest gift of all: My first baby, Jacob Miles, and I adore motherhood. As amazing as it is to sing for fans, nothing compares to seeing my child's face transform with an enormous smile at the sound of my voice. From the moment we brought Jacob home, we've been playing fantastic music for him and he really responds. I guess love for quality music is part of his makeup.

It seems as though spring is when the best things in my life take place. A few shorts days after I gave birth, Canada's True North label put out a "Best of" collection of my work called *Her Very Best... So Far.*

I'm in a great place and the future couldn't be more exciting. I've spent years touring the world with the best bunch of guys in the business and now I have an incredible family to ground me. I am and always will be a singer, but I am also a wife and, incredibly, a mother. There's a lot to sing about. I just love my life.

—by ***Sophie Milman****, Toronto, Ontario*

Saving Shoebox Memories

Taking old photos trapped in dusty albums and bringing them to contemporary light

I began my art career by accident. It started when my mom provided me with my first sewing lesson, around the age of ten, and I have been exploring how to create with needle and thread ever since. I also have to credit my father with introducing me to vintage photographs. He was an amateur photographer and, one day, I was presented with this small, cloth-covered box. Hidden inside were these amazing vintage negatives, circa 1920.

This small gift started my obsession with exploring the concept of what I call "sustainable memory." When you consider how a snapshot has many details and stories to tell, and how the photographic medium has changed so drastically in our current digital age, the preservation of memories through a tangible object has become less important than the story that is embedded in that object.

Stored away in albums, shoeboxes and scrapbooks, I have close to 100 years of family photographs. I have been tasked with being the family "Keeper of the Archives," and this responsibility has turned into an obsession to expose the trapped memories in these pictures and incorporate them into a contemporary art piece.

Primarily self-taught, I have attended classes at New Brunswick Arts and Crafts College, George Brown College and the Stratford Festival of the Arts. I have continued to study throughout my life, including working on an art degree at the University of Guelph.

Over the years, I have tried my hand at several artistic mediums, including sculpture, painting and printmaking; I even run printmaking workshops. I am always lured back to fibre, however, and so the stitch often appears in my mixed-media work.

My hybrid art begins with scanning an old photo or its negative into my computer. I then play with software, like Photoshop, to manipulate the photo into something a little more contemporary than the original image. The image is then printed on specially treated cotton fabric, using archival inks. Finally, I apply by hand my freestyle straight stitch to add texture and colour.

My imagery challenges people to enter my debate as to what is more important to salvage—the emotional memory or the physical memory. Our memories are fragile and precious and if we don't constantly and lovingly revive them, they soon become forgotten in an old shoebox. I've had great discussions with people, especially friends, about digital photography and how those photos never go anywhere beyond the camera chip; we debate the purpose of taking a photo, if not to form some physical memory of when it was taken.

I also occasionally challenge myself with installation projects where I encourage people to get up close and personal with—and add to—my perception of sentimentality. At a high school and later at a local library, I displayed my "Take a Memory—Leave a Memory" project. Photographs from my personal collection were displayed on a French bulletin board, a visual tool that facilitates the sharing of creative ideas. Visitors were asked to select a photo that triggered a personal memory of their own and write a letter to me describing the memory. In turn they could keep the photo printed in the size of a trading card. I was thrilled to receive almost 200 letters from the two installations.

I want viewers to know that art is both friendly and accessible; it can result in an amazing experience for all involved, from artist to gallery-goer. They are encouraged to fill in the blanks with nostalgia, emotions and memories of their own.

—by ***Mary Kroetsch****, Guelph, Ontario*

Woven in History

Barn quilts celebrate the stories of our creative and hard-working ancestors

As I biked through southern Ontario one day, a brilliant green emblem with geometrical patterns on a barn in the distance caught my eye. I wondered what the design signified—a family emblem, or a creative artist displaying his or her genius for all to enjoy? A few more kilometres down the road, I noticed another mysterious large panel of colour on the side of a church. It had a large acorn in the centre surrounded by orange and red leaves framed by a black diamond shape.

By the time I reached the hamlet of Sparta, I'd seen three more outsized geometric-design billboards. When I came upon yet another, I had to stop and take a photo of the blue, yellow and white block patterned board outside the Winter Wheat Folk Art laneway. With my curiosity piqued, I discovered that this is one of many unique, historical "barn quilts" and one of Elgin County's original 20 designed to celebrate southwestern Ontario's storied past.

Two four-foot-by-eight-foot plywood sheets make up one giant quilt block, each of which unfolds stories of communities, events in history and the region's families. Part of an initiative started in 2011 by the EON (Elgin, Oxford, Norfolk) Museum Association to increase tourism, barn quilts now cover the Sand Plains Region, encompassing five counties—Elgin, Oxford, Norfolk, Middlesex and Brant. There are more than 100 quilt locations along these roads devoted to preserving, recounting and drawing attention to our rich rural heritage.

The Elgin County Barn Trail starts in West Elgin with "Peace Star," located on the sixth-generation Ford farm. This quilt represents the story of Thomas Ford from Edinburgh, his family tartan colours and how the United States government forced him to fight against his countrymen during the War of 1812.

Travelling eastward along the trail through hamlets, historic settlements and townships offers more of these heritage-designated landmarks. One of my favourite designs is the intricate "Irish Star" on the barn at the Backus–Page House in Dutton/Dunwich. The house was built in 1850, but each point on the star represents one of the four founding families, who arrived in 1809.

"Bike Wheel," in Malahide, epitomizes the depth and influence southern Ontario had on life in Canada. Perry Doolittle built the area's first bicycle in Elgin County around 1860 with the help of a local blacksmith. He was a decorated racer and Trans-Canada road system advocate who also invented a widely used bicycle braking system and helped found the Canadian Automobile Association.

While following this Barn Quilt Trail, I ended up at the Sparta Church Museum and Cultural Centre, looking for a specific barn quilt called "Drunkard's Path." It looks like a psychedelic puzzle piece, but the noticeboard below it tells a different story. The Temperance Society used it as a symbol for sobriety after excessive drinking had become a major concern in the village of Sparta in the late 1800s. Not only did I find this barn quilt but I also found something quite extraordinary: the history of quilting laid out in an astounding array of collected artistry. The church had a temporary exhibit of 50 quilts spread out in front of me in a sea of colours, draped over large display panels, from decades of crafters and woven as early as 1850. It was as if time had stood still.

Here in Sparta, antique quilts represent a big chunk of history all the way back to the mid-1800s. These vintage quilts are much more than stitched fabric squares: They are stories of the lives and legacies of the women who poured their love into each tiny, handcrafted stitch. Their lives were not easy. They laboured to bring children into the world, struggled to keep them alive without modern medicines, and endured hardships in a world without technological conveniences; however, they still found the time to sew, often by candlelight.

Early settlers in Canada were poorly equipped and oblivious to the harsh climates that awaited them, but they had skills in piecing together any readily available fabrics. Based on warmth and survival needs, and not aesthetics, pieced quilts—or patchwork—consisted of simple geometric shapes stitched together to form a square and then sewn together to form strips. Finally, they were combined to become the finished top. There are several traditional styles of pieced quilts, including sunbursts, postage stamps, grandmother's flower gardens, eight-pointed stars and baby's blocks.

Quilts even united communities. In 1930, the ladies of the First Yarmouth (Plains) Baptist Church wanted to commemorate the

100th anniversary of the church by making a signature quilt. For ten cents, names were embroidered on a quilt that would be raffled off as a fundraiser for a new church roof. The names on the quilt reflect many of the families who had and still reside in the communities of Sparta, Union and Dexter—including the raffle winner's name, Billy Bobier.

The museum also has a prize-winning quilt on display. Made in 1984 by Hattie Lawton and entered in a friendly competition at the Aylmer Fair, "Grandmother's Basket of Flowers" won first prize. The appliquéd quilt has about 12 stitches per inch, which is remarkably fine. Hattie was a three-time provincial Canada Packers Quilt Competition champion, and the only person ever to achieve this honour. Her three winning quilts are on display at the Royal Ontario Museum.

I head next to "Garden Maze" on the Norfolk County Barn Trail. It begins at Sand Hill Park and travels along the lake on the waterfront trail up to Port Dover and then heads north to Wilsonville. The quilt block patterns in this geographical area are diverse but profoundly rich in history, denoting the War of 1812, among other things, and depicting early settler practices and stories of triumph.

As I sat and looked at "Star of Hope," located on Front Road near Turkey Point, I thought about those who endured hardships back in the early 1800s and how powerful this symbol's message is even now. It's a reflection of community and hard work, created by those who strove to build memorable artwork and recapture history for us all. It is hope that exists in the shadow of the past.

—by ***Patricia Kuhnen-Beaver****, Port Stanley, Ontario*

G'zaagin: A Gallery of Love

Taking her passion for Native arts and culture and sharing it with the world

I am passionate about Native art, so creating G'zaagin, an art gallery for Native arts and artisans, had been in my thoughts for many years. After experiencing a devastating car accident in 2002, the tragedy allowed me to look at my life from a new perspective. Spending two years in a wheelchair, overcoming critical injuries, frustration, anger and grief, as well as relearning to walk, I came to a point where I realized I no longer wanted to be a victim. I wanted to make a real contribution with my life. After five years of rehabilitation, I became even more determined to make my mark on the world and live larger than life. I opened G'zaagin, which translates as "I love you" in the Ojibway language, in October 2011.

I am an Ojibway-Potawatomi woman from Wasauksing First Nation and my name is Boshdayosgaykwe, meaning, "The first ray of sunlight that comes over the horizon first thing in the morning." My own artwork includes making quill boxes and sewing with leather, both of which my mother taught me, as well as working with fused glass.

I create abstract art with warm glass (heated in a kiln) and dichroic glass (showing two colours). Combining clear, coloured and dichroic glass, I make pendants for necklaces, earrings, bolo ties, ornaments and unity pins of the four colours of the medicine wheel (a sacred symbol). I etch various designs, such as fans and medicine wheels, into dichroic glass that represent my culture and heritage.

The gallery has been open for a while now. With small successes over time, I have had the opportunity to move into a larger space on James Street in Parry Sound, Ontario, which includes a workshop, a lounge for artists, a supply store and, of course, the gallery. This space will not only help my own artwork get out into the world but will also be a place where artists can work and gather and perhaps do projects together. I encourage artists of different mediums to come to the gallery. I would like G'zaagin to be an exciting place to visit with a wide variety of Native art exhibited and for sale that also provides a learning experience for visitors.

Through G'zaagin gallery, it has been a goal of mine to heighten public awareness about Native art and provide a venue for everyone to witness the insights, skills and creativity of Native artists. As G'zaagin grows, I have begun to work with local schools, museums and organized groups that have an interest in Native art and culture, and request tours and learning experiences.

The artists in the gallery are asked to conduct workshops and seminars in traditional craft work. Workshop topics include making traditional porcupine quill boxes, moccasins, dream catchers, medicine pouches, beaded barrettes and hand drums. The workshops are facilitated by myself and artists who rent space in the gallery. The purpose of these events is not only to preserve Native traditional artwork but also to garner a renewed interest in Native heritage and culture. I hope for G'zaagin to be a forum for artists to meet, share and create.

Even though it's been years since my accident, I still concentrate on managing my chronic pain, depression and post-traumatic stress disorder. I have, however, gained a sense of well-being from working on my art and on G'zaagin. I am still learning and creating opportunities daily, and I receive support and encouragement from Native communities and customers who come into G'zaagin with a willingness to learn and understand more about Native culture. It's my time to be grateful and appreciate all that's been given to me and I hope to leave a legacy for my children, family and community—a legacy that is filled with love.

*—by **Boshdayosgaykwe (Tracey Pawis)**, Parry Sound, Ontario*

Helene's Gift

A loving husband's tribute to his wife and her talent

My life truly began when I moved to Canada; I knew that I had found a home in this vast, beautiful country. I immigrated to Canada from Hungary in October 1957 and worked on farms in Saskatchewan for two years. In October 1959, I moved to Red Lake, Ontario, and it is here in this small mining town that I met my wife, Helene.

She was a beautiful young woman from Belgium who spoke Flemish and French. Neither of us spoke English, but we made it work. She arrived from Belgium on April 4, 1960, we met on April 14, I proposed on May 10 and we were married on August 6, 1960. Both our families thought it all was a little too fast and that the only reason could be a baby. It wasn't—it was true love and eventually the babies would come.

Together we loved Canada and knew we wanted to become citizens as soon as we qualified. Helene gave me our two beautiful children, a daughter, Lorraine, in February 1962, and a son, Jozsi, in April 1963.

This isn't about our love story or myself, however; it's an opportunity to honour my wife and her beauty as an artist, while I still can. Time passes, memories fade, talent and skills start slipping away, but traditions shouldn't. The present is essential for the past to be passed along, and it is through my family's generational inheritance that my wife's artistic talents will be remembered, even after she is unable to.

When God asked everyone to stand in line to receive his or her talents, I believe Helene line-jumped a few times. She is an amazing wife, mother, friend and hard worker. But her talent as an artist surrounds me in the home she helped to create for us.

When Helene arrived in Canada, she came with a diploma in seamstress textiles and design. Her dream was to work in the textile industries in Winnipeg and Montreal, but with marrying me so hastily, she followed my career and we settled in Kamloops, British Columbia.

Our quick trip to the altar meant I was to discover her talents as the years went by. Wow, did she amaze me! Helene received her first sewing machine from our best man as a wedding present. It was tradition in those days for many women to make their families the necessary clothing to survive the Canadian weather.

Yet Helene had the background and talent that allowed her to indulge in her "crafts," as she called them, creating and designing wedding gowns for local young brides, as well as bridesmaid and graduation dresses.

While her focus was on our family, she also worked managing a pharmacy and later as a receptionist for two doctors, so her crafts became her creative outlet. The smiles of the brides and happy moments created by these one-of-a-kind pieces were her reward.

She diversified her skills to include knitting and embroidery; she had the ability to take a design from a piece of wrapping paper and use it as the jumping-off point to create works of art. She was a quick study and soon learned crocheting, lead glass painting and tole painting. She often outshone her instructors, producing works of art that even they were in awe of. As an artist, she radiated happiness and excitement over a completed piece as she proudly displayed it in our home or passed it on to deserving friends and family.

In 1990, we retired to Nanaimo, which gave Helene all the time she needed to follow her passions. More wedding dresses followed: gowns, veils and trains all embellished with lace and embroidered with details that she designed.

Recycled materials were the inspiration for diverse canvases upon which she created beautiful painted West Coast Canadian scenes on old milk cans. These art pieces displayed a vast diversity in scenery and multiple cultures.

As her family grew and aged, she tried to pass on her skills and talents to her daughter and grandchildren. They, like many of us, were often too busy to make time for these moments to sit and learn from the artists among us. With the diagnosis of Helene's Alzheimer's, however, time became more precious and everyone wanted to learn what is locked up in Helene's mind. Her diagnosis saddened the artist inside her but allowed everyone else to take a step back and reach out to that artist to learn from her the joy of a paintbrush or needle and thread. Grandma's art, once taken for granted, became a sought-after treasure.

One specific piece cherished by Helene is a tablecloth with intricate details inspired by the flora and fauna in her garden. This tablecloth is painstakingly slow to complete, as it requires a lot of time and energy to repeat the pattern the length and width of our large family dining table. The tablecloth has become symbolic in ways beyond what she first intended. It is nearly complete, not just by Helene's hands but now those of our daughter as well. Thankfully, Helene's gift—her art—will remain.

—by ***Josef Mukli****, Nanaimo, British Columbia*

Towering Over the Prairie

Through years of hard work, what began as a children's playhouse became a full-fledged lighthouse

The whole idea began with the desire to build a children's playhouse—it would be made of stone, in the shape of a miniature lighthouse. The original plan was to have two floors, with a deck and railing on top. Well, as construction progressed, the plans grew—to the height of a five-storey building. The finished project is not a miniature but rather a full-sized lighthouse.

During the summer of 2005, I cleared the bush from the site and excavated into the bank of the Valley River to make a level spot large enough for the lighthouse. The riverbank was too steep to access with power equipment, so my excavating tools consisted of a pickaxe, shovel and wheelbarrow.

By fall, after a few backaches and much sweat, the site was ready. The cement forms were built in the shape of an octagon, with eight-foot-deep piles (holes drilled into the ground and filled with concrete and steel) at each corner. A lot of steel went into the cement to support the huge weight that was to go on top of it. A special type of gravel was dumped at the top of the bank, brought down the steep hill by wheelbarrow, and then mixed with cement and water in a small mixer run by a gas generator to produce concrete.

After that, the first eight wall sections were carried down the hill and assembled. I did the majority of the work myself but did have help from family and friends to complete certain tasks, such as carrying those wall sections down the hill and pouring the main foundation at the base of the lighthouse. Although none were qualified tradesmen, my two sons, son-in-law, two nephews, brother and various friends helped out at different points in the building process.

Most of the lumber in the walls came from spruce trees cut in my own pasture and then taken to a local sawmill to be cut into lumber. Oak was used on all exposed areas because of its resistance to rot.

In the spring of 2006, my wife, Reba, and I began gathering stones for the construction of the exterior walls. Reba picked thousands of stones from our fields at seeding time. When she unloaded them, she'd pick out the prettier ones for the lighthouse project, while the rest of them went along the riverbank to help stop erosion. The stones for the lighthouse walls were all washed with a high-pressure washer and hauled down the hill by wheelbarrow to a stockpile. The stones were mainly four to six inches in diameter and it took approximately 1,800 stones per floor. Cementing the stones was a slow process because only one layer could be done in a day. When that layer dried, the next layer was put up. The second floor was added, making the building 16 feet high at that point. As the weather got too cold for mortaring the stones, more stones were gathered and stockpiled for the following year. During the winter months, the interior was finished in knotty pine and stairs were built up to each floor.

The spring of 2007 arrived and I was pleased to find no cracks in the cement floor or the stone mortar. It was now getting too high to be doing stonework from a stepladder, so I built a small crane that pivoted from the centre of the top floor. An electric winch was attached and the winch cable was suspended from the end of the boom and hooked to a cage, which lifted me, 100 pounds of stone and two pails of cement.

That summer, the third-floor sections were pulled up by rope and fastened together. Next, I built the observation deck, which extended three feet over the edge of the walls. The crane was moved to the top of the deck and the stonework continued. By fall, the stonework reached 17 feet in height with the wood framework above it, making the structure 24 feet high.

In the spring of 2008, everything was still looking good, so the rush was on to complete the rest of the stonework. The progress was slow, but it was finally completed in early fall. I then applied a coat of stone sealer, which really enhanced the colours of the stone. The crane was no longer needed, so it was disassembled and brought down. The deck was sealed with fibreglass to allow rain to run off it.

The following year, in the spring of 2009, a fourth floor was built on top of the observation deck. Eight glass panels measuring six feet in height were assembled on the ground and the aluminum dome was fastened to the top of them. This section was about ten feet tall and would be lifted and placed on top of the fourth floor. As luck would have it, a large crane was working in our nearby town, so the operator came by, had a look and said he could do it.

On July 2, 2009, the crane pulled in with a crew of five men. The guys were quite eager to do something they'd never done before—how many lighthouses do you see on the Prairies? The crane operator swung the top section above the trees and gently set it on top of the fourth floor. After it was secured in place, the crane installed a ten-foot mast with a beacon on top of the dome. In the end, the total height to the top of the beacon is about 50 feet.

The fourth floor was finished with artificial river rock panels, which were easier to work with and much lighter than real rock. A sign above the door reads Meyer Lighthouse 2005; Indian hammerheads—oval-shaped stones with a groove notched around the middle that a wooden handle can be attached to—were placed on either side of the sign.

Unlike today's buildings, many of which have a lifespan of about 50 years, I expect this structure to be standing in 200 years. In 2012, it was hit by lightning, which caused some electrical wiring damage, and then in 2013, it survived a tornado. One time, a couple of young engineers toured the lighthouse and asked me if I'd had an engineer design it. I was proud to reply that it had all come from my own imagination.

The Meyer Lighthouse has become one of this area's best-kept secrets, but more than 300 people sign our guest book every year. We've never advertised it and there is no admission charge—it's been a labour of love and dedication.

—by ***Robyn Meyer****, Gilbert Plains, Manitoba*

Journey of Discovery

For this French Canadian, the process of becoming an author began in Yellowknife

The day my father passed away, a few years ago in March, was an eye-opener for me. I realized my own life was crumbling down. I was not happy anymore with my job and my relationship with my boyfriend seemed hopeless back then. I was sad. Lonely. And exhausted.

All my life, when facing tough choices, my father had always asked me, "What would make you happy?" So, I asked myself the same question. The answer came right away: writing and going to the North. Things I had dreamed of doing for years.

So, I quit my job as a French-language radio and TV journalist, packed up my car, and on a sunny but chilly morning in September—all by myself at the wheel—headed to Yellowknife in the Northwest Territories, a city I had never been to before and knew nothing about.

Eight days, four provinces and three time zones later, I found myself above the 60th parallel on a ferry near a place called Fort Providence, overlooking the majestic Mackenzie River. Shivering on the deck, I had lost my bearings already, but I knew I was on board for quite the adventure.

When I arrived in Yellowknife, just like every newcomer, I noticed the very peculiar beauty of the place right away. Rustic but breathtaking. This city sits, literally, on the Canadian Shield, and it shows. You can see the exposed rock everywhere, with its shades of pink. Yellowknifers say, "You either love the place or hate it. There is nothing in between." I fell in love with the city right away.

One thing you quickly learn when living in one of the northernmost cities in the world is to be open-minded. It's not what you're used to and will never be. It's normal to have a polar-bear-skin rug and a narwhal tusk in your living room, or to see your co-workers wearing moccasins at the production meeting, or to hear the mayor, at the end of each city council meeting, saying, "Stay warm."

My first day at work, at CBC North, was a shock. The topics we discussed, well, I had never given them much thought before: food prices, oil prices, the diamond market, Aboriginal elections. I was lost. A stranger in my own country. That's how the North can make newcomers feel initially. But I learned, and by Christmas, I could produce pieces on any of those topics as if I had been in the North forever.

It started to snow in mid-October as the temperatures were dropping. By the end of the year, it was –40°C, the lake was frozen solid and snowmobiles were passing by on the streets. It was as dark as dark can be. I had no real problem with any of that; I'm a winter person. There is nothing I like more than cold weather, snow and ice, but Yellowknife's winters are challenging. If you go out on the lake for a walk and get lost, you'll die. If you don't dress warmly enough, you'll be in trouble. Here, you have to adjust to nature, not the other way around, and that makes you feel humble.

Things for me changed the day I met Julie. She was from Vancouver and had been living in Yellowknife for a couple of years. All of a sudden, I had a friend to talk to. A friend who, just like me, had pushed herself out of her comfort zone. Julie and I would laugh about pretty much everything and, God knows, our laughter saved us from so many things. You never know what you'll encounter in the North. It could be coyotes roaming around town, an old-school bar fight spilling out into the street or some mysterious-looking stranger from who knows where running away from who knows what. The North really is the last frontier.

On Saturday nights, Julie and I would go for drinks at the Gold Range, a bar in downtown Yellowknife—a rough one. There, I heard so many stories; some sad, others simply beautiful. For instance, I heard how Aboriginal people "call the lights," by scraping their nails together to imitate the sound of deer hooves, which they claim attracts the northern lights. I also met an Inuk guy who was from a city by the Beaufort Sea. He told me how his culture and language were fading away and how different life was becoming in this part of the world. How kids there, instead of hunting or fishing like their forefathers had done for thousands of years, were constantly on Facebook. It was all they seemed to care about.

Then one day, it struck me like a bolt of lightning—I didn't want all these stories I was hearing to be forgotten. And I realized that the best way to keep them alive was to write about them, using my own story—my journey from Montreal to Yellowknife—as the foundation.

I wrote down everything I had experienced living in this unique, small town up north with its wonderful, brave, funny and sometimes odd people. So I started to write, one page at a time, one chapter at a time, and before I knew it, it became a novel. I called it *La saison froide* (*The Cold Season*). To me, that's what the North is all about—an endless winter with varying degrees of light and darkness, coldness and warmth, where one has to survive the harshness to be able to enjoy the beauty and peacefulness.

Eventually, after almost three years up north, I went back to Montreal, polished up my manuscript and managed to get it published via La Presse publishers, who liked the story. During that time, I also began to host a French radio show about the North. Based in Montreal, I got to travel extensively throughout northern Quebec for the program, which provided the creative spark and new subject matter for two more books, *Le retour de l'ours* (*The Return of the Bear*), and *Jusqu'à la chute* (*Until the Fall*). I'm still working in French broadcasting, splitting my time between Toronto and Montreal, with book number four on its way.

The North, as you can well imagine, is still in my head and in my heart. I appreciate what it has given me: the power to free myself of everything that is not essential to my well-being; the strength, patience and confidence to write novels, one page at a time, and thereby change my life for the better; and the humility to see that there is something bigger than our individual selves—this planet, which we all share and should not treat as badly as we do.

—by ***Catherine Lafrance****, Montreal, Quebec*

The Art of the Deal

Thanks to one collector, a master carver's work is returned to his family 85 years after he created it

In the realm of folk art, woodcarving is a popular collectible. The Ottawa Valley was home to a number of folk artists who worked in wood. One in particular, Charles Vollrath from Chalk River, Ontario, was immensely talented; his carvings of wildlife, and angels and other religious items, are highly sought after by collectors. He was active in the 1930s and '40s producing woodcarvings that he sold to tourists at a roadside stand. From that small stand, his carvings were distributed throughout Canada, the United States and beyond.

Recently, a great-grandson of Charles Vollrath read my book, *Folk Art in the Attic,* which included a passage about his great-grandfather. As it turned out, Chad Vollrath wanted to find a carving by his great-grandfather to give his father as a gift. It was nice to receive the email, but unfortunately I knew his search was going to be a difficult one. I certainly didn't have a Vollrath carving in my collection and it had been several years since I had seen one. But I told him I would keep my eyes open and would let him know if I came across any examples of his great-grandfather's art.

A few months later, I decided to make the rounds of a few antique stores here in downtown Ottawa. Popping in once a week to review a dealer's inventory is standard procedure for almost all collectors. I included one store that I visit infrequently. I'm not sure why; just one of those things.

In any event, I climbed the stairs to the second level, said hello to the owner and proceeded to wander through the maze of rooms piled high with all manner of books, paintings, antiques and various collectibles. Some antique dealers prefer the "jumble" approach: Pile the stuff everywhere and anywhere within the shop and let customers have the fun and challenge of looking for a particular item. This dealer took that model to a whole new level.

I wandered here and there through his store and returned to where he was seated in a chair near the entrance. We chatted for a few moments about the state of the antique business in general. My left foot was touching a stack of paintings piled on the floor. Light streamed in through the dusty windows behind me.

Just then, an elderly man emerged from the entrance hallway and took a few steps into the shop area, where he paused for a moment in front of the two of us. He was breathing a little heavily from coming up the long flight of stairs that led to the shop. He wore a beige overcoat that seemed a few sizes too large for him. In his left hand, he was carrying a paper shopping bag; jutting out from the top of the bag were the antlers and the head of a very large woodcarving of a moose. My eyes immediately locked on to the bag. I blurted out: "Hey, is that a Vollrath or Patterson carving?"

"Why, yes, it is by Vollrath," he replied, somewhat startled by my question. The old man crossed in front of me and sat down heavily in the armchair across from the dealer. He placed the bag in front of him on the floor. Slowly, he reached down and extracted the piece from the bag and held it briefly in the air in front of him. I knew immediately this was an impressive carving by Charles Vollrath and, of course, I was anxious to buy it.

The dealer reached over and took the carving and began to examine it. The old man explained that while bringing the piece down to the store, he had broken one of the antlers getting out of the car. Fortunately, he had the broken piece with him and I knew it would be a relatively easy repair.

Any doubt that this was a Vollrath carving was put to rest when we turned the piece over and there was a handwritten label tacked to the underside of the carving. In faint black letters were the words: "Made by Charles Vollrath, Chalk River, Ontario." Vollrath had also carved his surname into the base of the piece. "Are you going to sell that?" I asked the old man.

"Are you interested in it?"

"Yes, I am."

"Well, make me an offer."

I paused at that point because I knew it would be a serious breach of etiquette to attempt a direct transaction with the man, thereby removing the dealer from the process. I changed tactics. I turned to the dealer.

"Are you going to buy it?"

"I might," he replied.

"Well, if you do, I'm interested."

They continued to chat while I stood by and then wandered off several paces away to give them time alone to make their transaction. I realized that this might take longer than I thought. I retraced my steps and stood in front of them. "I tell you what. Why don't I leave you to it? I'm going to go for a walk."

The dealer turned to me and, reaching for pen and paper, said, "Give me your number so I can call you."

"Why don't I just come back in an hour?" I suggested.

"That's good," the dealer said. "Come back then."

I left the shop and continued my rounds of other antique stores and also made a trip to the bank to pick up some funds to complete the transaction, should I be fortunate enough to acquire the carving.

An hour later, I walked into the store. The dealer was still sitting by the front entrance. The old man was gone. There was no sign of the carving. We chatted for a few minutes and he confirmed—much to my relief—that the carving was now in his possession. I told him I knew the carver's great-grandson and I wanted to buy the piece so I could sell it to him and fulfill the dream he had of acquiring one of his great-grandfather's carvings. We quickly agreed on a modest price for the carving and he retrieved it from a room where he had it in safekeeping for me.

I drove home thinking about the fortunate set of circumstances that had occurred. Chad Vollrath contacting me; my decision to visit the shops on that day and choosing the one I don't patronize on a regular basis; the old man walking in with the Vollrath carving and, finally, being able to acquire that wonderful piece so Chad could give it to his father.

After arriving home, I took a photograph of the carving and then sent an email message to Chad. He replied a few minutes later and I gave him an account of what had just transpired. He was excited. Then I sent him the photo of the carving and he was over the moon. A few moments later, we completed our transaction. This majestic carving was going back to the Vollrath family. It was one of those magical and serendipitous moments that occur in collecting. I'm sure Charles Vollrath would be pleased to know that his creation was returning to a member of his family some 85 years after he created it.

*—by **Shaun Markey**, Ottawa, Ontario*

Making History

Writing plaques calls for accurate research, the ability to identify and convey key details succinctly, and a passion for history

When I retired from teaching in 1993, it was easy to remove the teacher from the classroom but not so the teacher from the man. I still had the desire to disseminate knowledge, so I volunteered to join the Hamilton Historical Board and its plaquing subcommittee. Thus I began a personal quest, drafting 16 plaques that present local history in ways that improved understanding and corrected misinformation.

I had a special interest in plaque writing because it meant putting history directly into our neighbourhoods. The endeavour called for accurate research and précis-writing skills—presenting ideas or information briefly, without overlooking any essentials. At the heart of every plaque, I tried to create a memorable "WOW" factor, so that the reader was compelled to say, "Wow, I didn't know that!"

Perhaps most meaningful to me, however, was that I successfully encouraged our city's cultural department to present plastic facsimiles of the community plaques we produced to the neighbourhood schools involved, giving the children there a sense of ownership of their own heritage.

One of the greatest challenges was correcting popular but sometimes inaccurate accounts of Canadian history often recorded in books, magazines and old plaques, or simply embedded in local lore. As one Roman orator once said, "Men are quick to believe that which they want to believe."

The three-year commemoration of the War of 1812 bicentennial provided a golden opportunity and a large stage to review and rectify misinformation that had accumulated during the past 200 years. A defining moment in Canadian history, and a war like no other, the War of 1812 preserved our Canadian identity and rejected a republican form of government. It doesn't get much more important than that.

During research, it soon became evident that there was a complete lack of clarity about the War of 1812. Most Canadians had no accurate perception of what the key was to the successful defence of Canada. And so our plaquing focus was aimed at two themes: the early British success, which gave Canadians confidence, and the essential control of transportation and communication on the Great Lakes, so vital to military success.

Our first opportunity to write a meaningful plaque came with the promotion of the "Brock Walk" program, tracing Maj.-Gen. Sir Isaac Brock's route to his spectacular victory at Fort Detroit in August 1812. En route, he rallied regiments, militiamen and Natives to the cause. At the Head-of-the-Lake, the future site of the city of Hamilton, 250 militiamen (all United Empire Loyalists) joined him, including several leading personalities of the region.

Our plaque commemorating Brock's route was unveiled by a Brock re-enactor at a 100-seat Loyalist dinner. Following the Brock Walk theme, the plaque is titled "Brock Stepped Here" and for a "wow" factor claims that the surrender of the Michigan territory was the largest territorial loss in U.S. history.

The second bicentennial plaque that I wrote was about the naval battle known as the Burlington Races, a daring military clash at the head of Lake Ontario for naval control of the lake that would determine the outcome of the war and the future of Canada. (Wow!) Incredibly, the information on an older provincial plaque was incorrect, based on pure fancy.

On September 28, 2013, an accurate version of the battle, titled "From Fancy to Fact" was unveiled with me wearing my 1812 naval uniform. The event took place beside a walking-trail observation deck at the Lakeview Banquet Centre, overlooking the Burlington shoreline. It was a beautiful day for an unveiling, but few official guests appeared. However, a wedding party and their 200 banquet guests joined us and became part of a joint celebration.

Hopefully, future generations of Canadians will have a better appreciation of the significance of the war on the water, and many other historical events.

*—by **Robert Williamson**, Hamilton, Ontario*

For Better or Verse

This "Limerick Man" turns a fine phrase, loves music and supports worthy causes

There's a hymn from my choir days titled, "I Love to Tell the Story." And I just so happen to have a story I'd love to tell. *For Better or Verse* was hatched when my close friend Anne Jarvis said, "You've got all these limericks; why don't you create some more and write a book?" So I did. Nine months later, in 2017, I self-published the book.

Many of the limericks I already had on hand were written back in 1997, and were inspired by the 350-voice choir I sang in. We'd spend a half an hour or so before practice showing off our literary chops and many of my limericks came into being right there, usually as a tribute to my fellow singers, like this one:

"Will you ever forget our wee Pat

She was known as a swingin' hep cat

Pat went out each night

Till dawn's early light

Then sat with the milkman to chat."

As was the case for just about everyone my age—I'm now in my 90s—my life was influenced by the Second World War. At age 15, I went to work in a pay office, as the men of age were off to war.

When my turn came, I served in the Army Depot Pay Office. After the war, thanks to the Army Rehab provisions, I was sponsored for three years' worth of high school in six months, followed by a Bachelor of Commerce degree, which took three years. I then immediately proceeded to become an articled student in a chartered accountants' firm. All this nonstop pressure subsequently brought on a nervous breakdown, but that's another story.

I married in 1954 and my wife Kate and I moved from Toronto to Victoria, settling onto a waterfront property at Prospect Lake, where I wrote many more limericks, like this one about our dogs:

"When Pedro brought Belle to the door
We wondered what next was in store.
Poor Belle was a wreck,
Kate said: 'What the heck,
We've plenty of love for one more.' "

Getting my book published was a learning experience, as the printing company was hung up on computers, and I was hung up out in dinosaur land. So, I learned about computers, at least what was needed for the book to see the light of day. In the initial stages, I was given more than 100 pictures to choose from for the cover. Snow-covered mountains just could not compete with the dog that won the job. Feedback from sales: "Love the cover!" Yeah, but what about the limericks, I wondered!

"If limericks bore you to death
Recall what the Bible has saith:
Don't do adultery
Unless she is sultry
Then go to the priest and confessth."

In case you want to know more about the "Limerick Man," as I've been referred to, I'm a guy who paid the rent by being an accountant, but my real passion was music. After the war, my first stint education-wise was at the Toronto Conservatory of Music. At the risk of name-dropping, a certain Robert Goulet was also studying there at the time. I lasted one month before it became obvious that putting bread on the table was not likely to happen for me via that route. So I switched to commerce.

The chartered accounting firm I was first hired at was actively seeking students and, believe it or not, the first question they asked me was, "Do you play ball?" Back in those days, many firms were so large they could field an entire baseball team from their latest crop of students. As a left-handed first baseman, I had it made! I still have a photo of our winning team hanging on my wall to this day.

On the music side, I ended up with a Grade 10 certificate as a baritone soloist and a Grade 8 piece of paper for the piano. During my stay at one church, the organist and I produced an LP, with all the proceeds going to the church, of course. I've also played the trumpet in dance bands, trios and community organizations. One of my early memories is of a trip to Williams Lake—my first flight ever—and it looked like we had landed in a farmer's field. Our house band from the Club Sirroco was scheduled to play for Princess Margaret. She didn't show, and I can't say that I blame her!

Forty years as a choir leader kept things busy on Sundays. In the big band I frequented, you'd catch me playing the trumpet and singing. We'd practice every two weeks on Thursday nights, and when the band went public, we realized we needed a name! We settled on Thirsty Knights, which seemed like a good choice.

One of the tidbits I've learned over the years is that music and poetry are a great fit, so I guess my love of limericks is only natural. I'll sign off with this one, about some guy named George:

> *"There once was a fella named George*
>
> *Who thought he could be Victor Borge*
>
> *Though he worked like a dog*
>
> *Really all he could log*
>
> *Was a one-nighter down at The Gorge*
>
> *(a hotel in Victoria).*

—by ***George R. Roberts****, Victoria, British Columbia*

Fine Felted Friends

Discovering this simple yet versatile pastime

Growing up on beautiful Manitoulin Island, I was surrounded by the works of many artists in the area, including family members. My cousin did beautiful beadwork, while my grandmother created everything from quill boxes to canoes. It was also not uncommon for me to see paintings by Leland Bell and carvings by Gordon Waindubence, both First Nations artists, also located on Manitoulin.

Some of my first memories are of creating art. I was forever drawing animals that I loved—there would invariably be horses or some kind of big cat sprinting across the pages of my school workbooks and any scraps of paper I could get my hands on. I carried this passion with me and, as I grew, my methods and mediums evolved. Now, I love to create in pencil, paints and wool.

I began needle felting, which is basically sculpting wool with special, barbed needles, about three years ago. I wanted a little wool creation of my cat and, after failing to track down another artist to make one, I went about gathering supplies such as wool, felting needles and protective gear. The gear includes foam to felt on to protect surfaces and prevent needles from snapping, as well as silicone or leather finger guards to protect yourself from the barbed needles.

After trying needle felting for myself, I fell in love with the craft. Needle felting is such a versatile fibre art. It can be used to create so many things, including ornaments, portraits or sculptures. What makes it so enjoyable is that the materials are fairly easy to obtain and the methods are pretty straightforward. All you do is take a bit of wool and either "punch" it through a piece of fabric with the needle, or use the needle to knot and form a chunk of wool into shapes. It is a very repetitive motion but the possibilities are endless.

I still love drawing and painting; however, working with wool has opened up new creative opportunities for me. I've had the honour of making several pet portraits and sculptures of people's current furry family members, as well as their beloved pets that have passed on. Often I am able to include a tiny tuft of the pet's hair to make these mementoes even more personal.

I have also begun exploring my roots through my needle felted work. I've begun creating pieces in the "woodland style," which is part of my Anishinaabe heritage on my dad's side. It has allowed me to storytell in a different way, in addition to working with a whole other palette of colour combinations than I normally do when working on pet portraits or other animals. My first pieces are made solely of wool, but I have a few new exciting medium combinations that I have begun experimenting with and hope to be able to share in the near future.

Being able to work with my hands and create all of these different pieces has been such a gift. It has allowed me to work with others in my community and build not only professional relationships but friendships as well. Most of all, I enjoy how it has given my mother and I a special activity to bond over—I treasure my "art visits" with her. I look forward to creating many more pieces and cannot wait to see what direction my work will take next.

*—by **Adrienne Assinewai**, Sudbury, Ontario*

Musical Ambassadors

A Canadian teen marching band wows an international crowd

You might think taking 150 teenagers across the Atlantic to a foreign country would be an exercise in chaos, but when that group is the Burlington Teen Tour Band, we do it with flying colours—and, in our case, that colour is red.

As a Canadian youth marching band—also known as the Redcoats—we tour the world performing in parades, competitions and other prestigious events. Founded in 1947 in Burlington, Ontario, we were originally known as the Burlington Boys and Girls Band. As much as we have changed since then, we still share the pride the original members treasured in both wearing our uniforms and representing Canada.

As Canadian musical ambassadors, we have had the honour of taking part in multiple worldwide events, such as the 70th anniversary of the attack on Pearl Harbor in Hawaii, the famous Rose Bowl parade in California, and the 20th anniversary of the twinning of Burlington and Itabashi in Japan. Recently, we had the privilege of participating in the St. Patrick's Day parade in Dublin, Ireland.

As members of this band, we were thrilled to have the opportunity to share our love and passion for music with the people of Ireland. Before our departure, we spent many months working as a team to create an end result that would, hopefully, impress the crowds and judges. Preparation included marching practice, fundraising, uniform cleaning, instrument polishing and more.

After a seven-hour flight to London, followed by a two-hour flight to Dublin, we finally arrived at the Emerald Isle full of excitement at getting the chance to enjoy what we had worked so hard to achieve.

Our ten-day adventure included excursions to notable Irish landmarks. In Cobh, we were blown away by the scenic surroundings, including multi-coloured houses, a historical cathedral atop the hill and the exciting Titanic Trail walking tour. We went around the city viewing different memorials and breathing in history and culture. Did you know that Cobh (then known as Queenstown) was the last port of call for the *Titanic* before embarking on its journey? We were all awestruck by the original dock the passengers had walked across.

At Blarney Castle, we trekked up the narrow spiral staircase to kiss the stone that inspired the "gift of gab." We don't know if it was just us, but the bus did seem louder during our castle departure! Our stop in Killarney consisted of a scenic cart ride around the Muckross House property. The Cliffs of Moher were picturesque and breathtaking and, despite the constant weather shift from hail to rain to sun, we were still speechless by the natural beauty—the gift of the gab must have worn off!

As much fun as the sightseeing was, no tour would be complete without plenty of performances. Our first was in Cobh, where we marched along the winding streets to the promenade bordering the sea. There we held a stationary concert. We were inspired to see people putting aside what they were doing, even closing down shops, to come and support us. The mayor of Cobh later personally thanked us for coming.

The next performances in Killarney and Dublin were small but rewarding. In Killarney it was awesome to see the crowd dancing and jumping to the music, and in Dublin we were personally invited to play at the Welcoming of the Bands for the St. Patrick's Day parade.

The next performance was our first competition parade and what a place to debut—the world-renowned Dublin St. Patrick's Day parade. Waiting around in the cold for two hours was quickly forgotten after stepping off and embracing the sea of green, cheering spectators and general festive atmosphere.

Although it was a long parade, nobody cared because we knew we were making lifelong memories. Up against top bands from around the world, we were extremely anxious to hear the results of the competition. All of our worries faded after we received word that we were judged to be the Best Youth Band—the category with the most competitors!

Proud of our accomplishment, we quickly had to turn our attention to our next competition in Limerick. During an opportunity to socialize with fellow bands before stepping off, we discovered a mutual interest in learning about one another. After a slow-moving but well-populated parade route, we reached the awards ceremony.

Although we were excited for other bands as they won their awards, we were slightly disappointed we hadn't heard our name called yet.

We applauded for every award until the last one, when our fellow competitors and enthusiastic spectators cheered for us: We had been named the All Ireland International Band Champions, the top award of the entire competition! We marched out after a celebratory concert and could not remove the smiles plastered on our faces for the rest of the day.

It was a whirlwind tour but one to remember. We were successful not only in competitions but also in representing our hometown and country. When we returned to Canada, local residents and even people who didn't know us had heard of our accomplishments in Ireland through multiple media reports. We were welcomed home by friends and family with congratulatory hugs.

The memories we made were not just of our successes but also of the considerable pride we gained knowing we were truly Canada's musical ambassadors.

*—by **Amy Longley and Emily Di Matteo**, Burlington, Ontario*

Artist and Dreamer

Through life's bumps and curves, there is always art

Even before I was old enough to colour inside the lines, I was amazed by what appeared on a blank page or canvas as I sketched whatever images came to mind. Throughout my eclectic working career, I have always tried to keep my creative side alive and consider myself a hobby-type artist.

I had a successful graphic and advertising business for many years. I also worked as an art director in television. During the '80s, however, my marriage slowly disintegrated and I went bankrupt. I did manage to somehow scrape up enough money to purchase and move onto a 42-foot sailboat called *Dreamer II*—a fitting name, and not just for the boat.

I think it was my artistic nature that drew me to the idea of living on the water, even though I had never sailed before. I lived at several marinas throughout the years, though my dream at the time was to sail to and live at Haida Gwaii, British Columbia, and get more into painting. I'd been to the islands before and, although it rained most of the time, I camped at the base of Tow Hill and felt a presence there I've never felt anywhere else.

I never doubted that I'd be able to learn to sail, but it wasn't until I crewed aboard a 27-foot sailboat, *Dove III,* that I truly experienced the sea, and boy did I! My friends Winston Bushnell, George Hone and I sailed the legendary Northwest Passage in a single season. Upon our return, I wrote and illustrated *Arctic Odyssey,* which was published in 1995, and many years later I self-published the book again as a limited edition.

While living on *Dreamer II,* I mostly earned a living by lettering signs, but I did paint a few murals and commissioned paintings and even did a stint at the ferry terminal drawing portraits for a couple of summers. The one thing I really enjoyed about living on the boat was not working five days a week with only two days off. With minimal needs, I took five days off!

I eventually sold *Dreamer II* shortly after getting married in 2007 and moving in with my wife, Sarah, and her two daughters. We both wanted to get back to basics, however, and with dreams of living on a farm, we crammed what little we could into a small trailer and hauled it almost clear across Canada to Fosterville, New Brunswick. Of course, upon arrival I had to build a small studio in the garage to continue my artistic endeavours. I later renovated other rooms in our house and turned the baby barn into a second studio.

Although we have 75 chickens, the farming idea didn't quite work out as planned. After I hit 70 years of age several years ago, my back and now some of my joints, plagued with arthritis, just won't allow me to bend over and work as hard as I would like. Having a large garden is like having a full-time job during the spring and summer months.

Sarah has been operating the kitchen at the local Woodstock Farm & Craft Market, plus the little café we opened in the front of our house. Neither of them are real moneymakers, but they help pay the bills. The market is year-round, but our home café is open just in the summer months when people who have cottages on the lakes arrive.

Both being artsy and enjoying other artists' abilities, Sarah and I started up the Golden Unicorn Arts Festival four years ago. The festival was my idea, but Sarah, being more of a social person than I, quickly embraced it. Between the two of us, we have turned the festival into a seasonal event looked forward to by the artisans who display their art and crafts and the musicians and singers who entertain the public.

The arts festival came into being because I have always enjoyed helping other artists achieve their dreams, either by hiring them when I was in business, buying their creations, or, when I used to own my own little gallery years ago, putting on exhibitions for them. The Golden Unicorn idea came from the old logo for my business called Unique Advertising, which stemmed from the fantasy world in my mind and my love of horses after spending ten years as a groom at Exhibition Park in Vancouver.

Since we started the festival, which takes place the second Sunday in August, the number of participants has grown—last year we had 700 people strolling through our place! It's hard to believe we will celebrate the festival's fifth anniversary next year, hopefully with a two-day event.

I still paint in my studio, but I have also recently begun a small monthly publication called *The Messenger.* I don't make any money at it, but people have told me they look forward to reading it. Sarah writes as well, so it's something we enjoy together.

When I lived on *Dreamer II,* my love for the sea and boats were depicted in many of my paintings, but now that I live in a semi-wilderness area, I try and paint the breathtaking landscapes around me, from colourful trees in the fall to the harsh yet dazzling winters. I also paint wildlife and unicorns, of course. Through ups and downs in my life, the urge to paint or write has never left me.

—by ***Len Sherman****, Fosterville, New Brunswick*

Our Canada, Our Country, Our Stories

STORY CONTRIBUTORS

FAMILY

Shirley Davidson Bonic, Regina, Saskatchewan ("Tapping the Trees")

Lynnae Ylioja, Macrorie, Saskatchewan ("The Curling Kettle")

Brad Nichol, Rosthern, Saskatchewan ("The Debonaire")

Louise Szabo, Nepean, Ontario ("An Occasion Fit for a Queen")

Bill L. Knibbs, Medicine Hat, Alberta ("Achieving Their Goal")

Ed Papazian, Kanata, Ontario ("The Georgetown Boys")

Adrienne Ulliac, Whitecourt, Alberta ("Family Ties")

Betty Moore, West Guilford, Ontario ("A-Camping We Will Go")

Gail M. Murray, Scarborough, Ontario ("Macaroni Sundays")

Anne Megahy, Toronto, Ontario ("When We Were Young")

Linda Sweeney, Miramichi, New Brunswick ("Frying Up a Feast")

Donna McAleer Smith, Bowmanville, Ontario ("Remembering Gram")

Kim Han, Kanata, Ontario ("Natural Beauty")

Judi Hannon, Terrace, British Columbia ("Gone Fishing")

Kenneth Sornberger, Dunsford, Ontario ("Marrying the Farmer's Daughter")

Melanie Saulnier, Fredericton, New Brunswick ("What Money Can't Buy")

KINDNESS

Jean E. Hubbard, West Vancouver, British Columbia ("The Wedding Dress")

Ardith Trudzik, Edmonton, Alberta ("Queen of May")

Doddi Reid, Palmerston, Ontario ("Water for Africa")

Eldora Baillie, Fort McMurray, Alberta ("Vanquishing the Fort McMurray 'Beast' ")

Janice Murphy, Hamilton, Ontario ("Born to Help")

Dale and Allan Bond, Grande Prairie, Alberta ("A Lasting Legacy")

Susan Debreceni, Toronto, Ontario ("Saving Our Shorelines")

Jayson Childs, Thunder Bay, Ontario ("Curling for a Cure")

Wesley Pitts, Hantsport, Nova Scotia ("Helping Blanding's Turtles")

Chris Robinson, Cambridge, Ontario ("Volunteer Veterinary Team")

Lynn Turcotte, Gamètì, Northwest Territories ("Sewing With Pride North of 60")

Scott Prevost, Elliot Lake, Ontario ("Paddling With Purpose")

Esther Meerschaut, Harrow, Ontario ("From Milk Bags to Bed Mats")

Beverlee Brown, Bridgewater, Nova Scotia ("From Rescue to Rescuer")

Connie Weinberg, Aylesford, Nova Scotia ("Flying High on Knowledge")

Maureen Littlejohn, Toronto, Ontario ("Making a Difference")

Anna Levin, Winnipeg, Manitoba ("Northern Manitoba Matters")

Janette Slack, Cobourg, Ontario ("PrimRose Donkey Sanctuary")

Brenda Keay, Coldstream, British Columbia ("Lessons Learned in Ethiopia")

Mike Christiansen, Edmonton, Alberta ("Racing for a Cure")

Jeremy Bryant, Edmonton, Alberta ("Turning Dining Out Into Helping Out")

Ward Burr, Forest, Ontario ("Generosity in Motion")

David Hill-Turner, Nanaimo, British Columbia ("Give Me Shelter")

John C. Hudspith, Toronto, Ontario ("Moulding Young Minds")

VALOUR

As told to **Bob Pearson**, Strathroy, Ontario ("Battle of Vimy Ridge")

Marion Fraser, Toronto, Ontario ("Lessons My Father Taught Me")

Catherine MacKenzie, Fall River, Nova Scotia ("Dodging Death")

Don Martin Jr., Melbourne, Ontario ("Noble Steeds")

Lynn Philip Hodgson, Port Perry, Ontario ("Camp X")

Gordon Baron, Dawson's Landing, British Columbia ("Legendary Flying Goose")

Mac Horsburgh, Winnipeg, Manitoba ("Making a Connection")

Annette Gray, Markerville, Alberta ("Canada's Dambusters")

Christine Cameron Emmett, Brighton, Ontario ("The Forgotten Ones")

Colleen O'Hare, Parry Sound, Ontario ("Canadian Kangaroos")

Harry Watts, Kitchener, Ontario ("Lone Rider")

Miriam (Atwood) Thompson, Pugwash, Nova Scotia ("Uncle Wilfred Remembered")

Irene Martin, Expat Canadian now residing in Skamokawa, Washington ("Accentuate the Positive")

Leonard "Scotty" Wells, Scarborough, Ontario ("Tales From the Sea")

Shirley O'Connell, Perth, Ontario ("Izzy's Story")

Sgt. Caitlin Yacucha, Winnipeg, Manitoba ("A Letter Home From Afghanistan")

Allan Cameron, Sylvan Lake, Alberta ("A Tribute to Our Vets on Remembrance Day")

Steven Doucette, Manotick, Ontario ("A War Vet's Best Friend")

Jim Lowther, Dartmouth, Nova Scotia ("Vets in Transition")

MEMORIES

Ugo DeBiasi, Nanaimo, British Columbia ("Memory-Go-Round")

Jeanne Emelyanov, Ottawa, Ontario ("Facing Off Against a Blizzard")

Carman Scherlie, Wembley, Alberta ("The Coldest Day in Canadian History")

Hilda J. Born, Abbotsford, British Columbia ("The Fabric of Her Life")

Jim Soul, Erin, Ontario ("My Early Education")

Gloria Barkley, Coquitlam, British Columbia ("Hockey Night in Hedley")

Leesha Nikkanen, Newmarket, Ontario ("Ice Dreams")

Sue Weiss, Bloomingdale, Ontario ("This Old Sugar Shack")

Cassandra Cardy, Minnedosa, Manitoba ("Summer Dreaming")

Hector M. Earle, Stoneville, Newfoundland and Labrador ("Larger Than Life")

Wyman Atkinson, Cottam, Ontario ("A Man Named 'Apples' ")

Leanne Smith, Calgary, Alberta ("Cowboys, Flapjacks and Fun!")

Bernard J. Callaghan, Charlottetown, Prince Edward Island ("The Saturday Matinee")

Jennifer DeBruin, Smiths Falls, Ontario ("Going Home to 'Lost Villages' ")

David Hooper, Port Alberni, British Columbia ("The Last Steam Donkey")

Jo-Anne Sheanh, Sechelt, British Columbia ("A Treasure Reclaimed")

RJ Goodfellow, St. Albert, Alberta ("Remembering RCAF Station Namao")

Dianne J. Beaven, Winnipeg, Manitoba ("Sowing the Future")

ADVENTURE

Darryl W. Lyons, Sayward, British Columbia ("High Hopes")

John G. Attridge, Hamilton, Ontario ("My Struggle With the Nahanni")

Leigh McClurg, Garibaldi Highlands, British Columbia ("Climb Every Mountain")

Marcia Lee Laycock, Blackfalds, Alberta ("The Yukon Is Gold")

Joan Prunkl, Edmonton, Alberta ("Life in Igloolik")

Barbara Leroy, Delta, British Columbia ("Beauty and the Barrens")

Tyler Dixon, Calgary, Alberta ("Searching for Wild Bill")

Gregory McNeill, Winnipeg, Manitoba ("Epic Winter Race")

Anne Hagerman, Picton, Ontario ("The Motorcycle Diaries")

Evelyn Godin, Saint John, New Brunswick ("Grand Manan, New Brunswick")

Shawn Hamilton, Campbellcroft, Ontario ("The Mystique of Sable Island")

Jill Yoneda, Victoria, British Columbia ("Swimming Great Bear")

Julie Birch, Didsbury, Alberta ("Wild About Horses")

COMMUNITY

Mary Derksen, Abbotsford, British Columbia ("Canada, Do You Have Room for Us?")

Gerlind Koesling, Edmonton, Alberta ("Salami and Popsicles")

Patricia Wilsenach, Fort McMurray, Alberta ("A Fairy Tale of Ice and Magic")

Surjit Singh Flora, Brampton, Ontario ("Reflections on Canada")

Mary Lou Beattie, Hudson's Hope, British Columbia ("Loving Peace River")

Ruth Morris Schneider, Baddeck, Nova Scotia ("Come From Away")

Janak Gautam, Edmonton, Alberta ("Journey From Nepal")

John McCurdy, Hamilton, Ontario ("A Pioneering Black Nurse")

Barbara Turner, Kelowna, British Columbia ("A Long Tradition of Service")

Cheyenne Stapley, Linden, Alberta ("The Show Must Go On")

Valerie Keenan, Winnipeg, Manitoba ("Forging New Friendships")

Tracey Rice, Grande Prairie, Alberta ("Breaking Boundaries")

Karen Taylor, Edmonton, Alberta ("Beaver Tails and Bear Paws")

Dorothy Hannah, Lacolle, Quebec ("Bilingualism at Its Best")

Waneek Horn Miller, Ottawa, Ontario ("Boot Camp, Indigenous-Style")

Maxine Noel, Stratford, Ontario ("Heart to Spirit to Hand")

Tanya Haye, North Vancouver, British Columbia ("Harmonizing Cultures")

Rob Rainer, Perth, Ontario ("Conserving Canada's Wild Species")

Ann Dwyer Galway, Paradise, Newfoundland and Labrador ("Recess in the Arctic")

John A. Gervais, Embrun, Ontario ("The Dream of Belonging")

Carmel McDonald, Garson, Ontario ("Hunting With Mémère")

TALENT

Marcia Godbout, Innisfil, Ontario ("Learning to See")

Sophie Milman, Toronto, Ontario ("Russian-Israeli-Canadian Jazz Singer")

Mary Kroetsch, Guelph, Ontario ("Saving Shoebox Memories")

Patricia Kuhnen-Beaver, Port Stanley, Ontario ("Woven in History")

Boshdayosgaykwe (Tracey Pawis), Parry Sound, Ontario ("G'zaagin: A Gallery of Love")

Josef Mukli, Nanaimo, British Columbia ("Helene's Gift")

Robyn Meyer, Gilbert Plains, Manitoba ("Towering Over the Prairie")

Catherine Lafrance, Montreal, Quebec ("Journey of Discovery")

Shaun Markey, Ottawa, Ontario ("The Art of the Deal")

Robert Williamson, Hamilton, Ontario ("Making History")

George R. Roberts, Victoria, British Columbia ("For Better or Verse")

Adrienne Assinewai, Sudbury, Ontario ("Fine Felted Friends")

Amy Longley and Emily Di Matteo, Burlington, Ontario ("Musical Ambassadors")

Len Sherman, Fosterville, New Brunswick ("Artist and Dreamer")

PHOTO: JAYSON CHILDS, HAMILTON, ONT.

SHARE YOUR STORIES AND PHOTOS AND GET A FREE 1-YEAR GIFT SUBSCRIPTION UPON PUBLICATION!

Our Canada is your magazine, written by and for Canadians just like you. Tell us about your hometown, adventures, handicrafts and collections, and show off those amazing snapshots you took on your vacations at home and abroad!

Written by and for Canadians just like you
Contribute today at **ourcanada.ca**